LIVE FROM **MONGOLIA**

LIVE FROM MONGOLIA

FROM WALL STREET BANKER _TO_ MONGOLIAN NEWS ANCHOR

PATRICIA SEXTON

BEAUFORT
BOOKS

Copyright © 2013 by Patricia Sexton

FIRST PAPERBACK EDITION

Paperback ISBN 9780825307973

Library of Congress Cataloging-in-Publication Data
Sexton, Patricia
Live from Mongolia : from Wall Street banker to Mongolian news anchor / Patricia Sexton. — First edition.
pages cm
1. Sexton, Patricia. 2. Women television news anchors—Mongolia—Ulaanbaatar—
Includes bibliographical references and index.
ISBN 978-0-8253-0697-6 (hardcover : alkaline paper)

Biography. 3. Americans—Mongolia—Ulaanbaatar—Biography. 4. Television news anchors—Mongolia—Ulaanbaatar—Biography. 5. Foreign correspondents—Mongolia—Ulaanbaatar—Biography. 6. Bankers--New York (State—New York--Biography. 7. Career changes—Case studies. 8. Sexton, Patricia—Travel—Mongolia. 9. Mongolia—Description and travel. 10. Ulaanbaatar (Mongolia—Biography. I. Title.
PN5449.M662S38 2013
070.4'3092—dc23
[B]
2013024833

For inquiries about volume orders, please contact:

Beaufort Books
27 West 20th Street, Suite 1102
New York, NY 10011
sales@beaufortbooks.com

Published in the United States by Beaufort Books
www.beaufortbooks.com

Distributed by Midpoint Trade Books
www.midpointtrade.com

Printed in the United States of America

Interior design by Neuwirth & Associates, Inc.
Cover Design by Lorin Taylor

For anyone out there who's got a dream, is following it,
or isn't quite following it but might one day follow it

But most especially—for Bunkle and our little copilot

CONTENTS

Dear Readers,

*I've sifted through a number of dusty old tomes spelling out
Mongolian history in great, if not somewhat confusing, detail.
While I've done my best to honor the ancient memories with what
I've written in my own tome, I admit I'm no historian.
So if you are, by all means by all means, email me at
LiveFromMongolia@gmail.com if you've found an error
and we'll correct it in the next edition.*

Some names have been changed.

LIVE FROM **MONGOLIA**

The anchor called in sick at the last minute. My boss, Gandima, head of English News, was desperate. The backup presenters were on vacation or not answering their phones; no one else was available. In desperation, she told me to comb my hair and put on some makeup. I was a summer intern for Mongolia National Broadcaster, and I'd just been tapped to present the evening broadcast to an audience of more than two million people.

There'd been no time for a rehearsal, so I muttered my lines over and over to myself as I was led into the basement studio. Mongolia National TV has been around since before the fall of Communism, and it's the oldest and most respected network in the country. Fully three-quarters of the Mongolian population tunes in to its broadcasts. As I ducked under the studio's low doorway, I let my eyes adjust to the bright lights. Once they did, I gasped.

None other than the station's top brass was waiting for me. Gandima was there with her boss, Enkhtuya, the network's news director. On either side of them stood a cavalry of senior producers, editors, and a handful of technicians. All eyes were on me, the summer intern, and nobody was smiling. Never before had this storied station allowed a foreigner to be promoted to anchor so quickly, even just temporarily, and Gandima had reminded me of just that before issuing a chilly command.

"Patricia," she said, "you *will* do a good job tonight."

To the crew standing solemnly alongside the network's bosses, I dipped my head in a slight nod, but their silence offered little encouragement.

"Come," Gandima said, a bit more softly, breaking the ice. She showed me to my seat in the anchor's chair, helped affix a mike to my lapel, and gently smoothed my hair. One by one, the spotlights snapped on. There I sat, frozen in the hot blaze, wondering how on earth I'd ended up here, anchoring a national news broadcast. Just a few months earlier, I'd been working at a bank in New York, wondering what might happen if I quit my job of nearly ten years to pursue a lifelong dream to become a foreign correspondent. I was about to find out!

CHAPTER 1

Making It and Breaking It

Mr. Ng stated that his organization's goal is to assist Mongolian labor organizations. He invited Prime Minister Enkhbold to participate in the deliberations of the Asia-Pacific meeting being held in the Korean city of Busan.

—*MM Today* lead story

"Are you deaf or just stupid?" a cantankerous senior bond salesman barked at me one morning my first year working on Wall Street. "I said peanut butter on *well-done* toast! This is *not* well done!" he raged, flipping his medium-rare toast into the trashcan beside him.

Fresh out of college, I'd been hired by Salomon Brothers as an analyst trainee. Like every other twenty-two-year-old on Wall Street, I'd come there for the money. But the big bucks were a long way off; first I'd have to pay my dues like everyone else there who'd already "made it." Wall Street's pecking order works something like a school playground: you're bullied until you become the bully or until you figure out how to outsmart the bully.

And "making it" was just what I was determined to do. Whatever it took—making well-done toast, picking up dry cleaning, fetching dozens of lunch orders, working dawn to dusk—this was the price I would willingly pay to make it on Wall Street. It wasn't the allure of opulence and glitzy excess that I was seeking, not then anyway. It was freedom I sought, something that my parents had never been able to afford. If I couldn't make it here in New York, I wouldn't have anywhere to go but home.

In Cincinnati, Ohio, on a salary of $15,000, they had raised four children. That they'd been able to do so at all left me feeling a mixture of awe and fear. I was in awe that they even could. And it was my greatest fear that I, too, would end up trapped.

In fact, my parents could have done better for themselves; they weren't simply victims of circumstance. Both of them had pursued something they were passionate about, and both of them had paid a price. My mom taught part-time and spent weekends with the local newspaper spread out in front of her, clipping and stacking coupons. On top of a full-time teaching job, my dad spent weekends and summers cleaning gutters, cutting lawns, and painting houses to make ends meet. And all that was before he got fired.

I was fourteen years old when my dad's boss, a nun, insisted he change a student's grade. It was a small request but an immoral one, since the student simply didn't deserve the better mark. My dad took a stand and refused to change it. His boss insisted, threatening to fire him for insubordination if he didn't follow her orders. This went on for months, with the nun visiting my dad's classroom to remind him that he had to comply—or else. Eventually, their disagreement erupted into a screaming match in the middle of the school hallway. That was when it became clear that this sweet little old lady, who belonged to an order of nuns so religious they still wore the traditional black-and-white habit, was holding my dad by the balls.

With three kids in school, a second mortgage on the house, a used car that had just died, and only $10,000 in savings, my dad reluctantly agreed to make the change. And when he did, the nun fired him anyway. Worse still, she refused to give him an official reason, which made it impossible for him to get another teaching job. No one hires a veteran teacher who comes without a recommendation and who has been fired without cause. In the end, my dad had fought for something he'd believed in, and he'd lost everything.

So it seemed, anyway.

Now, more than twenty years later, I still reflect on that story with the same admiration that I felt as a teenager. I admired my dad's passion for what he believed in and my mom's staunch commitment to him. I always longed for a career that I was so devoted to I'd be willing to risk everything to honor my commitment to its principles.

Instead, I chose a career that would pay the bills. Of course, this makes perfect sense when you consider what happened to my family next.

And what happened next was what happens to the lucky people who slide into poverty with the benefit of a support network made up of close family members. At first, we found bags of groceries left on the front porch. At the time, my mom was forty years old and had gotten pregnant again, just as their insurance was running out.

Being uninsured in America is certainly not ideal, but being uninsured in America with four young kids is just an ER visit away from financial ruin. So the groceries arrived anonymously to help my parents take the edge off their bills. Then it was money, tucked discreetly into an unmarked envelope and left in our mailbox when we were away. We never knew for sure who was helping us, because the anonymous benefactors would always deposit their gifts when we weren't home.

The only way my mom could express her gratitude was to create an enormous paper banner and hang it from the railing of our porch. In huge script, it read, "Thank you, Santa Claus!"

It was this experience that sent me to Wall Street and, eventually, from Wall Street to, of all places, Mongolia. If my greatest fear was of being trapped, I was willing to do anything at all to be free—financially free. But the funny thing about having money is that it creates its own sort of prison. It would take me nearly a decade to realize this.

▲

"Two dozen burgers, fries, and milkshakes," a head trader at Salomon Brothers instructed me on summer Fridays. I loved summer Fridays because I knew exactly what to do to do my job right. The burgers had to come from Burger King, the fries from McDonald's, and the shakes from either, as long as the hot food arrived hot, the shakes were still cold, and the fries hadn't wilted. Wearing secondhand suits that my grandmother had tailored to fit me, I raced out of the office at 7 World Trade Center into the scorching city heat and then back again, eagerly lugging heavy shopping bags of food. When the traders ordered in bulk like this, they always let me keep the change. And on summer Fridays, there was a lot of change. Besides, getting a food order right was the best part of the job because it was the easiest.

There were eleven other trainees in my group, and we were competing against each other for a few coveted roles at the bottom of the totem pole on various trading desks: mortgages, equities, government bonds, and so on. Most of the trainees had majored in finance. I'd "concentrated" in finance, a slight distinction but an important one when facing down a series of bond math tests.

"Think you'll pass?" Tyrone asked me one afternoon, and I was instantly annoyed. It wasn't just because my fellow twenty-two-year-old trainee impressed everyone in the firm with his quiet confidence. And it wasn't because he'd graduated somewhere near the top of his class at Georgetown. It wasn't even that he wore navy blue dress shirts to work, which we'd been told *specifically* not to wear, for it was a mark of seniority to wear blue on the trading floor.

It was because Tyrone had asked *if* I thought I'd pass the coming bond math test. Of course I'd pass! I'd just have to study—a lot more than he'd have to study. But I wasn't going to tell him that.

"I'll pass," I said firmly.

That week, I committed myself to learning bond math from scratch. I had to be at work at Salomon by six-thirty each morning, so I studied on the subway to work, studied while I made coffee and photocopies for the traders, studied on the subway from work, and I stayed up late, studying. The morning of the test was one of the hottest on record in New York City. I couldn't afford air-conditioning, so I chilled my suit in the freezer and dressed in front of the open fridge. I simply could not be distracted by the discomfort of a hot summer's day.

"How did you do?" Tyrone asked, after we'd gotten our scores back.

"I got a hundred," I said, trying to contain my own excitement. "What about you?"

"Ninety-eight," he said, and slapped me on the back as he added, "Good job!" Tyrone wasn't the only one who was impressed. That afternoon, Susan stopped by my desk. The head of Salomon's training program, she had the power to make or break our nascent careers. "Well done," was all she said, and I knew I'd aced more than just the bond math test.

But the going wasn't so good for some of the other trainees, who were being mercilessly hazed. Salespeople and traders made it their mission to "break" the juniors in order to see who could really make it in their world. "Survival of the fittest!" someone would remind us first-years, every single day. Often, the hazing some of the trainees were subjected to was almost diabolical.

One afternoon while the market was quiet, a salesman sauntered up to Gimp, one of the trainees. It should have been the kind of moment every junior was waiting for—being chosen by someone senior. Getting noticed. Getting a shot.

Instead, the salesman wore a smirk, but Gimp didn't see that. That's probably why his nickname was Gimp. Eager and desperate to please, he was always ready to show just how submissive he could be.

"I'll bet you a hundred dollars that you can't drink a dozen quarts of milk within exactly one hour," the salesman said, knowing all too well that, although the task was almost impossible to complete, Gimp wouldn't say no, for two reasons.

First, for a trainee earning barely enough to make ends meet in New York City, one hundred dollars was a princely sum, enough to pay for a month of groceries, a decent suit, or even an air-conditioning unit.

But far more important, this was Gimp's chance to prove his worth, to position himself as one of the "fittest." On a trading floor where bets are made professionally all day long, a personal wager was a junior's chance to show his mettle. And because it was customary for a senior guy to try to break a junior kid just for sport, absolutely everyone would be watching. From secretaries to senior bankers, side bets were already being wagered: if Gimp didn't finish the dozen quarts, how many would he finish? At precisely what time would he begin to vomit? If anyone was willing to measure how sick he got, how much vomit would there be? In other words, there was actually a derivatives market on Gimp's future performance.

"Done!" Gimp said earnestly, making use of his first opportunity to speak in official market vernacular. Accepting the unnecessarily large fifty-dollar bill to buy milk, Gimp set off for the cafeteria.

"Keep the change," the salesman shouted after him.

By the time Gimp returned, the crowd had gathered. One by one, he put the dozen quarts of milk on his desk and sat down, nervously wiping his hands on his suit pants. Fingers trembling, Gimp opened the first container. Around him, everyone was silent. Arms folded, they watched, their faces a mixture of pity, amusement, and anticipation of the foregone conclusion.

"Clock's ticking," the salesman goaded.

Gimp started drinking. Quart after quart he chugged, occasionally leaking dribbles of liquid out of the corners of his mouth. By the fifth quart, Gimp's eyes were squeezed tightly shut, and he was emitting malodorous milky-wet burps. I would know; I sat right next to him. It wasn't long before he vomited into the trashcan next to him. Not once, but over and over again. And not only did he regurgitate the milk he'd drunk, but we also witnessed his lunch follow suit.

"Don't worry about the hundred bucks," the salesman said with phony generosity as Gimp was heaving. "Keep it."

The next morning, the mail cart stopped in front of Gimp's desk. Charlie, the stooped old man who delivered packages to the traders and salespeople, was about to deliver some terrible news. Handing Gimp a manila envelope, Charlie nodded innocently and shuffled away, unaware of his role in the cruel prank that was unfolding. While the traders peered over the tops of their computers, sneaking furtive glances at their victim, Gimp tore into the envelope with his typical zeal. In it, he found a memo announcing that he'd been fired. In vain, he tried to compose himself, but the betrayal proved too much. As he burst into tears, clutching the memo in his hand, Gimp ran off the trading floor.

When he eventually discovered that word of his dismissal had been a mere joke, Gimp returned to his desk, trying to pretend nothing had happened. Sniffling and wiping his red-rimmed eyes, he combed through a stack of unfinished tasks. But at that moment, we all knew: Gimp had been broken. Of course, "breaking" a trainee was usually only temporary, so long as the trainee could pick up the pieces and stop crying.

Now, a decade later, I was about to be broken. But unlike Gimp's break, mine would be permanent.

By this point, I'd stuck with my banking job for longer than I'd expected. I'd left Salomon Brothers years earlier and moved to Credit Suisse New York, where I was vice president of Foreign Exchange Sales. I'd worked overseas in Asia for a few years before returning home to Manhattan and had been informally appointed Japan specialist. If anyone on the trading floor had an obscure question about the Japanese prime minister's history with the ruling Liberal Democratic Party, or wanted to parse the definition of "independence" when it came to the Bank of Japan, I was the one to ask in the New York time zone. And after nearly ten years of banking, I'd paid off all my debts and earned enough money to feel the freedom that my parents had never been able to feel. I'd even taken part in some of those wagers that had broken my colleague, Gimp, all those years ago.

While in Singapore, to the cheers of the entire trading floor, we'd all watched a junior derivatives trader try to eat ten Big Macs in less than an hour for a bet of roughly $700. (He managed to down only three.) In London, I'd bet a spot trader $1,000 that he couldn't chew and fully swallow a single slice of bread in less than thirty seconds. "Fully swallowing" was crucial, however, so he lost the bet on the technicality that the bread had turned gluey while he was chewing it and had stuck in the back of his throat.

Of course, I also participated in these wagers, rising to a challenge to eat a single spoonful of the second-hottest hot sauce in the world for $1,000. I won the bet but paid a hefty price for it later on that afternoon when my nose and eyes swelled during a meeting with a top European hedge fund whose business I was trying to win.

It had taken me a long time to pay off those university debts and save enough money to feel "free," and by the time I'd done so, I'd grown so accustomed to my job that I'd actually convinced myself I enjoyed it. And I could hardly argue that I didn't enjoy at least parts of it. There was nothing quite like the thrill of a busy market or of being the first to learn of breaking news.

But deep down, what I longed for was a career that I truly loved. And I knew what that career was; I was reminded of it every time I turned on the television to see Christiane Amanpour reporting live for CNN from Baghdad. Over the years, I'd managed to quiet that nagging, persistent voice telling me that I was meant to be doing something more with my life. After all, that meant taking a risk, and I was too afraid of losing everything I'd earned.

Besides, after all those years working in Tokyo and Singapore, my lifestyle had actually become more important than my dream. If you're looking for a surefire way to persuade someone to forget about pursuing her passion in life, ply her with business class plane tickets, a corporate apartment in an upscale neighborhood, and those high-tech Japanese toilets that wash and dry your bottom.

And yes, there was the money. I'd begun to make good money—*really* good money. So good, in fact, that I wasn't exactly sure how much I was actually making. Bankers didn't depend on their salaries to survive, at least not back then, before the post-recession reforms went into effect. Back then, a midlevel bank vice president was earning a base salary of about $150,000, not far off from a managing director's base. It was the year-end bonuses that counted for everything, and they were often so large that a Ferrari, or even two, could easily be purchased for cash.

Even so, I wasn't making nearly the kind of money that my colleagues were making. Although our "numbers" were strictly confidential, everyone seemed to know what the top traders and salespeople were earning, and their payouts were many multiples of what mine were. Of course, a job that pays so handsomely doesn't come without a price.

In fact, I'd gotten greedy. After moving back to New York, I'd bought a dream loft apartment in downtown Manhattan's Union Square. I ate out with fellow well-heeled friends at Michelin-starred restaurants and traveled to exotic destinations like Tibet and the Maldives. I'd grown quite accustomed to this lifestyle that had won me over, and I even felt a certain sense of entitlement to it. Without anything but work to define me, I had let it do just that.

And then Goldman Sachs called. The crème de la crème of investment banks, Goldman Sachs was where all bankers claimed they wanted to work. Just getting a single telephone call from Goldman Sachs suggesting they were thinking of hiring you was enough to negotiate a bigger pay package from your current employer. And I'd gotten more than a call; I'd actually gotten an interview. Sixteen of them, in fact, which was standard vetting practice at this venerable old Wall Street firm.

So one afternoon, after lying to my boss that I'd gone to the dentist, I sat down in Goldman Sachs' conference room, across from Bob, the head of foreign exchange sales. If Goldman Sachs bankers were supposed to look slick and exquisitely groomed, Bob didn't quite fit the image. His gray hair was tousled, he wore a boxy suit, and his tie was cheap. But he wore expensive angular eyeglass frames, and in typical Goldman Sachs style, he got right to the point.

We began to discuss money, and Bob didn't waste any time getting specific. Without even asking me what salary I'd be expecting in order for me to abandon Credit Suisse, he offered me nearly double what I was currently earning. I'd learned in my early days of banking how to maintain a poker face, but this time I was having trouble doing so. I was giddy with greed because Bob had just said "eight hundred fifty thousand dollars." It wasn't an official offer so much as it was a suggestion. But it was a starting point in our negotiations, and I was astonished that I could ever earn that much money, especially when I'd only just turned thirty.

However, I just couldn't do it. I couldn't go to work for Goldman Sachs. Long ago, I'd promised myself that I'd quit banking by the time I was thirty years old, and that time was now. I'd only interviewed with them because I was curious—and because nobody turns down an interview with Goldman Sachs. Turning them down would be like getting called up to the Major Leagues but not bothering to show up for the tryouts. Successfully applying for a job at Goldman Sachs, well, it was proof that you'd made it.

⚜

"Are you fucking *stupid?* Do you know what time it is?" Eric, one of my clients, growled at me down the phone line early one Thursday morning, shortly after my discussions with Goldman Sachs.

Although I'd met Eric only once, it had been memorable. Over a steak-house dinner with a Credit Suisse strategist in tow, Eric had made it clear that he hated salespeople. Throughout the entire dinner, he had addressed me only once, and that was to interrupt me. Worse, rumor had it that Eric's wife was in the process of dumping him, and he was infamous in the market for his impatience with women. Obviously, as a woman and a salesperson, I was in an unenviable position, trying to win his business.

Eric was thin in a wiry sort of way, and each time I spoke, the veins in his sinewy neck seemed to bulge, as if revealing a hypertensive testament to his revulsion for saleswomen. In the hierarchy of the trading floor, no one reigns more supreme than a client. Even the most belligerent senior traders and managers know that the client's word is always gospel, always final.

"It's just past eight–thirty a.m.," I responded quietly that Thursday morning, ignoring the rhetorical nature of the question, imagining Eric's veins bursting, one by one, in response to my insolence. Every weekday, government agencies around the world release statistical data revealing the health of their economies. Every Thursday at eight thirty a.m., the US jobless claims report is published. A weekly snapshot of the American employment situation, it often has the power to move markets.

"Jobless data have just been released," Eric notified me, feigning patience after loudly sucking in a deep breath of air. "The bond market is opening, and you're telling me about a fucking *rumor*?" He enunciated "fuck" and "ing" as if they were two separate words, his condescension audible.

Although Eric had a point about my timing, I had a point too. Moments earlier, a rumor had begun to circulate that the Japanese government was intervening in the market value of the yen. When a government steps into the market to buy or sell its own currency, it's a signal to traders around the world that officials have drawn a line over or under the value of their money.

In other words, this is breaking market news, especially for someone who is long or short of the currency, which was Eric's situation. As his salesperson, it was my responsibility to alert my client to the rumor. But it wasn't just that. I knew, almost for certain, that the Japanese were indeed intervening in their currency. When it came to Japan, I knew what I was talking about, and I knew I had to get Eric's attention.

"But," I tried to explain, "there's a rumor that—"

"*No buts!*" he screamed into the receiver before slamming it down.

Taking a deep breath of my own, I gritted my teeth and bit my lip until it bled, focusing all my effort on not crying. Obviously, on a trading floor everyone gets yelled at and sworn at. It's part of the job. That wasn't my problem.

My problem was that Eric's account was too big for me. Although I'd carved a niche for myself by understanding the intricacies of Asian current affairs, I was in over my head when it came to the mathematics behind large derivatives deals.

The currency market trades in tiny decimals: one one-hundredth of a yen, one ten-thousandth of a euro, and so on. Currency prices can fluctuate wildly within the space of a single second, so the minutiae of a change in the yen's value by just one one-hundredth can drastically impact the price of a derivative. The larger the derivative, the greater the risk. Eric often dealt in half billions.

Unfortunately, telling my boss that I couldn't handle Eric's business was simply not possible. On a trading floor, you keep quiet about your shortcomings until you overcome them. So I spent sleepless nights going over and over option math in my head. When I did sleep, I dreamed about making terrible mistakes—career-ending, newspaper-headline-type mistakes. This was all normal for a midlevel banker like me; I was simply facing a hurdle in my development. It was my job to overcome it, and if I did so, I'd have a shot at really succeeding in banking.

But that was just the point. I didn't want to succeed in banking. I wanted to follow my dream before it was too late. That nagging, persistent voice was only getting louder.

"Where is Japanese yen trading?" salesmen were shouting at traders, moments after Eric had hung up on me.

"Who is your client!" traders suspiciously demanded of the salespeople before delivering the yen quotes.

"05-08! 08-12! 15 bid! 30 bid!"

Something was happening in the currency markets. Whether or not the Japanese were actually intervening in the yen, the market was behaving as if the rumor were fact. But I wasn't about to call Eric to tell him so. I was about to break, just as Gimp had done, all those years earlier.

In a last-ditch effort to avoid crumbling, I concentrated hard on the activity around me, noting with only a hint of smug satisfaction that I'd been right to urgently call Eric earlier that morning about the yen. But then, a single tear fell, and several more quickly followed. I just had to get off the trading floor and dash to the ladies' room. There were only two paths to it, and both of them required me to walk past all my colleagues. With my chin buried in my chest, I slunk off.

Once inside, I locked myself in a stall and sobbed. It was a long time before I stopped. And when I did, I was able to see myself for who I'd become—someone who'd settled. With all the money I'd earned over the years, I had the privilege of choice—theoretically, anyway. But in the end, it was choice itself that I'd squandered. I'd wasted my time, depositing one paycheck after another, staying each and every year for "just one more bonus," ignoring the persistent call of my dream. This wasn't what I wanted to do with my life, so how had I gotten so caught up with money and lifestyle?

Trouble is, if you spend enough time in a place where everyone tells you you're lucky to be there, you convince yourself you're lucky to be there too. You're playing house with your dreams; you're only fantasizing about them. And then one day, you wake up and realize that your time came— and it went.

Mulling over all this, I sat in the bathroom stall, in one of those hang-your-head-in-your-hands moments, knees wet with tears, elastic strings of snot inching their way toward the tiled floor. *Is it too late?* I wondered as I returned to my desk.

"So what's with the waterworks?" Valerie asked, hovering over me. A senior saleswoman, Valerie was one of the few female managers on the trading floor. I didn't answer her, so she did for me.

"Come with me," Valerie ordered. "We are going for a cup of tea."

I wasn't looking forward to this cup of tea. Years earlier, Val had wanted to work in the fashion industry, or so I'd heard, anyway; she never would have told me that. Val certainly dressed the part, wearing perfectly tailored navy pantsuits paired with simple jewelry, even once appearing in the *New York Times* Style section. She'd had a difficult start in banking but had worked hard to make it. Back then, no one had thought she could hack it on a trading floor, and here she was now, a managing director and one of the most powerful women at Credit Suisse. I'd have to work hard to follow in her footsteps. Only thing was, that's just what I didn't want to do.

"Crying," she began coldly, as soon as we'd sat down in the tea salon, "is completely unacceptable on a trading floor. *Certainly* for a woman."

Valerie was blunt, and that was just what I needed, especially from someone who'd given short shrift to her own dreams. I had nothing to say because I knew she was right, so I stared down at my hands and kept quiet.

"But I can help you," Valerie offered, this time more kindly. "You'll need to start by expanding your client base."

While she continued talking, I began fantasizing. *What if I finally did it? What if I went as far away as possible to pursue that old dream to become a foreign correspondent?*

"By this time next year, you can even aim for another promotion." Val smiled encouragingly.

And if I went, where would I go? I returned to my thoughts, tuning in and out of what she was saying. *But was it crazy to leave behind a job this good after all I'd done to get where I was now? And just as I was being offered the helping hand of one of the most senior women bankers at the company?*

Suddenly, I knew with absolute certainty that this was it, that my chance was *now* to pursue my dream. Tired of all these years trying to imagine what would happen *if,* I was finally ready for *when.*

Valerie paid for our tea, and together we walked back to the office. While she strategized about my career, I did my best to pay lip service to her plans for me. But my mind was elsewhere, imagining the possibilities if I flung myself as far my dreams let me.

Back at my desk, I logged on to the Internet. On Google's Web site, I typed three words in the dialogue search box: "journalism," "internship," and "Asia." And a moment later, there on my screen, was my answer.

Mongolia.

CHAPTER 2

Taking the Leap

Finance Minister Bayartsaikhan added that the burden of reducing expenditures should be shifted from the public sector to the private sector, which would lend more clarity to the government in how to effectively reduce expenses.

—*MM Today* interview

"Broadcast journalism internships available in Ulaanbaatar, Mongolia," the ad read, and I was sold. I knew almost nothing about a career in journalism, and even less about Mongolia, but right then, the only thing that mattered to me was *finally* taking a leap of faith. I'd been standing on the edge of my own cliff for years, peering down into what could be my future, but always turning back to the safety of the known. This time, I promised myself, would be different.

Right away, and with a sense of inevitability that was more wary than excited, I applied directly to the station for the internship. But I never heard back. Of course, like any form of unrequited interest, the station's indifference left me absolutely certain that I wanted the job, even if I wasn't exactly sure what the job was all about.

Tinkering with my Google search to find another way in, I ended up on the Web site of a British volunteer organization located in the country. For a fee, the organization would find me a job. So that's what I did—I applied for the internship and begged for an undefined journalism role, for which I was not at all qualified. And then, I handed over my credit card details.

A few days later, while I was delivering a currency quote to a client, I got a response. The e-mail said, "Welcome" and "Mongolia," and it took me awhile to read the rest, which informed me that I'd been accepted for an internship at Mongolia National Broadcaster, a state-owned TV and radio station in Ulaanbaatar. Of course, it was unpaid, but why else had I worked all these years in a job that paid well, if not to spend the money I'd earned on a future I was actually passionate about?

For a long time, all I could do was stare at my screen in disbelief that I was on my way, that in the end *this* was all it took—firing off an e-mail, buying a plane ticket, and taking that leap.

So theoretically, I was all set. But still I hadn't resigned from my job. And I'd been playing it cool with Goldman Sachs. And worst of all, right now I was sitting next to Jamie, my boss and the head of foreign exchange sales at Credit Suisse. Jamie was jolly and Canadian and had a knack for making everything all right. But everything wasn't all right. I wanted to—I *needed to*—pursue this dream. It was now or never.

Naturally, I got cold feet about leaving. For the next few weeks, I created one Excel spreadsheet after another, concocting budget scenario after budget scenario, trying in vain to forecast every conceivable outcome. Thirty years old and single, I was in a much easier position than most to disappear from ordinary life. But that didn't change the fact that, like everyone else, I had obligations: a mortgage on my apartment, bills, parents who were getting older. What if something went wrong? What if everything went wrong? What if I got sick? What if my parents got sick? What if I never got another job and I ended up back in Ohio?

On the other hand, what could be worse than sitting in the passenger seat of my own life? If I took any more time deliberating about how to follow my dream, I knew I wouldn't pursue it at all.

One night not long after, a blizzard hit Manhattan. There's something kind of romantic about a heavy snowfall; it seems to create the very atmosphere where dreams become reality. As the storm painted the city streets in incandescent tones, I sipped tequila in a cozy Mexican bar with my best friend, Meghan. A pocket-size writer with an infectious giggle, she was out of place in Manhattan, but she was completely in her element giving heady advice to a rapt, if not confused, audience of one. Something of a modern-day philosopher, Meghan had survived a half-hearted suicide attempt brought on by a bad marriage and a worse divorce. Then, rising from her own ashes, she'd embarked upon three careers, written two books, and gotten married again, this time to the man of her dreams.

In other words, my best friend had good, solid perspective. Of course, you can seek advice from anyone you want and orchestrate for yourself whatever outcome you hoped to achieve. All you have to do is choose certain easygoing friends to advise you on certain difficult matters. Meghan, however, is not that kind of friend. Wise in her simplicity, she tells it like it is, whether you want to hear it or not.

After our fourth round of tequila, I was ready to seek the fruits of her wisdom. One after another, I detailed my concerns with every worrying scenario I could think of. Finally, Meghan stopped me.

"If you stay in banking, *one* thing can happen," she said, and paused, letting logic sink in. After some thought, she went on. "But if you go, *anything* can happen."

I stared at Meghan in that unblinking way you do when you've been served the truth or too much tequila or both. Numb with intoxication, I signaled to the waiter to bring our bill. Outside, the snow had left Manhattan completely silent, our crunching footfalls interrupting the echoing hush. Cars were tucked in for the night in blankets of soft white powder. Leaning onto a hood, I traced "I quit" in capital letters on a windshield. The next morning, head heavy with a hangover and body leaden with the realization that it was time to end a career, I walked to work just after dawn in the freshly trodden snow. I was nervous, but I was ready. Almost.

On the trading floor, nervously perched on the edge of my seat, I stood up and sat down, then stood up again. I tapped my foot and twirled my pen, dropping it repeatedly. I drank a third cup of coffee when the first had all but shredded my fraying nerves, and though I reminded myself that I could back out, I knew I wouldn't, not anymore. It was time to resign, time to take the leap of faith that I'd been putting off for so many years.

In a last-ditch effort to create a stay of execution for sensibility's sake,

I called one of my favorite clients, shaking as I punched the numbers on the keypad in front of me. A hedge fund trader who swore by his family and the suburbs, Frank had looked after me from the day he'd stomped on my slice of cherry pie, nearly ten years earlier.

"It's Lent; you have to give up sweets!" he had chided me that spring afternoon when I'd just begun my banking career. New to the trading floor hierarchy, I'd laughed at him, ignoring the experience gap between us. Frank was a senior trader and I was a junior nobody. In other words, I was supposed to obey him. At the very least, I wasn't supposed to question him.

"Pie doesn't count as a sweet; only candy does!" I'd insisted.

Giving me a look that suggested he was about to teach me a lesson, Frank removed the plastic pie takeaway container from my desk. Fresh from the cafeteria's oven, it was still warm and left behind a mark of steam. Nonchalantly, he placed the container on the floor in front of him, lifted his leg, glared at me, and stomped on my pie. Cherries burst out of the container's cracked sides and landed on desk drawers and the floor, leaving behind the edge of a footprint in the smashed piecrust.

Everyone around us was still; no one said a word. And it wasn't because everyone was shocked at Frank's behavior; it was because nobody was paying any attention. I was just one more junior kid being taught a lesson by a senior trader. But with Frank, the lesson didn't stop at the pie. From that moment on, he took me under his wing, teaching me the basics of trading and selling. Without Frank, I'd have been just another new kid on the block. With Frank, I'd been chosen to succeed.

So it was with some trepidation that Frank was my first call that morning, nearly a decade later. Without question, I knew he'd deliver the sort of advice that I wanted to hear—and didn't want to hear. Mostly, though, I wanted him to tell me I was crazy. In fact, he would do both.

"Frank," I whispered into the phone to him. "Do you really think I should do it?" I asked, not needing to explain any further. For years, I'd confided in him that my real passion did not lie in a career in banking. For years he'd listened, only stopping me to express his wonder over our differences—my passion for adventure, his for the suburbs and his wife and children. In turn, this had encouraged me, making me believe that there was a nugget of validity to my belief that I wanted, and maybe should try to have, something different out of life.

"I think you're fucking crazy," Frank said after a pregnant pause. "But do it."

"I'll call you back," I said as I hung up, steeling myself for what was about to happen.

I took a deep breath and rose from my seat. Putting one wooden foot in front of the other until I reached the glass wall of Jamie's office, I tapped on the door. He motioned for me to come inside, and I did so, feeling like a traitor. Awkwardly, I sat down.

"I think I'm resigning," I said abruptly. "To go work for a TV station in Mongolia."

Gathering my unrehearsed thoughts, I reminded myself that, for better or worse, *this* was the risk I wanted to take. That's not what I said to Jamie, though. Instead, I told him why I thought I was wrong to do what I'd been planning to do. Gripped by a sudden, overwhelming feeling of uncertainty, I was half hoping that he'd talk me out of it, that he'd tell me that dreams are only in your head. But Jamie just listened and I went on, telling myself that regret only makes an appearance when you're saying your good-byes.

"If I knew at your age what I know now," Jamie said solemnly, "I'd have done exactly what you're doing." Correcting himself, he added, "But not in Mongolia."

Incredibly, Goldman Sach's response was identical.

"Go," Bob, the head of sales, said to me when I called him to let him know I wouldn't continue negotiations. He'd sounded almost wistful. "Call us when you're back," he added, and I promised I would, hoping I'd never have to follow through.

CHAPTER 3

The Fortune-Teller

Environmental laws are being breached repeatedly. Legal discussions are under way to update these outdated laws. The first of these discussions took place today; nongovernmental organizations as well as government officials took part in the discussions.

—*MM Today* lead story

Mongolia is one of those destinations that isn't particularly easy to pack for. While the capital is full of trendy bars and nightclubs, the countryside is rugged adventure. You might find yourself dining on the top floor of a posh hotel during the week and roughing it on the back of a nomad's horse come the weekend. I tried to prepare for all of this. In a single backpack, sturdy hiking boots joined a single pair of high heels, mascara and eye shadow were lumped together with heavy-duty sunscreen, and a sealed Ziploc bag contained both diarrhea medication and a bottle of perfume. For my internship at the TV station, I packed one notebook and one pen. Finally and for good measure, I tucked Cat—my worn-out and shabby thirty-year-old stuffed animal—into the mix.

I was about to fling myself thousands of miles from the nearest designer juice bar or Starbucks, a time zone or so way away from a reliable salad. In fact, I'd be exactly 6,355 miles from my home, my friends, and my family. I'd be migrating from one of the most crowded cities in the world to one of the most remote capitals in the world. It was so remote, in fact, that I'd been required to purchase emergency evacuation insurance before departing New York. What had seemed for years little more than a fantasy was about to become a reality.

"Trishy," Netta said to me late one evening a week or so before I left. "You'll come back, won't you?" We were sitting in Astor Place on a giant metallic cube sculpture spinning round and round, reminiscing. I'd met Netta only a year earlier when we'd reached for the same cupcake at a mutual friend's thirtieth birthday party. From that point on, we'd been inseparable.

"I think so," I said, and we both got tears in our eyes. Over countless dinners, Netta and I had talked through the pros and cons of leaving behind a decent job. And Netta wasn't just talking the talk; she was about to walk the walk herself, from COO to a start-up. Netta understood that it wasn't a break I was taking; it was a break I was *making*. I was going from what I'd been told to want, to what I truly wanted, and from striving for more, to striving for something altogether *different*. Netta and I both knew that although I still could, it was too late to turn back the clock.

The night before I left, already feeling nostalgic for what I was about to leave behind, I meandered through the streets of Manhattan, saying a private farewell to all the people who didn't know they'd made my neighborhood feel like home: the matchstick woodworker in Washington Square Park; the crisply polite Englishman selling potato peelers in Union Square; and the resident black transvestite in Greenwich Village who flirted with passersby, flamboyantly flaunting his white plastic platform heels and matching white plastic suit.

As I began falling out of step with people walking quickly and with purpose, I eventually found myself sitting at a French restaurant on the Lower East Side with a tarot card reader, of all people. He was only a sideshow to the restaurant's cuisine, kind of a cabaret performer, and meeting him at all had been just an accident. But he was about to tell me something truly astonishing.

"You are about to embark upon an adventure," he began, and I rolled my eyes. Good guess, I thought. I don't know anyone who's paid a visit to a fortune-teller who hasn't received this prediction, along with the part about meeting someone tall and dark and good-looking. After all, an "adventure" can occur in plenty of places, even the Upper East Side.

"Draw another card," the fortune-teller instructed, and I drew one more. A hooded, faceless shape holding a scythe stood beneath a white rose. It looked like the Grim Reaper. Turns out, it was.

"Isn't that the death card?" I asked hesitantly.

"Yes, it is," he said, frowning in concentration, not exactly the look you're hoping for when someone is peering into your future. "You are going through a major change in life," he finally said. "An adventure that will result in the death of your old self, that will . . ."

Suddenly, he stopped short. Then, selecting a single card from the pyramid we'd created, the fortune-teller held it up.

"The love card," he said, and was silent a moment before speaking again.

"His name will begin with an 'E.'"

Without question, now he had my attention.

"'E'?"

"Yes, 'E,'" he said, trailing off. "Ed, Eddie," he went on quietly, talking more to himself than to me. "Earl?"

For some reason, he wasn't quite getting it, and he seemed to be growing increasingly frustrated about this, to the point of shouting right there in the restaurant, "Edwin? No, *NO*, that's *NOT* it. Ewan?"

"I can't. I just can't!" he finally said. "I can't tell you his name, but I can tell you this: E is American, he is several years younger than you, he's recently been a college student, and you will meet him on your adventure. Oh, and," he added as if it were something of an afterthought, "you may end up marrying E."

Really, I couldn't decide whether or not to take this man seriously. Staring at me intently while he stacked the cards back into the deck, the fortune-teller gave me the sort of look that makes you wonder if you're the last person to be let in on an inside joke.

"People who get extra time usually tip me generously," he said, tapping the face of his wristwatch and holding out his hand. I peeled off an extra five and left, walking home in the brisk chill of the late spring evening.

The next morning, I boarded a flight bound for Ulaanbaatar, Mongolia.

"Hey, where are you going?" a man's voice called out to me in an

American accent. On a layover in Tokyo's Narita Airport, I was as oblivious to someone talking to me as anyone is in an airport. Preoccupied with finding a cup of coffee, I ignored him, assuming he'd mistaken me for someone he knew.

"I said. *Where. Are. You. Going?*" the man repeated, this time standing right in front of me. He'd surprised me, and I didn't know what else to do but to answer him. Besides, he was blocking my path.

"Mongolia," I said. "I'm going to Mongolia." Even as I said it out loud, I could hardly believe it myself. *Mongolia?*

"Here," he said, offering me a piece of paper with a name and e-mail address written on it. "An American college friend of mine is working there right now. Tell him I said hello."

Dumbfounded because things like this *just don't happen*, and especially not in the anonymity of airports, I thanked him. What else could I do? Before I had a chance to come up with a reasonable response, like asking the man why he'd sought me out, he dashed off to catch his next flight.

"Good luck!" he called out as he ran. "Don't forget to e-mail Evan!"

Had he said *Evan*? With an 'E'? And American? And college friend?

Sure enough, on the slip of paper he'd given me was the e-mail address for a man named Evan. Fresh out of college, several years my junior, this man whose name began with an 'E' just happened to be living in Mongolia. Could this all just be a coincidence?

CHAPTER 4

The Arrival

It's impossible for the city to constantly administer to the needs of remote districts using domestic resources; that's why we try to involve foreign investment in this undertaking. For this purpose, we attempt to intensify our foreign relations and cooperation with organizations and persons in foreign countries who display sympathy of their soul for Mongolia.

—Interview with Ulaanbaatar mayor Mr. Batbayar, *MM Today* broadcast

The MIAT Mongolian Airlines plane thumped onto the runway of Genghis Khan International Airport, and we landed in a shroud of serene midnight darkness. Cupping my hands against the plane's window, I pressed my face up close as we taxied in, letting my eyes dart around to search for light that just wasn't there. Here, nightfall seemed to be absolute, and I'd have to wait a little longer to glean a first impression of my new home.

At Immigration, I waited in line for a very long time. It was two o'clock in the morning, and the plane had been delayed by twelve hours. Both its passengers and immigration officials yawned and wiped their eyes. Once it was my turn, I stepped up to the counter and handed over my passport. Waiting, I held my breath in anticipation. Grunting at me, the officer licked his forefinger and paged through my documents. Then, with a thud, he stamped me into Mongolia.

I stared at the Cyrillic inscription on my passport, the ink still wet, and I could hardly believe it. Finally, I was *here*. I'd actually done it; I'd left certainty behind to pursue a dream. Now, after all those years of asking, "What if?" I was about to discover the answer.

I collected my luggage and turned to scan the crowd for Urna, my local contact. Urna worked as a kind of ambassador for the British company that had arranged my internship with the Mongolian TV station. Responsible for everything from introducing me to my host family and explaining their customs, to showing me to my new job, she would be my first personal ally in the country.

But more important than anything else at just that moment, Urna was supposed to provide me with a ride. In a country without much of an official taxi fleet, it's important to know you're getting into town safely with someone who actually knows how to get you there. Especially when you're on your own—in the middle of the night.

An hour later, it was nearly three o'clock in the morning. The airport's crowd had thinned out, but Urna still hadn't arrived. Fearing she wouldn't come for me at all, I weighed my few options. Without any taxis or buses available so late at night, I could either hitch a ride with a local or sleep in the airport until morning.

"Urna?" I called out one last time into the quiet arrivals lounge. It had been two hours since my flight had landed, and I gave up imagining she was hiding behind a luggage rack, waiting to surprise me. As I rummaged through a sheaf of papers containing details of my host family's address, an old man approached. Dressed in a knit cap and soiled trousers knotted at the waist, he was grinning fiercely through a sparsely populated rack of teeth.

"I am Urna!" he declared with a giddy smile. "*Ger?*" he said, using the Mongolian word for "yurt." He wasn't Urna, but I was getting desperate. Obviously, the old man had been watching me, and surely he was only trying to help, but as a woman, you can never be too careful.

Before I'd left New York, I'd packed everything I thought I'd need in an emergency. So far, my emergency had been the delayed flight. And for that, I was well prepared: my teeth were freshly brushed; my face was scrubbed; I was wearing a clean pair of socks; and I was carrying a wad of cash, in bills both small and large. But no, I had not expected my ride not to show up, and no amount of toothpaste or dollar bills was going to get me safely into the capital at three o'clock in the pitch-black of a Mongolian morning.

And, I had only an address to rely on. Weeks earlier, the British company had provided me with the address of the host family with whom I'd spend my summer in Ulaanbaatar. I'd carefully tucked it into my knapsack, along with cash and toiletries. Of course, I'd never expected to actually need it, because they'd arranged for my transportation with Urna, their ambassador. In the end, though, it wouldn't have mattered because the address they'd sent me was the wrong one anyway. But I didn't know that yet.

Patiently, even graciously, the old man smiled a big, gummy grin at me. *"Ger?"* he asked again. So, I thought I'd give him a shot at helping me find my home. Surely I could try to pay him to take me there. Pointing at the address printed on my information packet, I shrugged and flashed him a shamelessly flirtatious damsel-in-distress grin.

"Bish," he said. "No." Pointing from me to himself and back again, he repeated, *"Ger."* Gers, commonly referred to outside Mongolia as yurts, are small portable homes. Built like a softer, rounder teepee, they have just a single room, which serves as the dining area as well as the bedroom. So, either I was jumping to conclusions, or this old man was asking me to spend the night with him. Generous as his offer was, I declined. After all, I had Evan to meet.

"Bish," I said, repeating back to him what he'd said to me. During my brief study of the Mongolian language, I'd learned what was proving so far to be one very useful word: no. As I backed away from the toothless old man, I eyed the women's bathroom, expecting to sleep there until daylight.

As if on cue, I dropped the folder containing my information packet, and its contents slid onto the floor beneath me. My arrival was going from momentous to comical. Just then, a small group of men rushed over and helped me collect the papers, examining each article carefully before returning it to me.

"Ger?" one of them asked, concentrating hard on one of my documents, reading it upside down.

Pointing at the same address I'd shown the first man, I made a big deal of pulling my shoulders up to my ears, miming a delayed flight, and acting the part of a missing Urna.

"My friend!" another one of the men suddenly cried out in English, peering over my shoulder, pointing at the address typed on the information packet. "Yes, it is my friend!" he declared with conviction.

"The man who lives at this address is your friend?" I asked. I was absolutely incredulous. In a capital city of about a million people, stuck in an airport at three o'clock in the morning, had I just happened to run into someone who personally knew my Mongolian host-father?

"Bish," he said, shaking his head. *"Ger?"* he asked, repeating his offer.

I gave up. Retreating from the men, I imagined how funny this would be—much later. Not only was I short a ride, but I was short any ride, and there wasn't a money changer in sight, even if I could find a taxi who knew where to take me. I had no Mongolian *tugrugs,* the local currency, and I had no place to go.

"Excuse me, miss?" a soft-spoken woman called out as she made her way toward me. "Do you need some help?"

Did I ever.

Smartly dressed in a crisp black business suit and high heels, Magvan, as she introduced herself, was the vice-chairwoman of the Mongolian Chamber of Commerce. She had coiffed hair, wore sensible rimless glasses, and had just the sort of matronly look that you're hoping for when you're in a real bind. Magvan peered at me over her spectacles and asked me to explain just what had happened.

"I've come from New York. My flight was delayed. And I got this internship here in Mongolia. And then—"

"Never mind. Where are you actually supposed to be?" she asked, cutting to the chase.

"Here," I said, pointing to the same address I'd shown the men earlier.

"Let's go," she said. "My husband and I will drive you."

Let's go? As in, You're taking me there? I thought, amazed by this woman's late-night generosity.

Eagerly, I accepted Magvan's offer to help, which wasn't so much an offer as it was an order. But either way, I was happy to oblige. In silence, she led me outside to her waiting car. Although it was June, it was cold, and I deeply inhaled my first impression of dust and car oil and a subtle fragrance that would take me a few weeks to identify as thyme.

Magvan opened the car door and began to vociferously address the man inside. Speaking like an auctioneer, she rattled off a long list of consonants, pausing only briefly to introduce me. "My husband," she said to me before resuming her dictating to the skinny, disheveled man sitting at the wheel. As we sped off over pockmarked roads, he finally interjected, returning fire with rounds of consonants. Both of them sounded as if they were speaking through semiautomatic machine–gun fire. It seemed pretty obvious to me that they were having an argument until Magvan explained that they weren't.

"The Mongolian language," she said when she turned around and saw the surprise on my face. "I know, it sounds like a quarrel, even when you're telling someone that you love them."

Through the stillness and into the night, we fell in a tired silence and drove in darkness so complete it was hard to believe that this capital city was not a sleepy countryside. At a gravel lot skirting a bare concrete building, we parked. Soviet-era architecture is imposing in the best of times, and this whitewashed structure didn't disappoint. Standing tall next to its dozen or so neighbors, it looked more utilitarian than home. Shivering in my shorts and T-shirt, I stepped out of the car into fresh frost and leftover snow. Even though it was already June and technically summer, it was wintry cold. Mongolia experiences some of the world's greatest temperature extremes, sometimes as much as sixty or seventy degrees in a single day, just enough to guarantee you'll leave behind a few vital wardrobe items when packing for just one summer.

"Fourth floor, third door," Magvan said, taking time to explain the numbering system for Mongolian addresses. Holding down a key on her phone, she used it as a flashlight, shining a weak light to illuminate a faint path inside the building.

Quietly, we climbed the crumbling staircase until we reached the fourth floor. At the third door on the landing, Magvan rapped loudly, as if it were anything but the middle of the night. Beside her, her husband offered me a mischievous smile, like he was used to his wife doing this sort of thing.

"What the hell do you want?" a middle-aged fat woman roared, poking her head just far enough outside the door to place her face an inch from Magvan's. Of course, I don't really know what the woman said, but at that hour it seemed a good guess that she wasn't offering us a cup of tea. After another heady exchange of thick consonants, the fat woman slammed the door in our faces. The good news was that she was not my host-mother.

"So, that is not your apartment," Magvan said with a measure of irony. "Shall we try the next?" Without any hesitation, she banged on *all* the doors on that landing, one by one. At the last door, a man with a bald paunch, dressed only in his underwear, looked completely bewildered. With steeply arched eyebrows and a tiny O-shaped mouth, he wore that surprised look that on some people seems permanent.

"Yes, this is the right apartment," Magvan translated what the man was saying, "but the family that lived here moved away a long time ago." By now, I'd realized that the address the British company had provided me was wrong.

At a loss and without a plan, it was about time to go to a hotel. It isn't often that you find yourself in a foreign country in the middle of the night, sneaking up crumbling stairwells and relying on complete strangers to help you locate your new home.

"It is time to take you to a hotel," Magvan said, as if she'd read my mind.

Magvan and her husband dropped me off at the Bayangol Hotel, in the heart of downtown Ulaanbaatar. After checking in, I rode a tiny, coffin-size wooden elevator to a lushly carpeted landing. Inserting my key into the lock, I pushed open a heavy wooden door to reveal a spacious room with a king-size bed, large TV, and generous bathtub. Too anxious to sleep, I switched on the tap and drew a hot bath, soaking in the steaming water until my fingertips and toes wrinkled into soft white creases.

I was already feeling a little homesick, wondering what Netta, Meghan, and my other friends were doing while I was traipsing around the Mongolian capital in a pair of shorts in the unseasonable June snow, searching in the dark for lodging for the night. I gave up thinking about what would happen the next morning, tucking myself into freshly laundered sheets, and fell fast asleep.

Just a few hours later, I woke to blazing sunshine, a golden yolk set against the backdrop of an eggshell-blue sky. Outside my window several floors below, children played tag in a dusty lot. I watched them for awhile and then unpacked my luggage, dressed, and headed downstairs to the hotel dining room for breakfast. I'd need a strong cup of coffee before making contact with Urna's boss at the British company. After all, at this point—without anyone to meet me at the airport, without an address where I'd be staying—I was beginning to wonder if I'd actually been taken for a ride.

The dining room was completely empty. Heavy white linen dressed several tables set for eight apiece, and a young Mongolian waitress offered me toast and a plate of scrambled eggs. It was just what I needed. Apparently, I was just what they needed too; the staff made sure to anticipate the needs of their only guest, refilling my coffee cup after each sip. Fully caffeinated, I returned to my room to make a few phone calls. Actually, I had only one telephone number, but I called it half a dozen times, leaving half a dozen messages, each one a little bit angrier than the last.

"Hi, this is Patricia Sexton—again," I said for the sixth and final time to the British company's answering machine. "As I said, I've just arrived from New York. I'm here in Ulaanbaatar, and I believe Urna, from your company, was due to pick me up. Well, she never showed, as I may have mentioned. I expect you'll be paying this hotel bill for me."

It was late on a Saturday morning, and no one was answering. So I gave up and bundled up, packed a daypack, and set out to explore Ulaanbaatar.

⟋

"Patricia?" a young voice called out from the hotel lobby, just as I was about to make my way outside.

"Urna?" I responded, squinting into the brightness at a young woman sitting on a sofa. "Is that you?"

She was thin, shy, and petite. With straight brown hair, brown eyes, and a fair complexion, she was pretty in an economical, nondescript sense. Nothing in particular about her stood out.

"Yes, I am Urna," the young woman said with a wan smile. "About last night," she offered, "I am sorry, but your airplane was many hours late. So I fell asleep. You will get your bags now. I will take you to your new home."

"Wait, you were *what?*" I asked.

"I was asleep," Urna said, as if I'd simply misheard her.

"Asleep?" I repeated.

"Yes," she said, actually managing to sound annoyed that I was recon-firming this detail.

"Do you know where I nearly spent the night? In a *toilet*," I spat. I didn't even bother to ask Urna how she'd managed to find me, although I suspected someone at the British company had checked their voice mail and she'd been dispatched.

"I hope you'll be paying for my hotel room," I said, and Urna just stared angrily back at me, as if a mere apology should make everything okay for leaving someone stranded in the middle of the night. I mean, this wasn't a case of accidentally oversleeping—Urna had actually chosen to turn off her alarm clock!

While I squared off with her, she said nothing, which was incredibly unsatisfying, so I stormed off to retrieve my bags from the hotel room. By the time I'd returned to the lobby, she had paid my hotel bill.

"Let's go," Urna said without looking at me. Walking outside into the cold wind and clear blue sky, we nestled ourselves between my luggage and drove to Sükhbaatar Square in the center of Ulaanbaatar. For de-cades, Sükhbaatar has witnessed some of Mongolia's most potent his-torical moments.

In 1921, under the military tutelage of a burly, handsome Mongolian general (who looked like a cross between Chow Yun Fat and Colin Firth), Mongolia stood up to China. Of course, it wasn't the first time this had hap-pened, and it wouldn't be the last. For a decade, ever since the Qing dynasty collapsed and Mongolia demanded independence from China in 1911, the Chinese had been hoping to reestablish sovereignty over Mongolia. They'd even signed a treaty granting autonomy to the Mongolians, but the condi-tions of the autonomy granted considerable power to the Chinese.

Really though, the Chinese and the Mongolians had been at odds for a long, long time. A millennium earlier, their rivalry had begun in one of those stories that you can't make up even if you try.

A thousand or so years ago, wary of his powerful adversary, the Chinese emperor invited the Mongolian chief to dinner at his palace to get on good terms with him. Hoping to get his cooperation on a few important issues, he plied him with fine food and drink. After awhile, the Mongolian chief became a little tipsy, so he did what any inebriated man would do. Clapping his hands, he lurched toward the emperor, grabbed his beard, and tickled his ear. Ironically, the emperor didn't seem too upset about this (afterward, he gave the Mongolian a flashy robe and a gold belt!), but the rest of the dinner guests were outraged, and they all happened to be high-ranking Chinese ministers who insisted that justice must be served to this barbaric dinner guest. By this time though, the Mongolian chief had already made his way home, so he had to be summoned back to the Chinese court. Of course, knowing the fate he faced, he refused to return, so the Chinese found him and poisoned him to death.

But that lesson wasn't quite clear enough, so the Chinese bided their time until they were able to capture one of the chief's nephews. Once they did, they nailed him to a wooden donkey and chopped him into tiny pieces—beginning with his fingers and toes—while he was still alive.

With a backdrop that spiteful, you can probably imagine that the Mongolians had harbored resentment toward their neighbors for some time. And so it was with a measure of this pent-up irritation that the dashing General Sükhbaatar teamed up with the Soviets, who didn't exactly have the Mongolians' best interests in mind. Together, they kicked out their common enemy. In return for the general's heroic leadership, the Mongolian government named the city's square after him. Better still, they built a statue in his honor, erecting it on a site considered to be auspicious because the general's horse may have urinated on the very same spot during a rally in the summer of 1921.

Now, still silent, Urna parked and led me to the square, as if she were paying homage to the general himself. The relentless brilliance of high noon sunlight reflected off the granite tiles, and I squinted into the distance at the rosewood-colored statue towering over the square. Next to it, a man stood on a makeshift stage and recited poetry to an audience of three, which included Urna, me, and himself.

"Let's love each other while we're alive," Urna translated. "It's about a father and a son," she added absent-mindedly, as if lost in a moment with only my presence dragging her back.

"What does that mean, though?" I pressed, musing aloud that maybe the poem was a riff on Genghis Khan's relationship with his father. It's impossible to overstate the reverence with which the Mongolians regard Genghis Khan, so I was hoping to invoke his name in order to curry favor with my new guide. It might have worked; although she didn't respond, she did buy me lunch.

"You are hungry," Urna pointed out. Her question sounded like a statement, but either way, she was right.

"*Buuz,*" she said to the waiter, who hadn't come to take our order so much as he'd come to get a number. As in, "How many *buuz* do you want to eat," instead of, "What'll you have?" At the most famous Mongolian fast-food restaurant in the country, which could have been named "Mong-Donald's" for its popularity, Urna and I were about to tuck into the nation's most popular snack. And at this particular restaurant, no one ever ordered anything but its namesake, *buuz.*

Greasy, hot, and savory, *buuz* are mutton dumplings. A little bigger than a Ping-Pong ball and about the same pale color, these pillows of chopped sheep meat are stuffed into miniature pillowcases of steamed dough, creating a pocket of salty succulence. *Buuz* are eaten year-round, but they're eaten with reckless abandon during the New Year, when matrons of the household make hundreds and hundreds of them.

It isn't immediately clear how to politely consume *buuz*, especially when you're the lone foreigner in a restaurant and at risk of making a spectacle of yourself in a lunchtime crowd. They're too big to eat whole, although I gave that method a try, and they're too hot and juicy to nibble. Eventually though, I hit my stride. Biting the *buuz* in half, decisively so, I tipped my head back and sucked the liquid out of the remaining half before it dribbled onto my plate. It was then that I noticed Urna looking off into the very important distance, as if I'd embarrassed her, but I wasn't about to quit while I was ahead.

When I finished, I peppered Urna with questions about my new home and my host family.

"So what's my host family like?" I broached.

"You will see," Urna responded.

"Have they hosted any other foreigners before?"

"Yes."

"Who?"

"Foreign people."

"What kind of foreign people?"

"People who are foreign."

"Interesting," I said, not meaning it, wondering how on earth it was my fault for having gotten off on such a bad foot with my very first acquaintance in Mongolia.

Urna said nothing, and we drove in silence to meet my host family. About a mile west of downtown Ulaanbaatar, we found ourselves in an expressionless neighborhood dotted with shops advertising in boxy Cyrillic letters. Soon, we turned left into a dusty lot alongside a stray dog, a series of nondescript apartment blocks, and a convenience store. Above us, stretching endlessly from horizon to horizon, the eggshell blue sky glimmered. Finally, we stopped and Urna got out of the car. I followed dutifully behind her.

"Hell-lo!" and then, "Well-come!" My host-mother seemed to be reciting, greeting me as she held open her front door. Plump and friendly, Batma had a warm way about her that could put anyone at ease. With a layered, bobbed haircut to match Jennifer Aniston's old *Friends* coif, Batma had a youthful, energetic look, as if she'd stopped aging when she was a little girl and had only grown bigger.

"I am sorry," she said, giggling, eyes creasing with her wide smile. "I do not speak English. Only little," she said, pinching her thumb and forefinger to illustrate just how little.

"Me neither," I said, pointing at myself and shrugging. "Well, Mongolian, of course," I added, trying to make a joke. Batma looked at me blankly for a minute, then laughed anyway.

While she served tea to Urna, I went back outside to collect my bags. The wind had picked up, and I stood still for a moment, taking in my surroundings. Sitting on a cement stoop in front of my host family's apartment building was a wrinkled old woman wrapped in a neatly pressed green-and-gold silk robe, her sagging bosom dangling down to her waist.

"Sain bain uu," I said to her. "Hello."

In return, the old woman tilted her head forward ever so slightly, offering me a vague nod, looking at a point just beyond me. The rich splendor of her evergreen-colored robe and gold sash clashed with the peeling paint of the apartment building's sea foam–colored exterior.

The woman turned out to be Batma's mother, and in just a few weeks I would spend a weekend with her in the Mongolian countryside, sharing a meal of boiled goat and fermented horse milk. For now, though, I regarded her with thinly veiled curiosity.

Crossing the gravel parking lot, I walked to Urna's car to gather my luggage. A couple of children sitting on a rusted swing set stopped what they were doing to watch me with interest.

Heaving under the weight of my backpack, I squeezed past the old woman and went back into the apartment building, climbing the four flights of stairs to my new home.

"Come, come!" Batma said, jumping out of her seat and beckoning me into the hallway. Built railroad-car style, like a series of small offices, my host family's apartment extended from a kitchen on one end to a child's bedroom on the other, a second bedroom and a sitting room in between.

"You," Batma said, pointing from me to the bedroom at the end of the hall. "You. Sleep. Here." Tugging on my sleeve and beaming enthusiastically, she led me to my new quarters. Spacious and decorated in varying shades of warm reds and bright blues, it was furnished with a narrow bed, a desk, and an old television. The bed was covered with a thick, furry throw rug, and the writing desk had been set up next to a window that looked out over a building construction site.

"Good?" Batma asked, surveying me carefully and suddenly looking worried. There was an innocent, generous quality to her, like an eager child you just can't bear to disappoint.

"Yes, good, very good," I said, smiling furiously to assure her.

"I will go now," Urna announced from the sitting room, bidding us an abrupt good-bye.

"You're leaving already?" I asked, wondering who was going to answer all the questions I had about how to live politely with my new family. So far, miming with Batma had been useful in being introduced to my bedroom, but I wasn't sure it would help me answer the more difficult questions, like where I should hang my lacy laundry to dry and what limitations I'd face flushing certain items down the toilet.

"Questions like what?" Urna said.

"Well, I have quite a few," I whispered, and Batma giggled again.

"Like *what?*" Urna said, scowling at me.

"Well, how do I get back into town, for starters?"

Slowly, she tore a tiny corner of paper from her notebook. Scribbling a note on it in Cyrillic letters, Urna pushed the piece of paper at me and left.

"Thanks," I called out, really meaning it, until I later realized that she'd played something of a practical joke on me.

"Hello," two quiet little voices said in shy unison, perfect replicas—a girl and a boy—of Batma. I'd later learn that Batma had another son, much older, who lived in America.

"My children!" Batma cried from the hallway. "They can speak very good English with you!" She sounded as excited about this as I was.

"Awesome!" I said with palpable relief, launching into a series of questions about household etiquette, like what I should eat and if I could share space in the refrigerator. The boy and the girl crouched down and sat in the doorway, politely smiling at me. Neither spoke, and it didn't look like they were going to do so anytime soon.

"So, about the fridge and the bathroom?" I said again slowly, obsessing over how I was going to share a single toilet with four other people. Because the Mongolian diet consists mainly of meat and dairy, I'd brought an entire bottle of fiber pills with me to remedy any shortcomings in my intake of roughage, and I'd already consumed three of the pills.

"We do not speak English," the daughter said. "Only little," she added, holding up two pinched fingers, just as her mother had done earlier.

"Patricia!" Batma said suddenly, as she leaned into my bedroom. *"Shul!"* She said it as if it were of grave importance. I unpacked my Mongolian-English translation dictionary and quickly thumbed through it until I'd found what *shul* meant.

"Soup?" I asked.

"Teem!" she nodded vigorously. "Yes!" Tugging on my sleeve, Batma led me into the kitchen, where, armed with my dictionary, I sat down at a small Formica table across from a man noisily slurping a bowl of dinner.

"Badaa," Batma said, introducing me to her husband. Hollow eyes in a cadaverous, bony face, Badaa looked up briefly to return my greeting.

Judging by the mutton soup he was relishing, Badaa liked his meat dishes. But he was emaciated and gaunt, and it would be a long time before Batma would reveal that he had a severe case of diabetes. After glancing briefly in my direction to return my greeting, Badaa grunted and left the kitchen to head for the sitting room, slurping from his soup bowl as he did so.

"Sit, sit," Batma offered, issuing another set of commands in Mongolian. Nodding, I did as I was told, and she ladled soup into a bowl and put it in front of me, watching my reaction expectantly. The broth was delicious. Thin and light, it was salty and savory, just like the juices that had squirted out of the *buuz* dumplings I'd eaten earlier that day with Urna. Made from stewed mutton, the flavor could have been a lot stronger and a lot more pungent. Most ovine dishes are. But because Mongolians tend to prize fatty, chewy gristle over leaner cuts of meat, which they regard as too soft, the country's soups have a delicately balanced flavor. Generous hunks of fat and thin slices of cabbage and carrot make for a kind of minestrone. Eagerly, I tucked into Batma's *shul*.

"More?" she asked, after checking the English pronunciation in my dictionary resting on the table.

"*Teem*, I said. "Yes," agreeing to just one more bowl. When she offered me a second refill, I pushed out my stomach to an exaggerated bloat and thanked her anyway. Besides, I didn't have time. It was time to meet Evan downtown. Earlier that day, we'd e-mailed each other and arranged to have a drink at a local bar.

"Me," I began. "Tonight. Airport. Friend—new friend! Bar. Ulaanbaatar. City. Meeting!" I finally finished minutes later, after looking up each word individually.

"*Bish, bish, bish,*" Batma said, either to my translation or my plans. "No, no, no." I couldn't think of a single reason why she would tell me that I shouldn't go, so I kept on trying to explain.

"I *have* to," I insisted, wondering how I was going to explain to her that, just weeks prior, back in New York, a fortune-teller had read my tarot cards and divined that I'd soon meet my future husband, whose name would begin with an 'E.' But now, bewildered by my hopeless attempts to pronounce the mangle of consonants in front of me, I tried to explain in as few English words as possible.

"Tonight, friend, bar," I said, waiting for Batma's blessing.

"Okay!" she finally declared in English, and walked off.

Weighing my options, I decided not to shower. It wasn't that I thought I didn't need to before my first night out on the town, and it wasn't even that I hadn't yet been given permission to use the bathroom or the shower. I'd just run into a situation requiring knowledge of protocol I didn't yet have.

In between my bedroom and the bathroom, which was all the way at the other end of the apartment, was the sitting room. That room now held my entire host family, and they seemed to be taking a special interest in everything I was doing. While I appreciated their attention, I had not brought a robe with me to Mongolia, which made showering, and then walking the length of the apartment to return to my bedroom, all but impossible unless I wanted to parade myself in front of my new audience.

Instead, I decided to brush my teeth twice and apply a lot of makeup.

"Good-bye?" I said hesitantly, armed with Urna's Cyrillic driving directions tucked into my pocket. Batma looked up from the TV program she'd begun watching with Badaa, shrugged, giggled, and returned to the program. Badaa grunted.

Outside, a rain of biblical proportions was coming down, and I hopped over yawning gravel puddles and into doorways, trying to remain as dry as my undersize and flimsy New York umbrella would allow. As I did so, I made mental notes of where I'd come from so I could find my way home again: Batma and Badaa's sea foam–colored apartment block, then the gravel lot next to the swing set, then the convenience store, and then the main road.

"Taxi!" I shouted into the roar of the downpour as I watched the only car on the road slow down to approach me, the driver poking his head out of its steamy window. He seemed to be debating whether or not to let me in. Most taxis in Ulaanbaatar are not actually taxis, but drivers of private cars who simply agree to take you to your destination for a fee. It's a guessing game whether you're in a taxi or a private car, but in the end it doesn't matter, as you usually end up at your destination and you always pay a fare.

"Please?" I begged, leaning into the open window. The driver reluctantly reached out to open the car door, and I quickly got in, dripping cold rain all over the front seat, although he didn't seem to mind.

Clutching Urna's soggy instructions as if they were a ticket to a sold-out concert, I pointed to the open road in front of us, urging the driver to begin our journey. Narrowing his eyes, he pointed from me to the road *behind* us. Both of us were bewildered, and it would take me awhile to realize that Urna had translated only the return portion of my ticket—the directions from downtown back to my apartment—but not the directions *to* my destination. Clearly, she'd had the last laugh with our morning altercation, but I'd have to deal with that later.

Now, I simply said, "Grand Khan Irish Pub," and we were finally on our way.

CHAPTER 5

The Unlit Spark

A lead consulting team of Mongolian and Japanese executives has undertaken a project to replace old and worn-out industrial steam-boilers. If the project goes as planned, by the year 2010, air pollution in Ulaanbaatar and surrounding areas is expected to decrease substantially.

—Lead story, *MM Today* broadcast

Apparently, nights out in this town began in just one place—at the Grand Khan Irish Pub. It was *the* place to see and be seen in Ulaanbaatar. Outside on a patio facing the main road, backpacking foreigners would sit at picnic tables and drink locally brewed Chinggis Khan beer. Inside, the mood was cozy and somewhat sophisticated, a modern Ian Schraeger version of a quaint Norman Rockwell setting. Against a backdrop of cherrywood paneling and dim lighting, local celebrities donned oversize faux Tom Ford sunglasses and sipped whiskey from heavy glass tumblers. Behind the bar, plasma TVs broadcasted the latest local news updates, reminding you in that jarring way that you were having a drink in a very foreign locale.

Sitting inside on a barstool was Evan. Dressed in a lime green polo shirt with an upturned collar and wearing pleated khakis, he had sandy brown, slightly receding hair. He wasn't exactly thin, but his frame was slight. Intellectual and bespectacled, he looked just like a twenty-something guy who was getting a second academic degree from a top American university, which I'd soon find out was exactly the case. In other words, it wasn't difficult to figure out who this mysterious Evan was.

"Evan?" I ventured coyly, pretending to be unsure that he was the right guy.

"Patricia?" he responded, looking up with a noticeable lack of enthusiasm.

"Hi," I said politely.

"Hi," he repeated politely. Apparently, we were off to a slow start. Neither of us seemed to be falling head over heels for each other.

"Let's get a table," he said as he gathered his belongings stashed beneath the barstool.

"Sure," I said, sneaking a glance at my watch.

It took a long time for the waiter to bring us two tall steins of very cold local beer, but it took him no time at all to deliver a plate of French fries so heavily salted it was as if the potatoes themselves had been an afterthought. By the time the beers finally arrived, I was so thirsty that I gulped down one lager and immediately ordered a second, as well as a round of water. The water never came, but another round of beers did, this time right away. It wasn't long before I was engrossed with Evan and his story.

Evan was twenty-six years old and from Texas. He'd graduated from Harvard University and had gone on to study law at Georgetown. But just after he was accepted at Georgetown, he'd had a crisis moment similar to mine. As Evan explained it, it was three o'clock in the morning and he said to himself, "What the fuck do I want to do? I've become an entitled nerd with soft hands! Is this all there is to life?" At the time, and in true nerd fashion, he was reading a double issue of the *Economist* cover to cover. In it, there was an article about Mongolia, and it was entitled "The—Best Place—Last."

Evan was sold. He deferred going to law school to enter the Peace Corps instead.

Applicants to the Peace Corps program are required to commit themselves to spending two years in a foreign country. They must also spend several weeks learning the local language once they arrive, and many of them stay with a local family. Although the Peace Corps makes the final decision, the applicant designates a region in which he'd like to live and work during those years. Evan was desperate to go to Mongolia. It was his dream. However, a technicality in the Peace Corp's application process forced him to apply to the Central Asia region, which did not include Mongolia. So he was sent to Turkmenistan, where he lived with a local family in a placed called Koneurgench and worked as an English teacher.

Two years later, after he'd completed his Peace Corps assignment, he was at Georgetown Law School and heard about a summer job clerking at a small private-practice law firm in Mongolia run by an American from New York. Finally, his dream had come true. Not long after, he found himself in Ulaanbaatar, and he'd arrived just a few weeks before I had.

Evan had moved from Turkmenistan to Mongolia, and he spoke fluent Turkmen as well as a little bit of Russian, both of which he'd picked up during his Peace Corps stint. He was certainly an intrepid adventurer, and I couldn't help but admire that. But still, our conversation was somewhat stilted, and it was getting late.

I sneaked another glance at my watch. "Oh, my God," I cried. "It's nearly midnight!" I flew into action, depositing my share of the bill onto our table, and bid Evan a hasty farewell. Although I had Urna's scribbled instructions to rely on, I still wasn't confident I'd actually make it home. The last two times I'd relied on her had not worked out so well.

"Coffee tomorrow?" Evan asked as we planted breezy kisses on each other's cheeks. "There's a French bakery called Michele's that serves a great cappuccino. Meet you there at ten?"

"Sure, I'll find it," I said as I dashed out the side door of the Grand Khan.

The cold, pelting rain had subsided, leaving in its wake enormous puddles. Tiptoeing around them in the pub's parking lot, I hailed a makeshift taxi, displaying again Urna's instructions to the driver.

It wasn't until after he'd begun driving that the driver made it clear he didn't know where he was going. Grimacing, he pulled over to the side of the road. Then, squinting one eye shut and then the other, he concentrated out loud, reading and rereading what Urna had written. Frowning deeply, he put the car back into gear and we drove off once again into the stillness of the night's empty streets.

A long time later, we circled back onto the road from which we'd just come. Maybe we'd done this several times before; it was hard to tell, but a few billboards had begun to repeat themselves. What should've taken five minutes had taken fifteen, and I was getting worried.

"Turn left at the shop in the fourth microdistrict," was all that Urna had written, which was something like telling someone in New York to meet you at a diner but not specifying which diner.

Finally, the driver pulled into a gravel lot and drove slowly past a rusty swing set, which looked just like the one I'd seen earlier that afternoon. As his headlights inched closer to the small apartment building on the edge of the lot, I made out its color. Sea foam green! I'd recognize that color anywhere!

Relieved that we'd finally managed to find our way, I gushed, thanking him, and tried to pay.

"*Naim,*" the driver insisted.

I wasn't sure what he meant, so I offered him what I'd been told the typical fare would be—1,000 *tugrug*—or about one US dollar.

Belligerently batting my hand away, he repeated, "*Naim,*" as he now poked his fingers into my wallet.

Obviously, the driver wanted more, but how much more I wasn't sure. His impatience was quickly turning to aggression, so I offered him double the fare in hopes of placating his fury. After all, he'd spent at least double the time trying to locate my destination. In fact, he'd probably spent three times as long as he should have spent to help me find my apartment. But at this point, he'd grabbed my arm and begun to twist. As a woman, I happen to have a stubborn policy of refusing to negotiate with men who use their physical strength to negotiate with me.

"*Naim, naim!*" he repeated, twisting ever harder.

Suddenly, I realized what he was demanding. During my long delay when flying into Ulaanbaatar, I'd made use of my time learning the basics of the Mongolian language. First, I'd taught myself to sound out Cyrillic script so that I could look up translations in my Mongolian-English dictionary. Then, I'd memorized how to say hello, good-bye, thank you—and numbers. From one to ten, I could count. Finally, I realized what the driver was saying; he was asking for "eight," or 8,000 *tugrug*, the equivalent of less than eight US dollars.

Now, eight dollars is nothing to get your knickers in a knot over, certainly not in a foreign country in an empty parking lot late at night with an angry man. But I was no longer just frightened; I was angry, angry that this man was using his physical strength to get what he wanted from me. And being angry usually results in the next move being reckless. So, I did what I probably shouldn't have done—I swore indignantly. Peeling off a second 1,000-*tugrug* note, I deposited 2,000 *tugrugs* on the dash in front of me and fumbled for the door handle. This took some effort; the driver's grasp was firm, and I was shaking. But at that moment, it felt like my life depended on it. So I gave it my all, finally breaking free of him, and ran off.

Shaking and frantic, I was terrified. Leaping over puddles, I fled his car toward the safety of my sea foam apartment building, not daring to look back. I felt just like I'd always felt in nightmares featuring me being chased, like I was running in a viscous slow motion. Just for a moment, I paused to listen for the driver's footsteps behind me. There was no sign of him. I didn't have a flashlight, and I wouldn't have used one if I did, so I had to count my steps in between each landing until I'd made it to the fourth landing, where my host family lived.

Once there, it was so pitch-black that I couldn't quite make out where their front door was. Blindly feeling around the perimeter of the hallway and the neighbors' doors, I managed to locate the right one and its keyhole. I was home!

Unlocking the door, I let myself in and locked it behind me. Once I did so, I bent over double, heaving and gulping for air. As I caught my breath, I leaned back against the door, sliding down it until I was resting on my haunches. Shimmering moonlight streamed into the hallway and sitting room. Quietly, I removed my shoes and placed them neatly next to Batma's.

"Patricia?" a sleepy voice called out gently. "Are you okay?"

"Yes, Batma," I whispered, still gasping. Gathering my thoughts and my breath, I decided that, from this point on, I'd have to be more careful. I'd made a rookie mistake and I'd acted foolishly. I couldn't let it happen again; this journey was far too important to me.

I tiptoed past the sitting room and the softly snoring outlines of Batma's husband and their children. They'd converted the entire room into a makeshift bedroom, and it was here that they'd sleep until I would depart at the end of that summer.

The next morning, I rose early to an empty apartment. Enjoying solitude and a hot shower, I dressed and made myself a cup of instant coffee. On a plate at the kitchen table, Batma had left a single fried egg for me next to a basket of Post-it–size slices of brown bread. As I tucked into my breakfast, I thought about Evan, pondering the evening before and the spark that hadn't lit.

CHAPTER 6

The Land of the Blue Sky

In addition to the construction projects, gers were distributed to twenty home-less families, greenhouses were built, and two Porter cars were donated to families who privately mine coal. During the summer months, the children of Nailakh are even able to attend Korean language classes, and participate in Korean cultural activities.

—Voiceover, *MM Today* broadcast

Mongolia is nicknamed the "Land of the Blue Sky" for one very good reason: the sky there is usually very, very blue. Mix cobalt with a pinch of tur-quoise, stretch out a wad of cotton until it's streaky and extend it over an endlessly vast horizon, and you have your Mongolian sky. The country is home to some of the highest atmospheric pressure in the world, which is the reason for its unusually sunny disposition.

Explained to me by a NASA ecologist, who also happens to be one of my little brothers, this pressure is due to the weight of the air above pushing down on it. Heavy, high-pressure systems tend to force air to sink. And in order for water to be released from air as rain, snow, dew, or even sweat on a beer mug, it has to cool. Short of a simple cold front, this would require the water-laden air to rise to an ear-popping altitude where the pressure is finally relieved.

Of course, in places like Mongolia, it can't do that with all that weight bearing down on it, so clouds and rain don't often form. During winter, this effect is even more pronounced because cold air is denser than warm air. That's why, on New Year's Eve in 1968 in neighboring Siberia, when the temperature dropped to an eye-popping minus fifty-eight Fahrenheit (minus fifty Celsius) and skies were crystal clear, scientists recorded the world's highest-ever reading of air pressure. That's also why the sun is forecast to shine in Mongolia for no less than two-thirds of the year. Basically, Mongolia's disposition is as sunny as a tropical island's, minus the beach and warm weather.

During spring and summer, the skies are just as dramatically blue, but navy—and ominous. In 2008, a violent snowstorm hit Mongolia. Hurricane winds whipped through at ninety miles per hour, destroying homes and killing dozens of people and an estimated quarter of a million animals. And that was at the end of May, when temperatures in most other places in the northern hemisphere are inching into summer!

I finished my breakfast and peeled back the curtains from the kitchen window to see heavy clouds hanging low in a leaden sky. Although it was early June, it was still cold, as if the seasons had simply stopped advancing back in February. Unfortunately, I'd packed only for spring and summer, so I bundled up in as many layers of T-shirts as I could find and set out to explore my new neighborhood. Into the blunt wind I walked, bent at an angle, burying my head in a pair of leggings I'd wrapped around my neck to use as a scarf. Picking my way through an alleyway, I navigated around last night's yawning pothole puddles until I came to the main road. At midmorning, it wasn't exactly early, but the streets were completely empty.

I crossed through the gravel lot, past the swing set, and headed for the same street where I'd caught a taxi the night before. Once I got my bearings, I headed east toward downtown Ulaanbaatar. On my way, shuttered shops promised Turkish kebabs, discount clothing, and something called *pivo*, which I'd later learn was the Mongolian word for beer. Few of the shops advertised their wares in English, and I retrieved my translation dictionary to look up everything from *pivo* to *makh*, or meat. So far, my first thorough glimpse of Mongolia by daylight suggested a capital city only recently free of Soviet Communism. Apartment buildings were monolithic and utilitarian; almost every sign was written in Cyrillic, and wide, crumbling concrete boulevards wrapped like fat ribbon around absolutely everything.

And then I saw it. Just ahead was Gandantegchenling, Mongolia's largest and most famous monastery—and surely its most resplendent. Sitting regally atop a low hill, Gandan Khiid, as it's commonly referred to, is what Mongolia used to be all about before the Russians came and insisted otherwise about their sense of identity.

Around the turn of the twentieth century, there were approximately nine hundred monasteries all over Mongolia, and tens of thousands of Buddhist monks—but not for long. Because Mongolian revolutionaries had teamed up with the Soviet Red Army to throw out the Chinese and the Russian tsarists, they'd made a pact with the devil, which wouldn't bode well for the country's faithful.

In 1938, in an effort to consolidate his power base, Stalin went on a rampage, making sure he eliminated his enemies, even if they were in distant Mongolia and especially if they were monks. So he bullied Mongolian officials into closing every monastery in the country, burning many of them to the ground for good measure.

And if that message wasn't clear enough, Stalin had most of the monks killed, jailed, or forced to join the army. Of course, because genocide is messy work, the monks were forced to dig their own graves and kneel in front of them before they were shot to death. Thus, when they died, they'd conveniently collapse into the graves they'd just dug. Few were spared, and by 1990 there were only 110 monks left in all of Mongolia. Incredibly, one monastery would be allowed to reopen and would even land itself a pretty snazzy paint job but only as a ruse.

In 1944, American President Roosevelt sent his vice president on an excursion to China and to what he referred to as "Soviet Asia." A grainy old video of his trip to Mongolia shows him smiling and shaking hands with officials and visiting with locals and their children, apparently oblivious to the genocide that had been taking place behind-the-scenes. It had been hidden so well that Vice President Wallace knew nothing about it.

Rushing to put on a dog and pony show that would cover their tracks of destroying most of the other monasteries in the country, the Mongolian prime minister ordered builders and artisans to reopen and refurbish just *one* monastery to show to the American vice president. At warp speed, they painted and polished Ulaanbaatar's Gandan Khiid, just in time for Wallace's visit to the monastery. Of course, around the same time, the United States and its allies were at war with Nazi Germany over the Holocaust. So it's incredible to think that the American vice president was on a friendly visit with a country in the middle of its *own* holocaust.

I made my way closer to Gandan Khiid. It was surrounded by the "*ger* districts," which couldn't provide a greater contrast to the monastery's glory. *Ger* districts in the capital are where some of Mongolia's poorest live. The *gers*, or yurts, much like rounder versions of tents, are set up in a haphazard fashion by families moving to the capital from the countryside, looking for a better life. There is no plumbing, other than a water pump, and few *gers* have electricity. In other words, they're makeshift tenements.

Gers don't have windows and feature just one door to help keep the elements out during extreme weather. As I walked through the district, I peered curiously into an open doorway. A young boy with roughly shorn hair and rosy cheeks peered back at me. He was neither smiling nor frowning, but he seemed just as curious about me as I was about him. I nodded at him as I passed and continued to make my way toward the monastery just ahead.

At the gate I paused, aware that I was about to set foot on hallowed ground. An old woman extended her knobby and wrinkled arthritic claw toward me, pushing a bag of birdseed into my hand. Slowly and silently, I passed beneath the ornate wooden entrance gate.

Once inside the main grounds, I could only stop and stare in breathless awe. At the edge of the cobblestone square, majestically overlooking the entire city, stood a cross between a temple and a palace. Carved into the whitewashed base of the building were tiny rectangular windows framed by intricately carved wooden awnings, neatly outlined in a deep blood red. Resting on top of the building's white base was a two-story wooden tower, painted and stained banana yellow, chocolate brown, and a wind-worn cherry red. Topping its mighty grandeur was a green-tarnished copper roof, pinched into ridges and tipped at its points with golden ornaments.

As I crouched down into a patch of shade, I made a point of noticing this moment, this *now*—so far from home, so far from what I'd known all my life.

Eyeing the palatial temple's main doorways, flanked on either side by Buddhist prayer wheels, I decided against entering the temple proper. Something told me to do so only when I'd had a special moment, when I'd earned it and could digest its history and its grandeur a little bit better. Lugging heavy camera equipment, a couple of tourists snapped a few photos and went inside. But I had a whole summer in Mongolia ahead of me, and it thrilled me to think that I'd be able to savor, at just the right moment, a visit to this storied old institution.

I'd end up waiting for that moment until the day I left Mongolia.

I stood to leave, and a flock of resident pigeons took flight, flapping away into the sky. Heading toward the eastern gate of the monastery, I threaded my way through another *ger* district on the monastery's edge, dotted with pint-size shops and tiny eateries. Just as I did so, I was mugged.

My would-be muggers, two teenage boys observing me with calculated scowls that easily betrayed their faux disinterest, approached me from either side. With military efficiency (although lacking military precision), one of them pulled a knife from a sheath while his friend held my bag steady. In a single swift motion, the boy wielding the blade poked its tip into the bottom of my knapsack to slice open its underside. Of course, all of this happened too quickly for me to react, or I would have—well, honestly—done nothing at all. Not with a knife staring me in the face!

Anyway, what was supposed to happen—eviscerated handbag spills its contents into muggers' palms, muggers take off with booty—didn't happen. And that was because I was wearing an old friend—a trusty, worn leather backpack that some manufacturer long ago had ingeniously fortified with rubber and kitted out with nylon. It was durable and wasn't about to end its long life at the point of a dull, rust-worn knife. In other words, the boys were going to have to do better if they wanted to relieve me of my wallet and everything else inside my bag. At this point though, I thought it would be best to run, full-tilt, toward Peace Avenue, where I'd been headed anyway. It seems the muggers had the same idea, and ran off in the opposite direction.

Peace Avenue is Ulaanbaatar's main street, the biggest and busiest thoroughfare in the entire country. Although Mongolia's capital is one of the most remote capital cities in the world, its main street certainly doesn't feel that way. Bustling with pizzerias, bars, Internet café, and one enormous department store, it's just as congested, cramped, and noisy as any other big city. There's no McDonald's or any other foreign fast-food chain, at least not yet, and rumor has it that there are no fences in the entire country. But there's plenty of commerce, traffic, smog, litter, and people.

Consulting my map, I located the French café where Evan and I had agreed to meet the night before. It was just before ten o'clock in the morning, and the city was slowly rousing itself from a deep slumber. Shopkeepers unlocked doors, produce sellers began to display their wares, and locals appeared here and there in the streets.

On the bite-sized porch of Michele's French Café and Bakery, Evan was sipping a cappuccino. I said hello and went inside to order a coffee, only to discover that real Parisian pastries were also on offer. This study in contrasts seemed entirely out of place with our surroundings, but I was only too happy to tuck into a buttery, flaky *pain au chocolat* while sipping a creamy latte.

"Best croissants and cappuccinos in the entire country, maybe even Central Asia," Evan said when I sat down. For just a moment, we regarded each other curiously, as if we both knew that something should've happened the night before but didn't.

Evan wanted to know why I'd come to Mongolia, so I told him all about my banking career and why I'd decided to leave it behind. If nothing else, I thought, we had our dreams in common. Together, we sat on the porch of this Mongolian Parisian café, two people bound by circumstances but maybe not destiny.

Now, not quite noon, the ominous sky had turned a shade of dusk, so I said good-bye to Evan to go shopping for a coat at Ulaanbaatar's most famous department store.

CHAPTER 7

"Frenemies"

Several projects are under way, or have already been completed. A children's library was built at a cost of twenty-seven million tugrugs, or twenty-three thousand dollars. Construction workers were hired to pave the road that would reach the library; these workers also dug a deep-ground well.

—Voiceover for lead story, *MM Today* broadcast

From skinny jeans to Dr. Zhivago-style fur hats that fold lengthwise like an envelope, Ulaanbaatar's State Department Store is the Bloomingdale's of Mongolia. Named *Ikh Delghuur*, or "really big shop," it sells an assortment of everything from Korean face creams to high heels, business suits, fur boots, and Genghis Khan knickknacks.

The *Ikh Delghuur* even offers an impressive array of knock-off North Face parkas, which was just the thing I was looking for. Like most good knock offs, these weren't immediately identifiable as such, and when I tried on a sky-blue parka, I was convinced I was wearing the real thing. Everything about it was authentic—the quality of the material, the colors, even the logo. And it fit like a glove. That is, until I tried to pull the hood over my head. It seemed to have been tailored for a head the size of a kitten's.

Since I'd already spent a weekend shivering in Ulaanbaatar, I made my purchase and, outside the *Ikh Delghuur*, cozy from the neck down in my new waterproof replica, I noticed an enormous sign tucked alongside the store that simply read "1921." I was curious, so I did some reading.

In 1911, China's last dynasty collapsed. For more than two centuries, the Qing dynasty had cleverly managed its relationship with its neighbors, the Mongolians. At first, the Chinese had needed the Mongolians because they were hoping to overthrow their own ruling Ming party, and there was no better enemy of their enemy whom they could befriend. In 1644, they succeeded, and the Chinese emperor hanged himself on a tree after a troop of peasants stormed the Forbidden City.

For the next two centuries, there was relative peace. Well, there were the Opium Wars, an outbreak of the bubonic plague, a few revolts, and some subjugation of neighboring lands, but still, there was some semblance of peace.

But by the twentieth century, things had changed. The powerful Qing dynasty had more important things to worry about than their fragile peace with the neighboring Mongols. Slowly collapsing under the crushing weight of a rapidly growing population, a shrinking food supply, slowing economic growth, and battle wounds from a recently fought civil war, it was the beginning of the end for them.

So in 1911, at the peak of the Qing dynasty's domestic struggles, the Mongolians saw their opportunity and took it. Determined to finally be free of foreign subjugation, the Mongolians demanded autonomy and were granted it—but only partially and not for long. Although the Chinese had signed a treaty with Mongolia agreeing to the terms of autonomy, the Russians were also involved, and crucially so.

In 1921, the same year that was displayed so prominently on the sign in front of the State Department Store, there was incredible turmoil in Mongolia. That winter, a Russian military commander stormed the capital and threw the Chinese out. This, of course, helped the Mongolians. But not all Mongolians wanted to team up with this particular Russian commander, who happened to be anti-Communist. Instead, by summer, their own General Sükhbaatar, who'd teamed up with the Soviet Red Army, threw pretty much everyone out. Having shrewdly sided with the Soviet Communists, Sükhbaatar had been determined to take back the future of Mongolia for Mongolians. It was no wonder there was a sign in honor of the year 1921, as well as the nearby town square that paid homage to General Sükhbaatar himself.

With a whole afternoon ahead of me before my first day at my new job, I decided to take in a museum. And then I'd go see about Urna, the woman who'd left me stranded at the airport earlier that weekend. It was just no good having an enemy, especially in a new country, so I vowed to right whatever was wrong.

Not far from the State Department Store and Sükhbaatar Square is the Zanabazar Museum of Fine Arts. The museum bears the namesake of Geghen Zanabazar, a descendant of Genghis Khan, who supported Manchu sovereignty over Mongolia back in the seventeenth century. Choosing the Chinese, he'd definitely bet on the right horse at the time and ended up being the first religious ruler of Mongolia under the Manchu government. And as it happens, the man was an amazing sculptor.

Painted a bright shade of turquoise, the museum is impossible to miss. In fact, during my entire summer in Mongolia, Zanabazar served as the "true north" point on my mental compass. If ever I was lost and in need of directions, that turquoise building always showed me the way.

Once inside, I paid 2,500 *tugrugs*, a little over two US dollars, and headed straight for the sculptures. I was one of the few visitors that morning, and my footsteps echoed in the hush. Behind a glass case sat a series of bronze Buddhas seated cross-legged on top of what looked like a platform of lotus leaves. Right hand resting palm up on the right knee, left raised in a sort of Zen-like peace sign, each Buddha wore an ornate and intricately sculpted crown. Gazing at a point just beyond, their serene faces and almond-shaped eyes looked to be deep in meditation. For a long time, I gazed in awe, and then I made my way upstairs to the *thangkas*.

Thangkas are Buddhist paintings. Presented on cloth or silk, they depict deities or scenes from religious or daily life and are often referred to as "scroll paintings" because they easily roll up into and are transported by monks as scrolls. What's fascinating about *thangkas* is that they manage to offer a peek into the window of a world completely foreign to someone from Ohio, who grew up knowing nothing about Buddhism. I took my time circling the displays of richly colored, utterly splendid *thangka* paintings. Their beauty wasn't the only reason why I took my time; I actually wasn't looking forward to what was next—going to see Urna.

Back outside the museum, I consulted my map and located the office of the British company where Urna worked. It wasn't far, and I made my way, trying to plan what I might say to her to make things right.

As I crossed through a small city park, two young Mongolian boys ran toward me, shouting, "Photo, photo!" in English. Panting and pointing at the puppy zigzagging away from them, they were scrambling to keep up. A shoebox-size terrier had been carefully spray-painted in racing stripes of green, white, and a faded orange—the colors of the Irish flag. His raspy bark sounded like a soda can being dragged across concrete, and I bent down to pet him, snapping a photo in the process.

"*Bayarlaa, bayarlaa,*" the boys called out as they ran off. "Thank you, thank you."

It didn't take me long to find Urna's office building, but it took awhile to find her actual office. There were no signs in the lobby and no security guard on duty. I climbed a few flights of stairs, knocked on a lot of unmarked doors, and, eventually, I found it and her. Sitting at a computer, she was smiling. And laughing. And twirling her hair. I barely recognized her, and I did a double take when I did.

"Urna?" I said.

"Oh, Patricia, hello!" she said sweetly.

"Hi, I just wanted to come by and talk. Do you have a minute?"

"For you, of course! But right now, I'm with someone else," she said, and began twirling her hair again. Out from behind another computer popped a blond head. Ruggedly handsome with bright blue eyes, he was unshaven and disheveled in that way that only young backpackers with goatees can be.

"Hi there," he said to me in a Southern drawl.

The backpacker, who didn't tell me his name, was from Alabama and was using Urna's office to facilitate a working trip to the Gobi, where he'd spend three weeks living with nomads. He seemed to be in his early twenties, about Urna's age.

"Patricia, would you like to check your e-mail?" Urna offered. "You can use my computer."

"Sure," I said, no longer feeling the pressing need to resolve my differences with her. After all, she was busy, and I hadn't exactly been looking forward to a shouting match.

Instead, I logged on to my e-mail and read a message from an acquaintance back in Manhattan. About my age, she'd married recently and was expecting her first baby. Really, though, that was all I knew about her, and I was surprised to have received any correspondence from her at all, until I read on.

First, she asked me how things were going for me in Mongolia. And then she confided in me that she was underwhelmed. That she wasn't sure she was taking part in a life that she'd ever wanted for herself. "What if I'd followed my own dreams when I'd had the chance?" she mused, wondering where she'd be now, instead of stuck where she was.

I couldn't help it—I felt so incredibly relieved I nearly turned around and kissed Urna. In a capital city in the middle of somewhere very far away, I'd at least temporarily extricated myself from the Match.com dating scene, ticking biological clocks, and duty-bound careers and relationships. For better or worse, sometimes all it takes to urge you on is reading about somebody else's regrets.

"Patricia?" Urna said, interrupting my glee. Her coquettish voice had been replaced with a nervous one. "My boss would like to see you in his office." Apropos of nothing at all, she added that his name was Oko and that his wife was pregnant, as if she were trying to quickly make idle conversation before I went inside to see him. It wasn't hard to guess that Oko wanted to see me about Urna.

I tapped on his office door and poked my head inside.

"Come in, come in!" Oko roared. "Have a seat!" Beckoning me to an empty chair across from him, I did as I was told. Behind a large wooden desk sat a fat, happy Buddha with earlobes so big and fleshy that they dangled like pendulums. Oko didn't just smile; he beamed.

"So, I know what happened the other night with Urna," Oko said immediately. "I listened to your messages. All of them." Grinning broadly, his rosy, cherubic cheeks pressed the creases of his eyes into long slanted commas. "I am sorry."

Oko assured me that this sort of thing had never happened before and would never happen again. He was affable and warm, and I liked him. So I forgave Urna and changed the subject.

"I heard your wife is pregnant?" I asked.

"Well, I suppose, perhaps," Oko said vaguely. His face darkened, and he appeared to regard my question suspiciously. Then, he seemed to make a decision. "Patricia," Oko began carefully, "in Mongolia, we do not discuss these things."

"What things? Babies?" I asked.

"Yes, things like that. Before those things are . . ."

"Born?" I guessed.

"Yes," Oko said, looking relieved that I'd said it and he hadn't. "It is— how do you say in English—taboo?"

"Oh dear, I'm sorry," I said.

"Don't worry. You didn't know," he reassured me.

I later learned that some families in parts of Mongolia wait until a child is old enough to ward off evil spirits (usually around the time it's able to walk), before he or she is given a name. In fact, the child will be referred to as "Not-here," "No-name," "Not-a-human-being," or even "Vicious Dog." This is a superstitious effort to discourage the spirits from kidnapping or killing newborns, especially in families that have previously lost a child.

Obviously, I hadn't known that, and I doubted even Urna was at fault for her belated attempt to make small talk with me. Oko and I shared a nervous laugh about the bad luck I'd nearly bestowed upon his unborn child. Fortunately, he had another son who was alive and well, and neither Oko nor his wife had exactly held back when they'd finally named their firstborn—after Genghis Khan.

"Oko, thank you for your time," I said, rising from my chair.

"And Patricia, best of luck to you tomorrow at the station."

Tomorrow would be the first day of my internship at Mongolia National Broadcaster. I thanked Oko again, left his office, and gathered my pack to head back home. It was only late afternoon, but I wanted an early night, and I had a long walk ahead of me.

"How is everything now, Patricia?" Urna said hesitantly as I turned toward the door. Her blond friend from Alabama was gone, and her concern seemed sincere.

"It was fine, Urna. Everything is fine." And it was. There's just no use having an enemy, especially when it's your opponent's boss who's doing the apologizing.

Outside, I headed toward Sükhbaatar Square. A few blocks from Urna's and her boss's office, the square was empty, save for a pair of artists sketching and painting the square's namesake, poised at their canvasses beneath the towering statue of the general astride his horse.

In 1990, nearly seventy years after General Sükhbaatar had teamed up with the Russians to eventually declare the Mongolia People's Republic, protests were held in the very same spot in Sükhbaatar Square, but this time to declare independence from pretty much everyone. Shrugging off decades, even centuries, of power struggles between their mighty neighbors, the Mongolians had finally, proudly, struck out on their own again, this time for good. The Communist Politburo government resigned and the Constitution was amended to allow for a multiparty system. In place of the old Communist Party, the Mongolians elected a new Communist Party, with no less than 85 percent of the vote. It wasn't the Communists they wanted out; it was domination that they were finished with.

As I strolled past the painters, crossing Sükhbaatar Square, I passed an unfinished statue of Genghis Khan, who looked just menacing enough to be an effective guard to the Parliament building entrance. I crossed the street and made my way toward Golomt Bank, the largest privately owned bank in the country, whose first one hundred deposit holders had been winners of the Mongolian lottery. With an ornate façade supported by columns and fashioned with balconied windows, its headquarters could have been mistaken for the headquarters of an old-fashioned European bank.

Turning back toward the congestion of strangled traffic on Peace Avenue, I made my way home to my host family's apartment.

"*Shul?*" Batma asked when I returned. "Soup?" There were guests in the sitting room, speaking English. They sounded American and like they were reading passages from the Bible.

I ate my soup slowly and accepted Batma's offer of a second bowl. The voices had begun to pray, and Batma left me alone in the kitchen so that she could join them. Between a rock and a hard place, I chose more soup, ladling myself another bowl of mutton *shul*. By the end of my third

helping, the guests were still praying and I could now hear Badaa partici-
pating. I wasn't sure what to do, but I knew I couldn't manage a fourth
bowl of soup. So I headed to my room, passing the visitors as I did so.

"Come sit," an older man said in English. Nondescript in that pleasant
way missionaries usually are, he managed to possess not a single memorable characteristic, other than his short shirtsleeves. But I accepted his
invitation and sat down, curious to learn what he had in mind.

"We are Mormons in this house," he said, even though his sleeves and
nametag had already given this away. Explaining that he was a missionary
from Utah and that he'd converted Batma and Badaa's family years ago to
Mormonism, the man offered me the book he was holding.

Mormons have been sending missionaries to Mongolia since 1992,
when they sent six couples to Ulaanbaatar to educate and proselytize.
Their timing couldn't have been better. The Russians had only recently
left, the economy was in the toilet, and religious freedom was making a
comeback. Within just a few years, those six couples had helped found
the first Mormon mission in the country, and just a few years after that,
they had enough members to dedicate a meetinghouse. As of 2011, there
were twenty-three congregations in the country, and nearly ten thousand
members. Of course, Mormons don't drink, and it suddenly occurred to
me that *that* was the reason Batma had tried to prevent me from going out
to a bar with Evan just a few nights earlier.

"Please, young lady, join us in prayer," the old American missionary
said.

Batma looked at me expectantly, as did Badaa, and with such an agree-
able grin that I almost did as I was told; it was the first time I'd seen him
smile at anyone at all. But I couldn't do it, not even to be polite. It's not
that I have anything against religious people or prayer—quite the contrary.
But I do have a bit of a bias toward religious people committing hos-
tile acts in the *name* of religion, such as fighting the Crusades, declaring
jihad, or firing my father all those years ago, leaving my family destitute.
Or showing up in a foreign country to inform the locals that their storied,
ancient concept of God has been dead wrong for so many centuries.

Besides, I felt as if I were on pretty good terms with the Man Upstairs.
After all, it was he who had spent years urging me to believe in myself

enough to embark on this adventure here in Mongolia. Silently asking his pardon for rejecting the missionary's efforts to win me over, I stood to leave.

"I'm sorry," I said lamely, retreating to my bedroom as I did so and clicking the door shut softly behind me.

A long time later, there was a tap at my door, and I winced. "Soup?" Batma asked through the door, offering me an olive branch the way an English grandmother would offer a cup of tea during a crisis. I opened the door and, as usual, Batma was beaming at me with a relentlessly cheerful disposition. Obviously, her adopted religion was working well for her, and I had to acknowledge respect for that. Thankfully though, the guests had left, and Batma led me back into the kitchen.

"Mar-gash?" she said. "Tomorrow? Tomorrow you work new job?"

"Yes, nervous!" I said, painstakingly translating each word one by one. "Tomorrow I begin work at Mongol Televit."

"Good, good," she said, clucking maternally and putting a bowl of mutton *shul* in front of me. It was the same soup she'd served earlier that week. Batma and her family never wasted anything and always made the most of leftovers, even after the leftovers had entered into a state of cellular degeneration.

"Good?" she asked in English.

"Amtai!" I responded in Mongolian. "Delicious!" And it was, sort of, although it had turned into a colorful mash.

"Bish, bish," she scolded. "No, no." *"Em-teh,"* she repeated back to me, slowly, correcting my pronunciation.

"Am-teh?"

"Bish. Em-TEH."

"Am-TEH?"

"Bish. Em-TEH."

"Em. Teh," I said one last time, remembering the last time I'd spent this long trying to properly pronounce a simple foreign word. Back then I was in Madrid at a Spanish appliance store, trying to ask the clerk where I could buy a "washing vagina" instead of the washing machine I'd come for. The salesclerks were doubled over, howling with laughter, and I left with neither item.

Bidding Batma good night, I retreated once again to my bedroom cocoon. Sleep was close at hand after a day of walking, followed by a heavy meal of four bowls of soup. Outside, a soft rain fell as I snuggled deeper into my blankets.

CHAPTER 8

The First Day of the Rest of My Life

A new bridge has been built at a cost of twenty-three million tugrug, or twenty thousand dollars, to replace the crumbling road in the third and fourth micro-regions of Nailakh. The bridge project had special significance, as it included not just construction workers, but local engineering specialists assisting with the design of the bridge.

—Lead story voiceover, *MM Today* broadcast

At dawn I woke with a start, exhausted from a night of restless, grind-your-teeth sleep. It was Monday morning, my first day on my new job, and I'd soon meet Urna, who would be the one to take me there.

Shutting my eyes tightly, I tried just for a moment to go back to sleep. But it was no use; I was full of anticipation. Today was the first day of the rest of my life. All these years I'd spent wondering what would happen *if* . . . was about to happen . . . *now*.

Tiptoeing out of my bedroom past Batma and Badaa, who were fast asleep on the living room floor, I crept into the kitchen. A few hours later and many hours late, Urna came to collect me to drive me to the station. Back in banking, we'd been told to be ready each morning to "bite the ass off a bear," and after three cups of coffee, I was ready for just that.

As we drove past a series of tiny shops with names like "Moscow" in bright, bold letters, outdoor beer cafés, *gers*, and Soviet apartment complexes painted in tropical pastels, I jotted down local landmarks, creating a second makeshift map for myself. When we passed Gandan Khiid and the grassy knoll that is its giant curb, I was finally able to recognize where I was and how to get from there to home and back. There's nothing quite like being able to connect the dots in new surroundings in a foreign land.

The oldest and largest broadcaster in the country, Mongolia National Broadcaster (MNB) is the biggest building in the district, towering over the tiny *gers* gathered at its base. Stretching nearly the length of a city block and with the administrative and clinical air of a hospital building, the station is planted on the flat top of a dusty hillside, its exterior the color of worn cardboard and its boxy windows patterned like a three-dimensional checkerboard.

Poking out from the roof and higher than anything else in the entire city, maybe even the entire country, its antenna spire is visible for miles around, something of a beacon reminding local residents just who is running the show when it comes to Mongolian news services. It has been around since long before the other half dozen or so private networks that sprouted up after Communism fell, and MNB has the implicit support of the government. Its patriarchal status affords its employees a certain kind of old-school respect around town. In fact, the station was responsible for live coverage of a February 1990 convention at which Mongolia's then-Communist government allowed the formation of the country's first opposition party. Just think, the second-oldest Communist regime in the world, which had been in power for nearly seven decades, was actually allowing *live* coverage of its own demise. If there's a better example of a smooth transition to democracy, I'd like to hear what it is.

"We are here," Urna announced matter-of-factly as she parked. She said this as if she drove a Wall Street banker to her new TV job every day. But I was damp with perspiration, facing one of the greatest life changes I'd ever undertaken.

"Thank you," I said to Urna, and she shrugged.

"*Sain bain uu,*" Urna said, "Hello," greeting the security guard seated behind a moon-shaped desk.

"*Sain, sain,*" he responded slowly and deliberately, as if he had to think about whether or not he'd go to the trouble of heaving himself out of his chair. With the broad, neatly lined face of a turtle and operating at a pace to match, the guard nodded idly and politely and remained seated.

"*Sain, sain,*" he repeated, eyeing me curiously.

"*Sain bain uu,*" I returned, wondering just how long it was going to take us to get past both the greeting stage and this dusty old man.

Turning his attention to Urna, he began to shout at her. Of course, I'd learned my first night in Mongolia to expand my definition of shouting, and so while they discussed my passage, I had a look around. The lobby was dark, shrouded in a permanent dusk. On the far wall was a set of old television screens featuring whatever was airing in Mongolia at that moment. The programs seemed to be heavy on soap operas. Behind the security gate was a wide staircase that I would soon find out led to the cafeteria. In between the televisions and the staircase was a dark and narrow corridor with low ceilings, which wound a circuitous route through the belly of the station.

Suddenly, Urna turned her attention to me. "Passport photographs?"

Uh-oh.

"I don't have any with me," I said, hoping I wouldn't have to wait until tomorrow to do this whole first-day thing again. "But I have my passport," I said hopefully.

Urna turned back to the guard and began actually barking at him, consonants tumbling from her mouth. Pretty and bossy, she appeared as if she were used to getting her way. And that's exactly what happened. She pleaded my case with such vehemence that the guard opened the latch on the gate and let us in.

I followed her down the long corridor. A single lightbulb dangled from the ceiling, giving the hallway a sort of Hollywood-thriller illumination. Several flights of stairs later, I was standing in my new boss's office.

"Patricia, Gandima is now your boss," Urna said, introducing us in very few syllables before she left. And just like that, my first day began.

Gandima, the director of the English news and of the *MM Today* English broadcast, was a seasoned journalist and her office showed it. Bursting with papers, magazines, books, and used cups, her desk and shelves looked as if they'd spent time in a blender. Trim and tall with sparkling, cheery eyes, Gandima wore a neatly pressed, conservative business suit and sported a carefully coiffed hairdo that was at odds with her cluttered office.

"Pleasure to meet you," she said, smiling warmly, sticking out her hand. "Our English broadcast is very important to us," Gandima began gravely, and proceeded to explain to me just how important.

In 1990, when Mongolia transitioned from socialism to a market economy, most of the local society's elite spoke only Russian as a foreign language. After a rather tumultuous past with the Russians, the Mongolian government set about changing this. In 2004, under the direction of a new prime minister, English was introduced as an official second language. The only trouble was, nobody really spoke it. Of course, the government had to do something about this if they wanted their decree to have any teeth. Luckily, the British embassy had already been helping MNB set up a news program broadcast entirely in English. With Parliament's support, it made air and the broadcast became a sort of surrogate English teacher for locals both in the capital and in the hinterlands. Of course, Gandima didn't tell me all of this right away, but she did spend the entire summer explaining the importance of these facts and thus filling in the blanks with the station's history. It was the reason she had a job and I had an internship.

"And then there are the tourists," Gandima added, explaining that MNB's secondary goal was to tap the growing market of foreign tourists visiting Mongolia. Fascinated that a national news broadcast took into account its foreign guests, I nodded, now very eager to begin doing whatever it was I was going to be doing.

"So, now you will meet *my* boss," Gandima said carefully after she'd finished her introduction. The director of the entire network, a woman named Enkhtuya, was the only person with the authority to give me a real shot at the station. Gandima could support me, but, ultimately, Enkhtuya called the shots.

Short and stout with broad, rounded shoulders, Enkhtuya was built like a British bulldog and leaned forward like one too. Her body tilted toward me, and resting on her knuckles at an angle on her impeccable desk, she welcomed me into her office and to my internship at her station.

"How do you do?" Enkhtuya asked, smiling heartily. She spoke in the throaty, husky voice of a longtime smoker and beckoned me to sit. Her office was very tidy and very dark. A shamrock-green table lamp glowed softly, the kind of fixture you'd expect to see in a library or cigar bar. Casting shadows on the neatly arranged contents of her desk, it created the hushed effect of a dimly lit movie theater.

"Patricia, do tell me about your previous work experience," Enkhtuya commanded, launching right into an interview I hadn't exactly expected. Although I'd been hired sight-unseen as an intern, Gandima and Enkhtuya still needed to place me in a suitable role.

"My experience in banking?" I asked hopefully.

"No, your experience at CBS."

"Yes, I interned at CBS," I said. "A few months ago, briefly," I added, murmuring that last word very softly. I wasn't sure how much experience they wanted me to have had already, and I knew enough to neither overstate my abilities nor understate them. The only thing worse than starting a new job for which you're overqualified is starting a new job for which you're woefully underprepared.

"Wonderful," Enkhtuya said. "We've partnered with CBS in the past."

Months earlier, I'd been put in touch with Magee Hickey, then a veteran reporter for New York's local WCBS. Taking me under her wing, Magee had invited me to join her for a few of her predawn reporting gigs that were being broadcast live. While she covered breaking news on camera, I watched and took instruction. Before I left for Mongolia, Magee was giving me one shot to learn what I should've spent several years in journalism school learning.

"Have you brought your show reel?"

No, I hadn't. I did have one; I just hadn't brought it. Although Magee had helped me create a show reel, it was the kind of reel I was pretty sure I shouldn't be showing. I'd spent a lot of time looking like a deer caught in headlights, reciting copy I'd written for myself for stories that Magee was about to report. And just once, at the scene of a smoldering blaze on Manhattan's Upper West Side, Magee had put the microphone in my hand and told me to ask the fire chief one pertinent question.

"Sir, were there any casualties?" I'd asked. On live TV, with the camera pointed straight at my hand holding the mike, I'd had my first brush with my dream. But it had only been that once.

"Never mind," Enkhtuya said when I admitted I hadn't brought my show reel. "You can correct spelling errors in the news scripts."

Now, this wasn't at all what I'd had in mind, but I wasn't about to tell Enkhtuya and Gandima that.

"Bayarlaa," I said. "Thank you." I was grateful for any opportunity to get my foot in the door. I was nothing if not determined to do this, and if it took me all day and night to be given a shot at reporting by correcting spelling errors in news copy, that's just what I'd do. Enkhtuya turned back to her work, effectively ending our meeting, and Gandima rose from her seat next to mine.

"Let's go meet Tobie."

Down the hall, we filed into a small office looking out over the station's parking lot. A brass plaque on the door read "MM Today English News."

Lanky and blond with bright blue eyes and gangling, bony features, Tobie had a mop of tight curls that barely shifted when he cocked his head to say hello. Eighteen years old and from London, he'd come to Mongolia for just the same reason I had—to intern for the television station. I'd soon find out that Tobie was extraordinarily gifted at all things technical. From editing video to speaking French and even writing computer code, he was just the kind of ally you want in your corner. But he was polite and shy, and I'd have to figure out later what to make of him.

"Yeah, hey," Tobie said gently with a posh British accent, sticking out his hand to meet mine. He smiled a distracted smile and went straight back to work.

"Tobie, from now on, Patricia will be taking over the spell-check," Gandima said after introducing us, adding that he ought to spend his time focusing on producing content. Now, this was quite a promotion for an eighteen-year-old intern. It would have been quite a promotion for anyone, but Tobie took it in stride. Barely looking up from whatever he was editing, his muted reaction suggested he was used to this sort of thing happening to him.

"So, how long have you been in Mongolia?" I asked Tobie after Gandima left.

"A week," he murmured.

A week? And he was already producing? My mind raced with

possibilities. If a teenage intern had been capable of pulling off the role of producer in a single week, wouldn't I have a shot at reporting?

"Where should I sit?" I asked.

"Dunno, really," he said. "Maybe at the other desk, but the computer doesn't work."

I sat down at the only other desk anyway, taking my time unpacking the contents of my backpack and slowly arranging the items on the desk. There were two desks in the room, three chairs, one computer, and no telephone. I'd brought nothing more than a pen and a notebook, so it didn't take me long to arrange everything. Eyeing Tobie's fleet of electronics, which included his own broadcast-quality Sony DV Camcorder and compatible MacBook Pro, I wished I'd at least brought a cell phone.

"So, what are you working on?" I asked him.

"Roaring Hooves," he said.

"What's that?"

"A music festival in the countryside." Clearly distracted, he didn't expand further.

An international music festival and music academy, Roaring Hooves is Mongolia's Woodstock, if Woodstock had offered classes. Musicians and scholars travel from all over the world to spend a couple of weeks doing what they do best but in a very unusual setting. Although the festival opens and closes in Ulaanbaatar in typical stately philharmonic fashion, most of the events are held in the countryside beneath the expansive blue sky. It's just the kind of event you'd never think of yourself—Mongolian fiddlers playing alongside Azerbaijani vocalists smack in the middle of the enormous Gobi Desert, attended by a crowd of nomads and their tethered horses.

But Tobie hadn't just attended Roaring Hooves. He'd actually been invited by Gandima to produce a story for the station on the event. With a photojournalist friend, he'd filmed and now was editing the piece.

"So are you in school? Or are you working? Or . . . ?" I asked. I needed a hint as to how he'd made such a good impression on Gandima, other than by the impressive fleet of electronics by his side.

"I'm starting university in the fall," Tobie said. "But I've worked for the Children's BBC. I was commissioned to produce two short pieces for them on remote foreign cultures. What about you?" he asked, pronouncing "what" like "wot" and drawing out "you" for several seconds.

"I interned for a little bit for CBS," I said, and suddenly I had his attention.

"What did you do there?"

"Mainly on-camera stuff," I said, even though the truth was a lie so white it could have been an advertisement for bleach.

"Wow, wicked!" Tobie said with sincere appreciation. "How long were you there?"

"Not *too* long," I said carefully.

"You're in my seat," a voice said from behind me. I turned around to see a handsome man with a round face and narrow eyes, the kind of face that looks like it might have a sense of humor hidden away. Unfortunately, the face wasn't smiling.

"Hi, I'm Patricia," I said, introducing myself. "I'm the new intern."

"I'm Chinzo, the anchor," he said. "And you're still in my seat." He stared at me wordlessly until I'd removed myself. Retreating to an extra chair leaning against the wall, I began shuffling and reshuffling scripts, neatly arranging them in and out of order.

"Hey, Tobie, why don't I get started on these script translations for tonight's news?" I suggested.

"I already did them."

Well, it was shaping up to be a long day. Tilting my head back against the wall, I wondered how I would make anything of all this, without much work experience or even a MacBook Pro.

Years before I'd ever contemplated leaving my banking job, I met a woman on a plane. A decade or so my senior, she'd left her banking job at Morgan Stanley to pursue her dream of becoming a photographer. While she told me her story, I scoffed, but wistfully. "What if it hadn't worked out for you?" I'd asked her. "What if you'd lost everything?"

Turning the tables on my own questions, she asked me, "What is it *you're* most afraid of?"

"Flipping burgers and cutting coupons," I'd responded. Terrified of leading the kind of life my parents had been forced to lead years earlier, I'd made financial security my top priority. But the funny thing about that sort of security is that it gets to be so secure it ends up imprisoning you. In other words, the things you own begin to own you.

"Then get a job at McDonald's," the ex-banker/photographer told me. I should embrace my fears, she said, encouraging me to realize that the things you fear are sometimes far worse than fear itself.

Many years later, with the best of intentions, I excitedly relayed my plans to my mother when I told her why I was leaving my paying job for an unpaid internship in a place as distant as Mongolia. She paused just long enough to let me know I wasn't going to like what I was about to hear.

"But what about your apartment and your mortgage?" she asked, stoking the flames beneath the steadily simmering worries that I'd spent years trying to cool.

Worse, my father's reaction had been one of abject disbelief.

"Mon-go-li-a?" he'd said, stretching out the word into four separate ones. "Why the *hell* are you going *there?*"

"What's wrong with your life in New York?" he wanted to know.

"Dad, I have a dream," I'd countered, wondering for the first time if I really believed what I was telling everyone else. Of course I knew that my dad, of all people, would eventually understand all this on a very cellular level. After all, it was he who'd skipped Christmas 1971 to hitchhike alone to Central America. And that was in the days before it was a good idea to hitchhike alone in Central America.

"O-*kay*," he'd finally said, emphasizing the word as if he were talking to me, the little girl, in what seemed to be half alarm at my reaction, half disbelief that I could do anything so foolish as to abandon all that I'd created for myself.

Now, as I sat across from Tobie and Chinzo in our tiny office, I made two decisions. One, I'd make the most of this. I'd have to. If it took correcting grammatical errors in scripts as if my entire life were staked on punctuation, then so be it. And two, it was time to have a look around the station to see what my work life was going to be all about.

Across the hall was the editing room, which Gandima had pointed out to me during her brief tour of the building. The door was heavy and wooden and shut tightly, so I knocked. No one answered, so I tried again.

"Hello?" I said, rapping a little louder. There was no answer, so I turned the doorknob and peered inside. Four faces looked up, all women.

"Hi," I said. "I'm Patricia, Gandima's intern."

None of the women said anything, so I went on. "Gandima said the computer in this room works? Can I . . . ," I began, trailing off. One of the women pointed to the computer and returned to whatever she was working on. I pulled up a chair and began to surf a few news Web sites. Occasionally, I'd glance out of the corner of my eye to see if anyone was watching and perhaps noticing just how interested I was in current affairs.

At most of the television networks I've visited, editing rooms are divided into little dens. A producer and correspondent work with an editor to cut a piece down to size. Each den is equipped with a lot of electronics: a miniature TV for playback, audio equipment, a microphone for voiceovers, and so on. At MNB, there was only one editing room, and it was big, the size of several dens, or maybe a school classroom. All four of the station's editors seemed to work together on almost everything. This wasn't immediately clear, but over the course of the summer, I'd watch them confer with each other over pretty much every piece, even when it came to the English news reports. And Gandima would always help out, especially when it came to the English news. Although it seemed unusual for someone as senior as she to discuss the particulars of a translation, or even to come into the editing room at all, she always participated, often staying late at night to do so.

The door to the editing room opened and a beautiful, heavily made up woman entered. I recognized her as one of the Mongolian-language anchors. Earlier that day, on one of the TV screens in the lobby, I'd watched her report. There was a lot of discussion among the editors and the anchor, and they were all looking at me. I had no idea what they were saying.

"I need to use this computer . . . now," the anchor finally said to me in English.

"Of course," I said, gathering my belongings and thanking the women before I left. No one said anything, so I shut the door behind me and headed down the hall, to the newsroom.

There is nowhere more exciting than a newsroom. Breaking news, the very latest in what's happening around the world, steadily filters in over the wires. When a story is big, reporters and producers will shout back and forth, trying to figure out the pulse of just what is going on and who will be sent to cover it. And beside all this, often on a large dais and always surrounded by lights, cameras, and action, is the anchor seat.

When Scott Pelley reports live from CBS's broadcast center in New York, he's sitting right beside all that action. If news breaks in the middle of the broadcast, he's right there in the thick of it to decipher what's going on and report on it.

However, things were very different in the newsroom at MNB. For one thing, it was silent. Usually a silent newsroom means a broadcast is being taped or is even live. But the anchor seat at Mongolia TV was on a completely separate floor, in a studio in the basement. The silence seemed to be due to people working diligently, but it had all the effect of being in a congressional library rather than in a bustling television station.

I poked my head in long enough to know I'd make a major disturbance by even trying to find myself a seat, and poked my head straight back out. During that entire summer, Tobie and I would get a chance to work in the newsroom just once, when we needed to use a working telephone.

I checked my watch and realized that it was a respectable time to leave for the day, so I began to head home. Outside, it was oppressive and moody. Although it was only dusk, the heavy-lidded sky forecast an early nightfall.

Walking alone in Ulaanbaatar at night is not exactly discouraged, but it's certainly not encouraged. The city is not the sort of place where you go for an evening stroll; it's the sort of place where you walk with purpose to arrive at your destination. Whether this was a cultural nuance or not, I never quite understood. Fact is, I never saw anyone, ever, *meandering* in this capital city.

Ignoring a persistent gut feeling that I shouldn't be doing what even the locals weren't, I cut through back roads and side streets, passing the Gandan Khiid monastery to get to the Soviet microdistrict where I lived. After awhile, and without any trouble, I arrived home, pleased with myself in that way you are when you manage to find your way in a new neighborhood. I still hadn't bought a flashlight, and by this point it was growing dark, so I felt around the stairwell's landing and counted each step as I climbed in the pitch-black. While I fished for my keys, Batma opened the front door a crack, peering out from behind the chain lock.

"Patricia?" she asked. Her voice sounded hesitant and unusually timid as she whispered into the dark.

"Yes, Batma, it's me," I said. "Is something wrong?"

Shutting the door, she unchained the lock and opened it up again to let me inside. And when she did, I realized she'd been hurt. Badly. Blood had dripped from her chin to her earlobe and was drying on her neck and blouse.

"Mongol book," Batma said, pressing her palms together, like she was opening and shutting an imaginary tome. Smiling at me nervously, as if to reassure me that, really, everything was fine, she giggled sheepishly. I took the translation dictionary out of my bag and gave it to her. Flipping through the Cyrillic section that translates to English, she sounded out one word at a time.

"Men."

"Four." She held up four fingers.

"Rob."

"Wound."

With that, she drew her fingers across her neck in an off-with-his-head cutting motion.

"Jewelry, *bish*," she said finally, showing me where her necklace and earrings had been.

Apparently, four men armed with knives had mugged Batma in our stairwell. They'd stolen her jewelry, and from the looks of the dried blood crusted on her neck, they'd tried to slit her throat as a parting gift. Batma would later explain to me that because she'd turned her head trying to break free, they'd missed her throat and instead had "only" cut off a sliver of her chin.

"Police?" I asked.

"*Bish, bish,*" she said, dismissively batting her hand at me as if I were crazy to have even asked.

"You are okay?" I felt impotent asking her this, but I didn't really know what else to say.

Pointing at me, Batma ignored my question. "You," she said, switching between Mongolian and halting English. "Those men were waiting for you."

Now, wait a minute. What on earth had I done wrong? Yet, I knew *exactly* what I'd done wrong. Some of it was naïveté; some of it was circumstantial. For one thing, ever since I'd arrived in Mongolia and plopped myself down in this working-class neighborhood, I'd been grinning at my new neighbors as if I had some sort of affliction. Nodding my head, greeting them in my feeble attempts at their own language, I'd allowed myself to arrive at the comfortable conclusion that I *belonged* here, that an affable grin was all it would take to undo the disparity in our situations.

And that was the other thing. Although the disparity was neither my fault nor necessarily my responsibility, it *was* the common ground my neighbors and I were forced to share. And in the end, really, wasn't this just a game for me? Couldn't I go back to New York, to Wall Street, to a life of preposterous excess? Of course I could. Would my neighbors know this or even care? No, but they'd *notice* the disparity in our circumstances. And it takes only one person noticing to grow resentful enough to, say, commit a robbery.

Later that evening, Badaa returned home from work. Expecting to see shock and concern, I was disappointed. With one look at the bloodied bandage on his wife's neck, he merely grunted. Whether he was expressing disapproval or stoicism, I couldn't tell, and I wondered what they said privately to each other, this bubbly, charming woman and her dour, quiet man.

Retiring early, I shut my bedroom door behind me and leaned out the window, peering at the ground just a few floors below, wondering if intruders could scale the wall to break into our apartment. Cooking up unpleasant and improbable scenarios, I shut the window tight to the sudden summer heat wave outside, locking myself in the sauna I created. I lay down on top of the soft rug blanket Batma had given me and tried to fall asleep. Sweating all night, I slept only fitfully.

Just before sunrise, I woke to banging and hammering coming from the construction site next door. In the dim light of very early morning, I lay completely still, not wanting to disturb the muffled peace of the day's first sounds outside my locked window.

You can either stay, or you can go, I thought, reminded of the advice my best friend, Meghan, had delivered just months ago, before I'd quit my banking job. Ironically, the last time we'd had this conversation, it was the going that was supposed to lead to endless possibilities. This time, it was the staying.

And with that, I decided to stay. Sometimes the best way to make an important decision is not to make it at all. Besides, it was either that or leave Mongolia to return to a banking job where I'd spend the rest of my life with my tail between my legs.

So I got dressed and paid a visit to the tiny supermarket sandwiched between the neighboring cement apartment blocks. If staying was going to be what I'd do, there was no better place to start than with breakfast.

Later that afternoon, at an Internet café, I checked my e-mail. There I found a message from CNN's Christiane Amanpour, the woman who'd been so instrumental in inspiring me to pursue my dream. In the e-mail, she wished me well and told me I had the motivation it would take to follow this path. And that was all it took to make me forget about leaving.

CHAPTER 9

Butchering Goats and Vowels

Our aid project has been working with the people of Nailakh since 2004. We found that the most immediate need for the district was creating temporary employment. During this fiscal period, a total of one-hundred-fifty-thousand dollars has been donated to the cause.

—Interview clip, *MM Today* broadcast

During the winter months, it can be very difficult to get fresh fruits and vegetables in Mongolia. A quick glance at the CIA World Factbook reveals that most countries in the world that experience four seasons (instead of countries in the tropics with just rainy and dry seasons) have about a fifth of their land available for decent farming. A third of both France and Germany is fit for farming, about of a fifth of the United States, and even a tenth in mountainous Japan. By comparison, less than one percent of land in Mongolia is suitable for raising crops, which can be a big concern for a country whose livelihood depends on its pastures having good fodder for the cattle to eat.

To add insult to injury, those who do work the pastures, called "the steppe," must endure some of the harshest weather conditions on earth. Sometime between 1999 and 2009, Mongolia experienced a few winters that were so long and so cold that many herders lost their *entire* herd of livestock due to starvation; six million died in the winter of 2009 alone.

It didn't help that just a decade earlier, when the Soviet Union had gone, they'd taken their aid money with them.

This was a real problem; they'd contributed as much as a *third* to the Mongolian GDP. Basically, Mongolia was weaned almost overnight; aggressive economic reforms taken on by the fledgling democracy caused a serious recession. By the time the current century had rolled around, they weren't in good enough shape to be weathering another catastrophe. Over the years, Mongolians learned to rely on themselves and on what they could produce at home in the steppe. Which is to say, they tend to eat a lot of meat, at least from what I was seeing in the capital.

I crossed the lot adjacent to my host family's apartment building and made for the local grocery store. Inside, I discovered an arrangement not unlike any other grocery store I've ever been to. There were rice and grains and produce and meat and liquor. It's just that the process was a little different from what I was used to.

Rice didn't come in its own prepackaged box; it came in enormous burlap sacks, and you chose how much you wanted. Eggs weren't sold by the dozen in their own crates; you selected the number of eggs you wanted, at about ten cents apiece, and they were deposited into a clear plastic sack drawn shut with a knot. It was as if each section in the store had a product, but not necessarily a brand.

Then, I came to the butcher, who seemed to be an entity all his own. As I may have mentioned, Mongolians living in the country's capital seem to have something of a penchant for meat. So it came as no great surprise to me that there was a line waiting for his services. But what did surprise me was just how intimate his job actually was. Right in front of me and the other shoppers, without the usual panes of display-case glass between us and the butcher's victim, lay a dead goat. The goat lay on top of a Formica table, and seemed to have a warm look about him, like he'd only recently lost his life. I wondered if I looked hard enough, if I could see his heart still beating. Up and down, in a very methodical fashion, the butcher brought his cleaver to and from the goat. Staring straight ahead, rather than at his work, he whacked and whacked. Little bloody bits of flesh and bone landed on the floor all around us, but no one seemed to mind or even notice. It was like witnessing a live murder scene.

Then, one by one, the butcher handed each customer plastic bags filled with bones and diced fatty flesh. I moved aside before it was my turn and headed straight for the produce section, where I bought a couple of bananas.

"Khoyor banahn," I said to the cashier, putting my goods on the counter in front of her.

I'd practiced this a few times in my head and was sure I had the pronunciation just right. There's something intoxicating about traveling to a new country, learning to speak fragments of the local language, and finally, one day, experiencing the moment where you achieve the mundane without incident. In other words, you blend in.

"Khoyor banahn?" I repeated, pointing at the "two bananas" I thought I was asking for. Of course, the outcome in these situations is strictly binary: either the cashier ringing up your purchase goes about ringing up your purchase as if you're a regular, or she looks at you as if you're crazy.

Squinting disapprovingly like a strict schoolmarm, the cashier looked at me as if I were crazy and repeated back to me what I should have said, sounding it out slowly. *"Kh-yr-bn-n,"* she said, waiting patiently for me to get it right before releasing my breakfast to me.

"Khoyor bin-in?" I mimicked, amputating the vowels just as she had.

"Bish, bish," she chided, slowly sounding out the words one more time as she rang me up and handed me my purchases anyway.

"I'm covering the Roaring Hooves festival again today," Tobie said as soon as I arrived at work that morning.

I tucked into my bananas and nodded approvingly. I'd just begun to look over the scripts for grammatical and spelling errors, and I had my work cut out for me.

"Want to come with?" Tobie asked.

"Really? Why?" I asked.

"Gandima's busy, and I need a reporter."

"You mean," I said as I put my peels in the trash. "You need a *reporter*?"

"That's right," Tobie said, and I took a deep breath. This was it. This was my first shot. It had come earlier than I'd expected, but I was ready ... sort of ... almost. But that was good enough. When does the opportunity of a lifetime ever come at just the right time? I'd had just enough schooling under Magee Hickey to make do, and that's just what I'd do. Tobie was already packing his camera and gear.

"Let's go," he said.

"Where are you two going?" Gandima asked as we made to leave. She seemed like the type of manager who wanted to be asked first, rather than told.

"Patricia is coming with me to cover the Roaring Hooves concert," Tobie responded. The way he said it was the way he said everything else—with simple logic that trumped any misgivings about his age. "Besides, there's no one else who speaks English to cover the story."

"Patricia, do you even know anything about the festival?" Gandima asked, looking at me skeptically.

"I do," I said, and I actually did. Although our office didn't have an Internet connection, I'd managed to find some old news scripts that had run the story a year earlier, which I'd already dug up in order to write that evening's script.

"I hope so," she said, as she turned on her heel and left.

In a taxi with Tobie, I read through the old scripts, jotted down some notes, tried memorizing them, put on another coat of mascara, and did my best to exhibit the grace under pressure I wasn't feeling. Although I wasn't about to tell Tobie this, I had an old childhood fear nagging at me.

In primary school, I'd been given the part of narrator in a rather verbose production of a play. One night, while delivering my opening lines to a packed lunchroom auditorium, I promptly forgot the rest. From behind the curtain, the director whispered, quietly at first. Although I could hear her and the lines I was supposed to be reciting, my lips were frozen. Even after her quiet whispers turned into stage whispers, I remained completely immobile and mute, and the show went on without me. At eleven years old, I'd experienced public shame for the first time, and I'd never forgotten it. My opening line, the only one I'd not clammed up on, has always been an indelible reminder of my embarrassment: "There's a but; there's always a but."

I didn't mention to Tobie how nervous I was. This was my first chance to really make something of my dream, and I wanted to keep it that way. Besides, the stage fright I had experienced as an eleven-year-old had happened two decades earlier. Whatever had happened to him when he was eleven hadn't happened very long ago. Obviously, I didn't need to remind him of that. Besides, we'd arrived.

The State Philharmonic is grand. It's decked out with columns and arches and elaborate moldings, and you almost feel as if you've walked into another epoch, a time when a dapper gentleman would dress for a performance in a freshly pressed waistcoat, smoking a pipe, holding the elbow of his impeccably dressed female companion. Inside, the Philharmonic is just as stuffy as any other concert hall and nearly as grand, despite its worn carpet and peeling paint.

At the door, we furnished our TV ID badges and were suddenly shown a considerable amount of deference. The security guards led Tobie and me to a quiet corner where we'd be allowed to film. It occurred to me that I was already a foregone conclusion, at least to those guards and the curious crowd who'd begun to gather around us. The only difference between success and failure was, simply, taking action.

In no time at all, Tobie had set up the shot and was asking me if I was ready to roll. Facing the inky depths of the camera in front of me, I wasn't quite, but it was now or never. Besides, I had a little trick to help me out. During one of my visits to CBS, an *Evening News* producer had confided to me that all novice reporters squeeze the cheeks of their backside tightly, very tightly, until they're numb, and then let go. Apparently, this takes the edge off the anxiety. Miraculously, it was working.

"I'm rolling in three," Tobie said.

Licking my lips and my teeth the way I'd seen other reporters do to moisten their mouths, I began. My heart was thumping so vigorously that my entire body jolted with each beat.

"Here we are—" I opened, and Tobie stopped me.

"Patricia," he said, peering out from behind the camera. "We aren't live. You can't say 'here we are' to viewers that aren't here." Tobie and I had quickly come to an unspoken understanding that he would be the one to call the shots, which was just as well. Not only was I unsure of what I was doing, but he was very sure of what he was doing.

"Of course," I said, taking a deep breath to start over. Behind Tobie, the small crowd that had drawn to watch us was growing ever larger.

"This week," I said, pausing just long enough to see if Tobie would emerge from behind the camera to correct me again. When he didn't, I continued. "The Roaring Hooves Music Festival makes its way from the idyllic countryside to Ulaanbaatar." Behind me, the crowd was completely silent. No twitters of laughter, no one reminding me of my lines, just silence. Emboldened and full of adrenaline, I went on to explain to the camera the festival's cultural and historical significance.

"Good," Tobie said as he switched off the camera.

"Really?" I asked, hoping he'd elaborate.

"We need to interview an official from Roaring Hooves," Tobie said. "While I move us to the hole-why," he said, pronouncing "hallway" in his polite English accent, "see if you might find someone who will talk to us," he directed as he adjusted the shot to take in better light. Giddy, I skipped the length of the concert hall to where the performers were.

Backstage, officials from the Music Association were silently mingling with the musicians, who were waiting their turns on stage. Pointing at my ID badge to identify myself, I whispered that I'd come from MNB, and that I was looking for someone to interview. Immediately, eager hands flew into the air. I'd hardly needed to ask. Waiting for noisy applause to mask our departure, I collected an English-speaking official from the association and headed back to where Tobie was waiting.

"Tobie, this is Mister . . . ," I said, trailing off with good reason, as I'd forgotten the man's surname.

"Mister," the man began, picking up where I left off, following for several seconds with an uninterrupted stream of consonants.

Just what I was about to say, I thought, before Tobie gave us an authoritative thumbs-up, cuing us that he was ready to begin rolling. The official began gulping and smoothing his hands on his pants; he was so nervous that I nearly told him about the *Evening News* producer's method for relieving anxiety.

"How long has the Roaring Hooves festival been running?" I asked after signaling back to Tobie that we were ready. Behind us, at the entrance to the concert hall, one of the guards had opened the double doors just wide enough so that he could peer out, watching us in action.

A long moment later, the nervous official had answered my question and then some. After explaining the ideology of Roaring Hooves, he'd gone on to describe in detail the festival's goals to incorporate other art forms into the music program. And he didn't stop there. Answering questions I hadn't even thought of, he'd clearly hit his loquacious stride. On and on he went until he gasped and ran out of breath. When we'd finally finished, the security guard standing just outside giggled and waved, poking the length of his arm out just enough to transmit the message and add a thumbs-up.

After interviewing one of the musicians, Tobie and I settled into the back of the concert hall to listen to the music. A hush fell over the crowd as a Mongolian fiddler stepped onstage and began to play the country's most revered instrument, the *morin khuur*. Like most things in Mongolia, it stems from a legend involving a man, his horse, and some shedding of tears. A boxy violin, the *moorin khuur* has only two strings, is played from the front like a cello, and has a horse head carved into its handle.

Legend has it that a heartbroken nomad had gathered the remains of his beloved flying horse, whose wings had been clipped by a witch, to create the instrument. Legend also has it that the sauntering, moaning strains of the melancholy music have the power to make grown men cry.

I sneaked a peek at Tobie, who was nowhere near tears. Neither was I; I'd *done* it! I'd overcome my fears. I'd *reported*! I'd corresponded!

I could hardly believe what was truly possible when I'd spent so many years in banking doubting just that.

CHAPTER 10

Currying Flavor

Japan ranks fourth for aid donation to Mongolia. Due to successes Japan and Mongolia have had working together, implementation of other projects is being considered.

—Evening news voiceover, *MM Today* broadcast

Batma had news for me. Soon, I'd have a roommate. In fact, very soon—she was due to arrive that evening. Now, Batma had sort of sprung this on me like I shouldn't mind, and I didn't, not really. But I admit to feeling just a tad jealous at the thought of some interloper usurping all the attention Batma had lavished on me thus far: giggling over my attempts to pronounce Mongolian words, giggling over her attempts to pronounce English words, eating endless bowls of mutton soup in the kitchen while she looked on, and breakfast of that single fried egg waiting for me every morning.

However, business was business, and for Batma and her family, I was a paying boarder. She'd hinted that they'd needed to augment their income, so that's just what she and Badaa had agreed to do.

Late one afternoon, I found my way downtown to the State Circus, where I'd meet this new roommate. She'd just arrived from the airport, along with a few others who'd come under the auspices of the

British company's internship program. Urna had arranged for Meg to be taken home to meet Batma first, and then driven back into town to meet me. And from the looks of it, Urna had even managed to do all this on time!

"Patricia, this is Meg." Urna introduced us cordially, but in her usual unceremonious monotone. "She's your new roommate now."

And that was pretty much that. Meg and I shook hands and smiled at each other uncertainly. She had fair skin; eyes that seemed to be colored green or gray or blue, depending on the light; and long, lustrous, fiery red tresses, which I'd soon find out didn't match her gentle personality. In a word, Meg was just gorgeous. And she didn't appear to have spent much time working at it; she was sporting worn-out clothing and even more worn-out gear.

Meg was just twenty years old and a pre-med student from a small town in Maine. This was her first experience living overseas. She'd also come to Mongolia to intern but at the State Second Maternity Hospital in Ulaanbaatar, where she'd begin work in just a few days. In the meantime, it was up to us to get to know each other, as we'd be spending time in pretty close quarters for the rest of the summer.

"So, what's it like here?" she asked softly.

Urna was ushering us into the State Circus for a performance, and there wasn't much time to talk.

"Want to come to quiz night with me after this?" I whispered, looking forward to showing off my newest friend to my week-old friends. Tobie would be there, and so would my friend Evan and his colleagues, whom I'd met a couple of times.

"Sure," she said, flashing an appreciative smile.

Every Thursday evening, Dave's Bar hosted quiz night. On the eastern edge of Sükhbaatar Square, with a view of the statue of the general himself, Dave's was not just popular; it was a religion. And it was about as packed and emotional as a Sunday service in Harlem. A week or so before each quiz contest, Dave himself singled out one of the regular patrons to perform the very difficult task of moderating quiz night. It was an honor bestowed on the few that could ask humorous, yet intelligent questions to a raucous and bellicose crowd.

But that was only half the battle for the moderator. He was also required to *compose* the quiz himself. With a crowd made up of an eclectic mix of backpackers, expats, local Mongolian celebrities, and a smattering of children, this was no easy task. With just a week to prepare, moderators could often be seen pulling all-nighters at local Internet cafés, drafting quiz questions to suit everyone's taste. In fact, in just a few weeks, Evan would be tapped to moderate.

The circus performance didn't last long, and Meg and I left the hall, heading east to quiz night at Dave's Bar. Just as we arrived, Evan was telling a tale I'd heard him tell before. He'd obviously mastered this particular one, and absolutely everyone within earshot was positively spellbound.

"This. Is. Not. Good," he was saying in a mock Borat accent, his tone invoking gloom and drama. Pulling his glasses down the bridge of his nose and peering over their top with an air of wise, imposing authority, Evan had such good command of this story that I listened to it all over again. Meg and I sat down at the picnic table across from him.

In Evan's second year working for the Peace Corps in Turkmenistan, he'd been saying, after he'd learned the Turkmen language and grown close with the family he'd been living with, he began occasionally preparing elaborate Sunday-dinner-type meals for them. One weekend he would make pizzas, another burritos. Ingredients for these dishes were not easy to come by, and often his meals required days of preparation and experimentation. And then he decided to make an authentic Indian chicken curry.

It took weeks to procure all the ingredients. He even called a friend living in India to order just the right curry spices, which of course had to be bought, shipped, and then checked through Turkmen customs. This was a long, slow process. When his package from India finally arrived, Evan still needed to buy a local chicken.

"Which was more difficult than ordering the spices, paying for them, having them shipped, and then getting them through Turkmenistan customs—combined," he added wryly, and went on.

Once Evan had gathered all the ingredients, he spent an entire day cooking. Proud of his result, he served the curry to his waiting dinner guests. The cries of pleasure that had honored his efforts after the burrito and pizza meals were replaced with silence. Finally, the patriarch of the family spoke up. Gruff and plainspoken, he looked at Evan for a long time before he finally delivered his verdict in English, "This. Is. *Not*. Good."

With raised eyebrows, Evan nodded slowly and deliberately, still peering authoritatively over the rims of his glasses, and finally finished his monologue. And none too soon, as the quiz was about to begin. In the meantime, Evan's audience was in hysterics. Every time he told that story, it got the same reaction.

"What was the name of Genghis Khan's wife?" the quiz moderator asked, and we were off to the races! There were half a dozen teams competing, with half a dozen or so people in each team. Huddling and whispering, we wrote down our answers on a sheet of paper.

"Name four British politicians to have served as prime minister in the last century."

"Who invented the printing press?"

"And in what year?"

"What color was Genghis Khan's hair?"

Genghis Khan's *hair*?

Although it's definitely not a widespread belief, in parts of Mongolia a person with red hair is thought to be either a devil or some sort of witch. Meg, my new roommate, was a redhead, and we would spend a lot of time discussing the color of her hair. During the course of the summer, she would often face particularly antisocial behavior from locals.

On one occasion, while she was stopped at a crosswalk on her way downtown, a man on a motorcycle pulled up, glared at her, revved his engine, and drove into her legs. Not once, but twice in a row. Another time, a man sidled up to her, and hissed, "Go home!" in English, directly into her ear.

Meg and I would both be ultimately interested in getting to the bottom of this behavior, but at that moment, she'd only just arrived in Mongolia, and we were short one final quiz question. As it happened, I'd done some reading on Genghis Khan before arriving in the country, and I'd discovered something astonishing about the man.

As it turned out, one of Genghis Khan's ancestors may have had an affair with a redhead. Generations before he was born, a woman from a clan from which Genghis Khan would eventually descend, slept with a "golden-hued man," as redhead men were called back in the day. The woman had been widowed, and shortly afterward had begun a passionate affair with this mystery man. Apparently to explain away the scandalous nature of the affair, the woman claimed that the man entered her *ger* through a hole in the roof and departed on the rays of the sun! Of course, divine intervention isn't frowned upon like a lusty affair with an unwed woman is frowned upon, and the widow might've needed a good explanation. Because with this mysterious heaven-sent prowler, she bore three sons. She even referred to them as "children of heaven."

So, to keep all her children from arguing with each other over paternity issues, the widow sat them down and told them a parable. To each son she presented an arrow and told him to break his arrow in half. They did as she'd instructed, and the mother then tied all five arrows together and gave each of her sons a chance to break them.

None of them could, and she had made her point: a family's strength comes from sticking together. Incredibly, thousands of years later, at modern-day weddings and family reunions in the Western world, we hear this very same folktale.

But back to Genghis Khan's hair. After the widowed mother died (presumably to join her deity boyfriend aloft the sun's rays), the brothers ignored her advice to stick together, looted the inheritance, and kicked the youngest son out of the family. Off on his own, the exiled brother kidnapped a couple of wives, founded a few clans, and participated in a few wars. Eventually, he had children and grandchildren, one of whom married a real shrew called "Monalun."

One season, some of Monalun's relatives were defeated in battle by another clan. The few survivors fled to her land and set up a little refugee camp. Monalun was very unhappy with these unwanted houseguests, so she hopped on her horse, rode to their camp, and trampled them to death. Of course, that led to another battle, which left pretty much everyone dead, aside from just one of Monalun's sons and his baby nephew. The man and boy stole away to safety and lived happily ever after.

Years later, the uncle's descendants would save Genghis Khan's life in a decisive battle, and the nephew's great-great-great-grandson was none other than Genghis Khan's father!

All this, supposedly, from illicit sex with a redhead!

Of course, the very fact that Genghis Khan is so revered in Mongolia and may have been a redhead himself would leave Meg and me with more questions during our summer in the country. After all, why would a local man drive a motorcycle into someone's legs who happened to share a characteristic with his adored national hero? Meg and I told ourselves that the Mongolians probably had assumed she was Russian, which was a more plausible, if not slightly less interesting, theory. After all, plenty of Mongolians still harbored resentment for the way they had been dominated by the Soviets until just a few decades ago.

"Time's up," the moderator called out, collecting quiz papers to tally the scores.

"But Genghis Khan's *hair*! How the hell would anyone know *that*?"

By the time the quiz drew to a close, everyone was so full of beer and local vodka that we took the verdict very, very seriously.

"And the winner is . . ." The moderator paused for effect, taking a leisurely sip of his tumbler of Bolor vodka. "Is . . ."

"Come *on*, mate," a saucy Australian backpacker called out.

With a cash purse of at least twenty dollars, the stakes were high.

"Team number four," he finally said. Although we'd nailed the question about Genghis Khan's hair, team four had just squeaked past us when the scores were tallied. While they erupted in cheers, the rest of the crowd resumed their garment-rending disappointment.

"That's *bull*shit!" someone called out.

"They *cheat*ed!" another team accused.

And then things died down, and everyone went back to their beers and their conversations.

"You must be just *yearning* to pop a kid out," Pimples said to me, apropos of absolutely nothing. "How old are you, anyway?"

Twenty-four years old and from the United Kingdom, Pimples was teaching English at a local school in Ulaanbaatar. He'd gotten his nickname "Pimples" because he had a lot of them. Pimples wasn't particularly popular, but he always seemed to be around. And he always seemed to be asking people things that were none of his business—without the benefit of an inflection point at the end of his question. In other words, he tended to state as fact whatever he'd already assumed to be true about the target of his interrogations.

"I'm right, aren't I?" he pressed, smiling a hard smile. "You must be just *desperate* to have a baby."

Pimples and I hadn't liked each other from the moment we'd met, and our relationship had gone straight downhill from there. At a bar one night, feet propped up on the seat across from him, he picked at his toes as he laughed at a recent accusation. Earlier that day, someone was saying that Pimples had been hanging out with the guys, taking a break from his teaching job.

"Close your eyes, everyone," he'd supposedly said while producing a small plastic bag from his knapsack. To my surprise, everyone had done as they were told. "Okay, now," he went on, "put your hand into the bag and guess what's inside." Just as unbelievably, one of the guys obeyed, and as quickly as he dipped his hand into Pimples's bag, he yanked it right out. Inside was a collection of wet, used condoms.

Laughing so hard he could barely choke the words out, Pimples finally managed to admit, "Yep, that was me. *Brill*-iant, wasn't it?"

Truth was, no one much liked Pimples, not even the girl with whom he'd made use of all those condoms. But everyone was afraid to say so, because when it came to seeing a person for who they really were, Pimples wasn't always right, but his shot was sharp. He often hit at some deep insecurities, and he even dared to follow up with unsolicited therapy. He was the kind of guy you meet while traveling whom you'll never forget but wish all the same that you could.

Actually, though, this time Pimples had gotten it all wrong. Just because I hadn't followed the usual script of marriage and kids didn't mean I wanted to join the ranks of the vast majority. Truth was, I was still ambivalent about all that stuff. The closest Pimples had come to accuracy was in detecting that I'd *wanted to want* all that, but I wasn't sure I *actually* wanted all that. Nevertheless, it was a sore spot, and he'd found it.

"Let's go," I said to Meg, shrugging Pimples off. Quiz night had ended abruptly for at least one of us; it was time to leave. In a protracted silence, Meg and I walked home together. The sun was dipping into the western horizon, a quivering orange light framing the outline of the Soviet housing blocks off in the distance. Behind us, our shadows tagged along, elongated versions of ourselves and just as quiet.

CHAPTER 11

Off the Beaten Puddle

The team of executives is currently discussing cooperation between the fields of geology, mining, transport, trade, and investment. The Japanese representatives offered proposals on intensifying Mongolian-Japanese relations, while the Mongolian representatives considered as their priority the availability of trade with . . . Asian countries as well as opportunities to penetrate the Russian market.

—Evening news voiceover, *MM Today* broadcast

That night, it rained hard, and I woke up the next morning to the tinkling sound of a storm that was just ending. The sky shone a leaden silver, relieved to have finished emptying itself. Outside my window and down the alley leading to Peace Avenue, enormous puddles had formed in the pockmarked pavement.

After sharing a breakfast of fried bread, an egg apiece, and instant coffee, Meg and I headed downtown. Batma had already shown Meg the ropes around the apartment, and it was my job to show her the way to town. I decided on a quirky shortcut.

Circumventing the main road and its traffic and dust, Meg and I ducked into the alley extending from our apartment block to Gandan Khiid monastery. From one end to the other, it was the length of a couple of city blocks. We passed an underground billiards hall, a local schoolyard, and a milk seller living in a rusted train boxcar. Taking this off-the-beaten-path route into town, I felt I was getting a sneak peek into the real Ulaanbaatar, and this was what I wanted to show to Meg. After all, anyone can go for a stroll along a main road in any town, but finding the side streets that pass in front of people's homes and through their lives is, to me, what adventure is all about. Besides, Meg and I were able to score points with local cabbies by explaining our shortcut to them in their own language—when we'd finally learned enough Mongolian to do so.

The alleyway zigzagged from one ex-Soviet apartment block to the next, linking parking lots and rows of brick storage sheds. At its center was a puddle so enormous and so permanent that cars occasionally sank deep into it, especially after a hard rain. Mongolian sewers seemed to have been designed with Mongolia's "Land of the Blue Sky" nickname in mind. That is, sewers were few and far between in the residential neighborhoods, and while there were plenty of them downtown, they were usually occupied by homeless people rather than rainwater.

There are no official statistics on the number of homeless in the capital, but, like any capital city, there seemed to be quite a few. And during winter, they were forced to make the sewer system their home. Of course, sewer dwelling is fairly common in big cities, especially New York. In fact, it's estimated that some twenty-five thousand "mole people" live in the tunnels of New York City's subway system. Likewise, in Mongolia, hundreds of people, many of them children, scratch out a miserable existence living beneath the surface of society, huddled closely in large drainpipes. With winter temperatures hovering well below freezing for months at a time, getting out of the cold can be a matter of life or death.

In fact, conditions in the sewers are so bad that death is always present and often imminent. Unbelievably, it's often steam that is responsible for killing many of the underground homeless. After what is frequently a violent fight for a coveted sleeping spot near the warmth of the city's hot water pipes, the victor must figure out from which direction the industrial-force steam will come. If he chooses wrong and sleeps headfirst toward the steam, he'll die. Otherwise, he'll end up with scorched feet.

So, without sufficient drainage systems in place in the Soviet microdistricts, where Meg and I lived, rainwater runoff was left to collect in dusty gravel parking lots. Since gravel isn't absorbent and dust is, those lots and alleys looked like a miniature version of an English lake district after a good, hard storm. And for whatever reason, there were plenty of rainstorms that summer. As the weather assaulted us relentlessly, puddles grew to epic proportions—especially our puddle.

On the puddle's south side was a high wall, sort of an embankment that kept it from leaking into the neighboring primary school's playground. The drop-off between the puddle and the schoolyard was about fifteen feet, just enough to kill you if you fell off it. And you might, because walking this tightrope was the only way to cross it. Of course, you could head back to the main road and altogether avoid the exhilarating danger of this pockmarked ribbon of concrete, but what would be the fun of that? Besides, there's no better roommate bonding exercise than facing down the fear of injury and death.

"You go first," I said to Meg, after explaining that we should take turns traversing the twenty or so feet across the puddle, in case one of us fell.

"Okay," she said a little uncertainly, looking as if she was about to risk much more than she intended. With her back turned to me, shoulders raised, I could tell she was holding her breath, terrified. Then, very carefully, Meg tiptoed across, stepping over and around the many cracks and divots in the pavement. Before I had a chance to wonder what I'd do if she tripped, she raised her arms in victory and whooped loudly.

Following cautiously in her footsteps, I reached our finish line and inhaled deeply, that intoxicating swell of adrenaline and relief that is the aftermath of any unnecessary but successful gamble. Meg and I high-fived each other, only to glance back and see a Mongolian woman actually trotting across the wall in a pair of unbuckled strappy kitten heels!

We were early for a lunch date with Evan, so we paid for a ticket to the Choijin Lama monastery in the south of the city. A complex of several temples with upturned, pointy-tipped roofs and rich red doors, it looked like a toy version of Beijing's Forbidden City. Built during the first few years of the twentieth century, it was one of the many monasteries shut down during the Great Purge, but it was never demolished because the Soviets wanted to use it to "demonstrate the 'feudal' ways of the past," as the *Lonely Planet* guidebook describes it. Located just a short walk from Peace Avenue, Choijin Lama took up little more than a city block and had a kind of boutique feel of grandeur.

Aside from a security guard, Meg and I were the only people at the monastery, so we roamed its grounds aimlessly, which seemed to fit well with the ambiance of the place. Tufts of tumbleweed and dry shrubbery blew in the unseasonably cool breeze that day; an eerie silence smothered any attempts at conversation. Unable to absorb the heavy weight of its atmosphere, Meg and I glanced at each other and wordlessly agreed to leave, then headed to meet Evan at an American-style deli.

One of Mongolia's most popular restaurants, the American- and Cuban-owned Millie's Café, prided itself on its fare as much as its clientele, who came from all over town to eat their Philly cheesesteaks and club sandwiches. In Mongolia, where things like seasonings are regarded with some suspicion (locals always shook their heads when I'd try to put even a little salt on my mutton), the mere thought of smothering sautéed beef with Cheez Whiz, onions, and mushrooms was positively sacrilegious!

So, as usual, Millie's wasn't just crowded, it was packed.

Backpackers, camera-clad photojournalists, and diplomats hunched over cheesesteaks and burgers, probably discussing things like foreign policy or adventure. Occasionally, you'd overhear a snippet of conversation from a nearby table and realize your hunch was right; everyone *was* discussing adventure and diplomacy. Once Meg and Evan and I landed a much-coveted table, we paid homage to Philadelphia and ordered cheesesteaks.

But it wasn't the food that was on our minds or, for that matter, diplomacy. Adventure was. The following weekend, we'd all head to a place called Khustain, a national park southwest of Ulaanbaatar, which, long ago, used to serve as hunting grounds for the khans of Mongolia. Now though, it's home to a rare breed of horse and is something of a destination for newly arrived expats looking to dip a toe into their very first Mongolian countryside voyage.

Khustain wasn't far from Ulaanbaatar, only about sixty miles, but this trip would still require some planning. We'd arranged to go with a group. Meg was on a tight budget, so she decided to camp in the steppe with a few others, not far from where Evan and I would stay in a traditional *ger*. It would be my first chance to stay in one of the round, felt, teepee-like structures so endemic to Mongolia. Tobie would also be there, as well as one of Evan's colleagues. It was our first order of business to plan the logistics of this adventure and research just who knew what about Khustain who we could tap for information. Halfway through lunch, it dawned on us—we knew just the person to help us out. Right away, Meg and I arranged a meeting. And one night soon after, Meg and Tobie and I sat down to dinner with a horse researcher.

Like many of us, the horse researcher had come to Mongolia under the auspices of an internship because she'd wanted to work in the country. She loved all things equestrian, and there are few better places to study horses than Khustain, which hosts some of the world's only surviving truly wild horses.

Tobie, Meg, and I met the horse researcher at a steakhouse. This would turn out to be a terrible mistake.

She greeted us, but it was hard to tell that she'd done so at all. Plump and fair-skinned with hazel eyes, she was so soft-spoken and so shy that it was almost impossible to hear what she was saying. In fact, she didn't actually speak; she whispered. Just as I leaned in to ask her to tell me her name, the waiter arrived to take our order.

Page after page, course after course, the steakhouse menu offered just one item in varying forms—meat. Meat with "special sauce," meat with Korean kimchee, sheep meat, cow meat, yak meat. And horse meat—but none of us knew that yet.

"I'll have the 'Strong and Hard Man,'" I said to him without looking very carefully at the menu. I was more interested in finding out about Khustain's horses. Tobie and I were hoping to pitch a story about just that to Gandima, and the researcher was our best shot at gathering information before we left for our trip.

"Are you sure?" the waiter asked, pointing at the menu's description of the "Strong and Hard Man" as a "flaming plate of grilled steaks fit only for consumption by a strong and hard man."

"Of *course* I'm sure," I said, always eager to flex a bit of culinary bravado, especially when it's on behalf of strong and hard *women* the world over.

"I came here to study the horses," the horse researcher whispered. She might've said her name was Heather, but I couldn't be sure. "But mostly I came here to spend time with them." She had a nervous way about her, eyes darting from us to her hands in her lap. "I'm really shy, but the horses seem to coax me out of myself," she said, trailing off and smiling weakly. Just as Tobie began to tell her about our pitch to Gandima regarding the Khustain horses, our food arrived.

"For you!" the waiter said with a flourish as he put my food in front of me. "The 'Strong and Hard Man'!" The platter of grilled meats was dotted liberally with red and brown sauces and an awful lot of kimchee, a Korean side dish made of spices and fermented cabbage. In the center stood an erect meat bone, nestled into, and supported by, layers of steaks. The tip of this phallic display was wrapped in aluminum foil and doused with a strong-smelling alcohol.

"What type of meats *are* those?" the horse researcher asked, leaning into my plate, carefully scrutinizing its contents.

From his breast pocket, the waiter produced a book of matches. "Cow meat, sheep meat, and"—he paused as he lit the top of the bone—"horse meat."

With the tip of the bone alight, my plate turned into a sort of layered birthday cake of steaks, with an upright bone as a candle.

"I'm sorry," I said quickly and feebly to our guest. "I didn't know about the horse." I wasn't sure which steak was horse steak, but I quickly pretended just the opposite, using my fork to disdainfully push one of the cuts to the far side of my plate.

The horse researcher daubed the corner of her mouth with her napkin and looked as if she might cry. I really wished someone would change the subject. Meg did just that and told us about her first day on the job at her internship at the State Second Maternity Hospital.

"You won't believe what happened to me yesterday," Meg said into the awkward silence.

Meg had spent her first day at her internship performing abortions.

This. Is. Not. Good, I thought, having already heard about Meg's first day on the job. If just one story could make dinner conversation go from awkward to excruciating, this would be it.

"Back and forth," the doctor on duty seemed to be instructing as he demonstrated what to do with the long, thin rod he'd inserted into a patient's vagina. Because Meg had only recently arrived in Mongolia, she hadn't learned much of the language yet, and she certainly hadn't learned any medical jargon. Thus, she and the doctor she'd been assigned to were relying on pantomime. Lying on her back on the gurney in front of them was a young woman, legs splayed out in front of her, wincing in pain.

"Harder," the doctor mimed, taking the rod back from Meg and thrusting it into the woman with exaggerated urgency. Once Meg seemed to have gotten the hang of what the doctor was teaching her to do, he left her alone with the patient to finish the job.

Meg was shaken, but what could she do? She'd been given an awful lot of responsibility, especially for someone who'd not even been to medical school. Besides, she was alone with one woman after another and had been given orders. So, whether she felt right about it or not, she did as she was told.

"So many vaginas, so little time," Meg quipped, tittering politely, finishing her story.

Still, the horse researcher was silent, and so were the rest of us. Dinner had all but ended, and it seemed best that Tobie and I research our pitch on our own. Of course, this was disappointing, but little did we know that the horses would serve as only a backdrop to an adventure in Khustain that would change a few lives. For now though, we needed the check.

"Check, please?" someone said to the waiter, and wallets were quickly produced from pockets.

CHAPTER 12

Dreams Come True

A famous local academic is the second Mongolian to be awarded the Asian Cultural Prize of Fukuoka. Just days ago, Mongolia's Mr. Bira was honored with the state title of "Hero of Labor." During a press conference at the Ministry of External Relations, the announcement was made by the Secretary-General of the Fukuoka Asian Cultural prize committee.

—Lead story, *MM Today* broadcast

The next morning, I walked to work in the flawless brilliance of an azure summer's day.

At the station, Tobie was already at his desk, head hung low and mouth slightly open. Deep in concentration, he was editing the Roaring Hooves piece we'd filmed earlier that week at the State Philharmonic Hall. Lifting his head briefly to mumble a hello, he immediately went back to work. I gathered up a stack of scripts and began my task of correcting spelling errors.

"Patricia?" Gandima said as she poked her head into our office. "Come with me; I need to speak with you."

Hearing "we need to talk" is rarely a good sign, especially when your boss summons you, but Gandima had a playful look on her face. This was very unusual. Although I'd known her only a few weeks at this point, I'd known her as nothing if not stern.

I followed Gandima to her office and sat down opposite her. "You are doing good work here at the station," she began. "In fact, your spell-checking is really very good indeed. And I know you want to do more," she went on as I held my breath.

"So," she said, pausing before she delivered her grand finale, "Enkhtuya and I would like you to begin teaching English to the staff here." With that, she broke into a wide grin and waited for me to follow suit.

Teach English to the staff? I thought. Surely if I'd wanted to teach after leaving banking, I'd have found myself somewhere sunny and warm and tropical in which to do it. But I kept my thoughts to myself and vowed right then and there that I would do whatever she asked in order to get a shot at doing what I'd actually come to Mongolia to do, which was to report.

"So, would you like to teach?" Gandima asked.

"Absolutely," I said.

Strangely though, this was the first and last time I'd hear of it from Gandima or anyone else at the station. Whether it was her test of my commitment to MNB, I never knew, but she didn't mention again the subject of teaching.

"Good, because I'd also like you to begin reporting with Tobie."

"What, really?" I said. "Seriously?"

"Yes, really."

"Thank you!" I said, jumping out of my seat, grasping her hand to shake it.

"Starting from today," she began, smiling as she had before, and I sat down again. "You and Tobie will work together on stories for the English news broadcast. You will pitch them to me, and if Enkhtuya and I agree that they should make air, Tobie will produce while you report."

"Thank you, thank you!" I cried.

The English news broadcast aired only three times per week, and the entire show lasted only about twenty minutes. Segments were of standard length, about two minutes apiece, and most of them focused on the English translation of the already-aired Mongolian news features on political and cultural events happening in Ulaanbaatar and around the country. In other words, Tobie and I would have very few chances that summer to get one of our stories aired. So, I wanted some direction on just how to go about increasing our chances of success.

"What did you think of my reporting on Roaring Hooves?" I asked hopefully. Because Gandima had handpicked the story herself, before I'd even arrived in Mongolia, she obviously already supported the content. And because she'd often asked Tobie to produce, I knew she was happy with his work. But I had only reported for her once, so I needed her opinion of my skills on camera.

"It was," Gandima stopped, choosing her words carefully. "It was . . . okay."

"Okay?"

"Yes, Patricia, it was *okay*," she repeated.

"How 'okay'?" I pressed.

"Just 'okay,'" she responded. "Now then, you should get to work," Gandima said, ushering me out before I could ask her how to get from "okay" to exactly what she wanted.

"Gandima, thank you again!" I said, beaming, before I headed back to the office Tobie and I shared.

This was a moment I'd never forget, and I took my time enjoying it, basking in what suddenly felt like endless possibilities. Just months earlier, I'd been staring at computer screens on a trading floor, mindlessly going through the motions of "just one more year, just one more bonus."

For nearly a decade, I'd counted the minutes until the day's end. And of those days, I reminisced, it was actually Friday that had always been the worst. Finally out of the office and free for an entire weekend, I'd already developed the Sunday blues as early as Friday nights. But here I was, pursuing my dream, and my dream was actually becoming my reality.

"Tobie!" I nearly shrieked when I'd returned to our office. "Guess what?"

"I know," he responded with a genuine smile. Normally economical in his reactions, he looked only a little bit less exhilarated than I was feeling. But he had to get back to work, and so did I. Earlier that week, Tobie had learned about an Irish couple from Dublin with such an unusual story that he'd already confidently pitched it to Gandima, and she'd just as readily agreed to let us produce it.

With Tobie's camera gear in tow, together we headed downtown. On the way, he briefed me on what he'd heard about them. And what he'd heard was a story that sounded very familiar to my own.

On the steps outside of a hotel in central Ulaanbaatar, Anne and Jonny O'Brien told us their story, in their own words. Some months earlier, they began, they'd decided to quit their corporate jobs to follow a dream. Now, this wasn't your average dream of, say, working in television. Instead, Anne and Jonny hoped to bicycle all the way from Ireland to Mongolia—and that's just what they did.

If that had been the conclusion, it would have been interesting enough. But it wasn't. Midway through their circuitous 20,000-kilometer journey, somewhere in Kazakhstan, Anne discovered that she was pregnant. At this point, it was obvious what they should do; they should quit and fly home. But, they explained, this trip had been their dream, and they were determined to continue on. So Jonny came up with a genius idea. He'd hook Anne's bike to his and *drag* her to Ulaanbaatar. A few weeks, and no fewer than 1,000 kilometers of effort, later, they made it. Anne and Jonny's story practically told itself, and I had little trouble preparing for the interview. In no time, we got started.

Soft-spoken and heavily pregnant, Anne sat down in front of the camera. She looked comfortable, as if being interviewed for cycling across a continent was just part of a regular afternoon for her. With Jonny and their bikes in the background, I crouched next to Anne and began asking her the same questions I'd asked myself and had only just begun to answer about my own life.

"Anne, tell me *why*," I began. "*Why* did you cycle from Ireland to Mongolia?"

Calmly, Anne nodded, but she didn't answer right away. She seemed to be gathering her thoughts.

"It was our dream," she said finally, and went on to explain that their dream wouldn't end in Mongolia. One day, she told me, they hoped to cycle through North Korea!

After we'd finished the interview, Anne pulled me aside. "Why are *you* here?" she asked abruptly, looking at me with the intensity of someone who already knows the answer to the very same question she's been asked herself.

"I have a dream too," I said, and stopped suddenly. I'd gotten a lump in my throat and found I could hardly go on. "I left behind certainty and money," I said when I could finally continue, "to risk pursuing something I'm passionate about."

"That's amazing," she said so earnestly and with such sincerity that I really had to fight back tears. It isn't every day that you share a dream with a pregnant woman who's just biked across nearly two dozen countries.

Back at the station, Tobie and I began gluing together his footage fragments with my interview notes. In no time, we'd put the finishing touches on our first piece. That week, our story went on the air.

After nearly ten years' working in management consulting, Anne and Jonny O'Brien decided it was time for a change of pace. They laid out plans to embark upon a journey that would last for months, span nearly twenty countries, and ultimately provide for them a new and very unexpected adventure.

In early 2005, the O'Briens set out from their home in Ireland to cycle here to Ulaanbaatar to raise money for Cancer Research U.K. While spending the winter in Kazakhstan, Anne discovered that she was pregnant. Instead of turning back, Jonny hooked Anne's bike to his and pulled her the last 1,000 kilometers to the finish line in Ulaanbaatar.

Upon arriving in Mongolia, the couple realized that their favorite Irish baby name is also the namesake of the Buddhist goddess who represents enlightened energy. In less than three months, Anne and Jonny will bring baby Tara into this world. But their adventure does not stop at parenting. They plan to one day cycle through Japan and possibly North Korea. The O'Briens have so far raised $7,000 for Cancer Research U.K.

CHAPTER 13

A "Washing Vagina"

The team meeting saw the signing of agreements between the ANU Service of Mongolia and the Carbon Financing Company of Japan. The goal of this inaugural agreement is to invest in better development mechanisms in Mongolia. Within this framework, contacts were also signed to provide for the replacement of old steam-boilers and the improvement of greenhouse air quality.

—**Evening news voiceover, *MM Today* broadcast**

It was time. Meg and I could no longer put it off. Our adventure into the Khustain steppe would begin in just twenty-four hours, and neither of us had any laundry left. I'd dreaded this moment and had avoided it by wearing each pair of undies twice, once inside-out. I simply could no longer in good conscience go on; there's just no turning back to an outside-in thong.

While we waited for Batma to wake up, Meg and I revved ourselves with three cups of instant coffee, a stack of Batma's handmade knots of fried dough, and the Mongolian translation dictionary to look up the words for "wash," "washing machine," and "long overdue." Most important though, we would need to communicate an apology. Batma hated doing the laundry, and she made this plain by deeply frowning. It was the only time either one of us would ever see Batma display any sense of displeasure—and that included the time when, a few weeks later, she cheerfully spent an entire evening pumping my stomach!

"Sain bain uu!" Batma greeted us with a broad smile. "Eat!" she commanded merrily, placing an extra knot of bread on each of our plates.

"Batma," I said, pausing to search for the right words. "We. Clean. Clothes. Need."

"Ah," she said, and her face darkened. Meg and I were ready, even if Batma wasn't.

There was a good reason this odious task put Batma in a bad mood. It would've put anyone in a bad mood. Slightly archaic, the family's washing machine was such an old Japanese model that the last person to use it actually might have been the last samurai. It had two speeds: off and rattle. In fact, its very simplicity was what made it complex. With an awful lot of hesitation, the three of us got started. It would be several hours before we finished.

After unplugging most of the electrical appliances in the apartment in order to feed the upcoming spin cycle, Batma ran an extension cord from the kitchen to the bathroom, plugging the washer into the stove's outlet. With the entire household on hold and duly inconvenienced, Batma now held up a finger at a time, explaining what we'd have to do.

Holding up one finger, she pointed at our clothes, which Meg and I had lumped together into a single enormous mound on the living room floor. Holding up two fingers, she pointed at the washing machine. Flipping the power switch, she turned on the motor and helped us insert our first load into the drum.

Then, holding up three fingers for the third cycle, she hooked a hose extending from the bathtub faucet to the drum and turned the water on full blast. When the drum was about half full, Batma poured detergent in and shut the lid, selecting the swish cycle.

Once she'd detached the hose from the bathtub's faucet, she turned on the tap, filling the bathtub with cold water, and held up four fingers. While she waited for the machine to finish swishing, she pawed at her chest and pointed to the cold water in the bathtub, and pawed at her chest again. Either she was suggesting we take an ice-cold bath while our clothes were being washed, or she was demonstrating that we'd have to repeatedly hand-rinse our clothing.

Moments later, Batma switched the washing machine dial from the swish cycle to the spin cycle. Quite unlike any other spin cycle I'd observed, this particular machine was committed to its task. The floors shook. The walls shook. My teeth chattered and my eyeballs rattled. Ten minutes of violent racket later, Batma shut off the power and peered inside. Pasted up against the walls of the drum, our clothing looked as if it had been transformed into used paper towels.

One by one, Batma yanked each article out and deposited them into the cold–water bath, creating a makeshift rinse cycle. Following her lead, Meg and I knelt in front of the bath and put our arms into the frigid water up to our elbows, creating an immediate sensation of arthritis. Individually, we rinsed each article of clothing. As soon as we did, the water turned a brackish brown, and we started all over again, from the very beginning. Until, as Batma instructed us, the water ran clear. Hours later, we giddily hung our clothes outside, the fifth and final step.

While our laundry dried in the late afternoon sun, Meg and I sipped cups of tea and relished the completion of this epic task. During that entire summer, we'd only resort to it twice. The rest of the time, we'd wear inside-out undies, and sometimes even outside-in ones.

"So," Meg said, staring into her empty teacup. "Is everyone meeting at the pub tonight?" Was I imagining things, or had she just said "everyone" like she meant "Evan"? As it would turn out, I was imagining things, but it would take me two very long and embarrassing evenings to come to this conclusion.

Meg and I had never discussed the subject of Evan, and I'd never told her about the fortune-teller, mostly because, by this point, I really didn't think much of his prediction. Sure, what he'd foretold was astonishing, or could've been, but maybe he'd just picked up on the fact that Evan and I would meet, rather than fall in love and marry. In any case, the spark between us just wasn't there. Well, not until right at that moment when Meg intervened. There's nothing quite like jealousy to turn indifference into desire, if only temporarily.

"I'm not sure who will be there tonight," I lied. Of course, I knew exactly who would be there; I'd been the one to make the plans with Evan. At the time, it had been a platonic afterthought of an arrangement, just a few friends getting together to flesh out the details of our pending adventure to the wilds of Khustain. But now, as my mind raced, I wondered if it was actually something more.

"Well, we should leave soon," I said, excusing myself to get ready. It was a Friday night in June; temperatures had risen steadily to guarantee warm summer evenings and nights out at the few bars and restaurants that featured patios. From the clothesline, I chose the only shirt that had dried, and it was perfect: lacy and sweet and low-cut sexy. Whatever Meg's intentions toward Evan, I'd been the first one to meet him. And, of course, with the fortune-teller as a backdrop, I did have a modicum of serendipity on my side. Obviously, I would pull rank.

In my bedroom, I shut the door behind me and stopped for a moment to gather my thoughts. *Was* there something more to my feelings for Evan? After all, it isn't often you meet someone whose dream to go to Mongolia is so important to him that he spends two years in Turkmenistan as a consolation prize. And it's exactly *never* that you meet someone who goes countries out of his way to cook up an inedible curry. Since I'd arrived in Mongolia earlier that month, Evan and I had spent an awful lot of time together and shared an awful lot of otherwise-intimate moments—cappuccino dates, quiz nights, lunches, dinners; we'd even taken in a museum or two. Had I been missing something all along? But then again, if I had been missing something, I hadn't been the only one to do so. In any case, there was only one way to find out.

I slipped my pièce de résistance over my head, which had been transformed in the vigorous spin cycle from gleaming to a shade of drab. But still, it was perfect enough. Just as I was deftly applying a third coat of mascara, there was a tap at my door.

"Are you there?" Meg's voice asked from behind it.

"Uh, yeah," I said, quickly applying a squirt of perfume to my nape. "Hold on just a sec," I stalled, surveying myself in the mirror with satisfaction. I was ready.

"Hi," I said as I opened the door, and stopped short. Meg looked radiant. Flecks of amber peeked out from her roaring red tresses like softly glowing embers. As she stepped from the dark hallway into the brightness of my bedroom, sunlight kissed her freshly scrubbed face, as if light itself had been created for her.

"Wow, you look great," I said, and meant it. It was the first time I'd seen her wear makeup, and she was more beautiful than ever.

"Thanks," she said sheepishly. "But my shirt looks terrible. Do you maybe have one I can borrow?"

She was right; her shirt did look terrible. But I wasn't about to dress her in something that improved on that. Instead, I rummaged through my closet until I found a shirt that would . . . fit.

"Thanks," she said, tugging it self-consciously over her head and smiling. "It's perfect."

Together, we set off to meet Evan downtown.

Every day at dusk, the Gandan Khiid monastery reinvents itself. The morning is hustle, as if the glare of bright daylight were itself a call to action. Monks briskly sweep the stone pavement outside the temple grounds; resident pigeons flutter nervously in their flock, preparing breakfast from yesterday's crumbs.

By afternoon, an ambling serenity sets in with the waning light. Businessmen and nomads pass each other by, the businessmen in smart-looking suits, the nomads dressed in vivid silk robes cinched at the waist with brightly colored sashes. Sporting dark sunglasses, the businessmen look a little bit like gangsters. Sporting fedoras, the nomads look a little bit like businessmen—but only from the neck up.

And finally, as the day relinquishes its own spotlight, dusk descends into evening in Gandan Khiid, meeting halfway with the curvaceous rooftops of the temples themselves. The effect of this handshake between light and dark creates a visual sensation of vibration.

Absorbing the electric dusk, Meg and I cut through the monastery in complete silence. I still wasn't sure if she had designs on Evan, but I was sure about one thing: I'd decided I did.

⚜

"So," Evan was saying to the crowd gathered on the outdoor patio of a local pub as Meg and I arrived. "My friend described the wine as 'perky' but never 'insouciant.' In the middle of recounting another legend, he caught my eye as Meg and I arrived and looked at me a little longer than

I'd expected him to. "And then," he concluded sotto voce, still staring at me as if it were the first time he'd ever seen me, "we agreed it was 'busy' yet not 'precocious.'"

As he slowly drew out the words embellishing the wine he'd drunk, everyone laughed. No matter how pedestrian his tale, Evan never failed to get a laugh out of his delivery.

"Have a seat," he offered us solemnly, making room for just one of us on the bench next to him. I sat down next to Evan and glanced at Meg for just a split second. I had to acknowledge it was still entirely possible that I was imagining our sudden rivalry. Still, I didn't want to take any chances.

"Zuhn gram vodka," Evan said to the waitress, and held up two fingers, ordering a pair of shots for us. Saying nothing, I caught Meg's eye once more as she ordered her own drink.

"Cheers," she said with her usual equanimity, which was now maddening, once our drinks had arrived. Raising her glass to mine, she smiled genuinely.

"Cheers," I said in return, reluctantly and guiltily.

Hell must have a table reserved especially for the manufacturers of vodka, and ex-Communist-nations' vodka, in particular. Abrasive, raw, and biting, it's like drinking nail polish–flavored rocket fuel. And we all know a thing or two about rocket fuel—it's strong enough to power a rocket. And like rocket fuel, Mongolian vodka burns your nose before it even touches your lips. You're as likely to sip it as you would be to sip lighter fluid. Holding my breath, I downed the acrid poison in a series of nervous, jagged gulps. Feeling like I'd just swallowed a lit match, my eyes bulged and watered.

"Another round?" Evan asked.

"Bring it on," I confirmed, narrowing my eyes seductively.

"Zuhn gram vodka!" he called out to the waitress again, ordering another pair of shots for both of us.

"Another round?" Evan asked a third time.

He hardly needed to ask. "I'm only getting thirstier," I quipped.

Obviously, we were both about to take the easy way out of confronting the evolution of a platonic relationship into a romance. But that wouldn't last long. In fact, it wouldn't even last through the weekend.

"Let's go for a walk," I said suddenly to Evan. I'd had just enough liquid courage to broach the subject I'd spent the evening pondering.

It was late, nearly midnight, and it hardly seemed unusual to anyone that we were leaving, although we did field a few raised eyebrows for leaving together. Meg just waved me off and said she'd see me back at home. In fact, she seemed even less interested in our joint departure than the rest of our friends. Obviously, I'd misunderstood her intentions, but it was too late to turn back the clock. Anyway, I didn't necessarily want to.

Once Evan and I had gone, I tried to gather the courage to say something, anything at all, but I just couldn't. The only thing worse than talking about your feelings is being told that you're the only one feeling them. Kicking at the dirt, we both seemed to try in vain to strike up a conversation, but it was no use. The weather had grown unbearably, sweaty-upper-lip hot that evening. There was only one place to seek some relief, and obviously it wasn't at my Mormon host family's apartment. Evan's apartment was near Peace Avenue, and without any discussion whatsoever about where we were going, we made our way there.

Once inside, we kissed. It was a slightly drunken kiss, the sloppy kind that is not exactly born of sincerity, and we both knew it. But we didn't figure that out until we'd ripped each other's clothes off, only to find that neither one of us was ready to go on.

"Mac and cheese?" Evan said, interrupting the otherwise awkward moment.

"I'd love some," I said, wondering where on earth he'd managed to obtain a box of American Kraft macaroni and cheese.

While he cooked, completely naked, I got dressed and sat in an armchair in his living room, watching him. What I couldn't deny was that there was something to him, but what I just wasn't sure about yet was if there was something to us.

Evan drained the pasta and mixed it with the cheese and butter. Turning back toward me, he held out a bowl of strategically placed late-night dinner that covered what his missing boxer shorts didn't. We both laughed.

"I have a girlfriend," he said suddenly into the choking silence of abruptly ended giggles. "Sort of," he added, as if either the girlfriend or the "sort of" was something of an afterthought. Explaining that they'd only recently begun dating, he said it was too early to tell if there was a future in it.

"We're deciding whether or not," he paused, considering his words, "to care more."

Carefully, deliberately, I put my unfinished dinner onto his coffee table. Considering my own words, I wanted to tell him that his macaroni and cheese was too salty. Instead, I looked at him for a long time, wondering just what to make of meeting someone so far away, under such unlikely circumstances, with such a serendipitous backdrop. Was this all that would come of it?

"The thing is," he added finally, "I think I love her."

"To. Care. More." One by one, I repeated those three words back to him, gravely, wondering if they'd sound as baffling to him as they did to me. But they didn't. He meant what he'd said; his brand of relationship wisdom was his truth. After all, he'd explained, he'd only just met her. While he was here, she was there, back in the United States, finishing up a law degree. He and his new girlfriend simply hadn't had the time to think about their feelings for each other before he'd left for Mongolia. But now, well, now he was more certain of what he felt.

Still though, I was thrown. I've always thought that love, like destiny, happens to you. You don't happen to it. So I told him all about the fortune-teller and his prediction. Evan just shrugged his shoulders, and I was left no clearer. The only thing I knew for sure was that it was time to go home. After all, we had a weekend in Khustain to resolve what was left of this. And that's just what we'd do, although not in a way I'd have exactly expected.

Outside, it was nearly two o'clock in the morning, but I managed to find a taxi quickly. Back at home, I slid under the covers and fell fast asleep. Just a few short hours later, I woke up to the clank of breakfast dishes and running water. This could mean only one thing: it was time to forget about the night before and get up to prepare for my very first adventure into the Mongolian steppe. I peered outside at a glorious summer dawn. The sun was rising, rimming buildings and trees in radiant orange and ruby.

CHAPTER 14

The Steppe

Anika Moarzing, President of the Federation of the World Anesthesiologists'
Association, organized a series of training courses for local Mongolian doctors.
These courses were aimed at enhancing the current practices and profession-
alism of doctors here in the country.

—**Evening news voiceover, *MM Today* broadcast**

Meg and I arrived at the bus stop, early and eager. Standing alongside our
transportation, waiting for the others to arrive, we tapped our feet in the
stillness and sipped cups of hot coffee. Finally, everyone arrived, and we
were off. Evan and a friend had booked a car and were already on their
way.

Politely, Meg had asked about my night with Evan, and I'd simply
shrugged. "We'll see," was all I said.

As we drove west along Peace Avenue, the pavement gave way to
a bumpy dirt road, which would soon give way to just bumps. I hung
my head out the window, ingesting as much of the scenery as I could.
Standing beside a wooden table at a street corner, an old man peddled
an unlikely combination of fur pelts and cassette tapes, with a sign that
simply read *"KACCET,"* handwritten in Cyrillic on a flap of cardboard.
Trailing behind a clunky, cheddar-orange Soviet oil tanker, we watched
the trappings of city life slowly exhaust themselves. Wide wooden plank

boards mapped out property lines, but those, too, disappeared as we drove deeper into the countryside. Here, emptiness spilled out onto endless emptiness.

I dug through my pockets until I found my iPod. Listening to it was something of a luxury that had to be rationed. Without reliable electricity in the host family's apartment, I was never sure which moment might be my last to listen to my music. Often, it seemed to complete the thoughts I couldn't always complete on my own. I scrolled to find Bach's cello suites and closed my eyes. As bow dipped into string, the swell of Yo-Yo Ma's cello served as the perfect backdrop to the adventure we were embarking upon. The drawn-out notes rose and fell, just like the verdant hills and valleys.

All around me, the color green exploded, over and over again, wafting scents of rosemary and thyme as the van turned onto a dirt path. Not for the first time, I silently and incredulously remarked to myself, I'm *here*; I'm not *there*. Still, I could hardly believe it all, and opening my eyes once again to the brilliance of the beauty and the steppe only made it that much more incredible to me.

Five hours later, Meg and I were still pressed up against one another, feeling a little less eager, a lot less poetic, and definitely impatient. Finally though, we arrived. Although we'd driven only about sixty miles, the rough terrain made the trip slow going.

Khustain National Park is home to the Przewalski horse, a breed of horse so endangered that it's already extinct—at least technically. In the wild, the Przewalski *is* extinct and has been since 1969. But in captivity, where breeding programs have all but saved the species, there are only about fifteen hundred horses left. And those horses, once they're set free in a special protected zone in Mongolia, roam as if they owned the place all along.

Built like professional wrestlers, the Przewalski horses are short and squat with brassy blond or auburn coats and taupe-colored mullet manes that are so scrub-brush stiff that they don't swish in a breeze. Frankly, they have the burly body of Hulk Hogan and the haircut of Vanilla Ice.

What's remarkable about the Przewalski horse is that it's the only wild horse on earth, and you will be reminded of just that by anyone who's ever come in contact with these majestic beasts. They look nothing like the lean and tall American Mustang, a breed that's often given the dubious distinction of being wild, despite having once been domesticated. To put this into context for those of us who know little about horses, most animals on this planet are used as our food, our food's food, our transportation, or for target practice. The Przewalski, however, has succumbed to none of these fates and has remained, all this time, wild.

We collected our bags from the bus and huddled in a group under the weight of a dense, sodden sky that had turned moody during the long drive. It was misty and unusually cool, a late-summer afternoon in the Mongolian steppe that felt more like early autumn in the Lord of the Rings. A neighborhood of *gers* dotted a dip in the valley surrounding us. From a distance, they looked like gigantic aspirin, neatly lined up in rows on a pharmacist's counter.

Our group was large, about twenty people, and most of the travelers had decided to strike out on their own and camp. At thirty US dollars per night for room and board in a traditional *ger*, the fee was steep for most of the backpackers. On the other hand, camping was free, but it was also illegal. And because it was prohibited, there were no facilities. So even if you could sneak around the restrictions, the threat of rain was going to make a warm fire difficult to come by.

The solemn sky began to empty itself on us, and we fled to our accommodations—Meg and the rest of the group to set up their makeshift campsite, and Evan and Tobie and I and a few others to the *ger* camp. Evan and I were very clearly avoiding each other and the previous night's conversation, but that wouldn't last for long, because each of us needed a roommate in order to stay in a *ger*. Ours wasn't the only group here, and accommodations were in limited supply.

"Pick a roommate!" someone shouted into the din of the noisy drizzle. Evan and I looked at each other, shrugged our shoulders, and gave each other a thumbs-up—a gesture of convenience, not of romance. Partnered up and hauling overnight packs, off we trotted to find our assigned *gers*.

All over Mongolia, *gers* are built with their doors facing south. This is done to keep out the intense heat of the summer sun and to keep in the warmth of sunlight during the cold winters. No matter where you go, you can tell which direction you're traveling just by seeing a *ger* and the location of its front door.

Crouching into the low painted entryway of the little round felt house, we deposited our bags on two of the three beds that lined its rear wall. An old-fashioned stovepipe was at the center, made of a thin aluminum. Although the *gers* in our compound were used as permanent hotel accommodation, nomads use them as portable homes. From the stovepipe to the felt walls, everything is lightweight enough to be carried by people and horses to fresh grazing pastures, season after season, year after year. While Evan and I unpacked, we made just enough small talk to assure each other that, really, everything was just fine. But not long after, the silence became unbearable. Mercifully, there was a tap at the door, and we both rushed to answer it.

"We're all going for a hike," one of the other group members said, inviting us to join them. The rain had stopped for a little while and the fragrant steppe was hushed.

Low stone ridges gave way to gentle craggy peaks. As I inhaled the subtle scent of herbs in the shifting wind, I marveled that maybe—just maybe—I was hiking one of the very trails that Genghis Khan had roamed eight centuries earlier. After all, given my surroundings, it wasn't exactly a stretch. Although Mongolian cities have modernized extensively since the fall of Communism, the countryside's prairies were left just as they had been long ago. With few roads, fewer modern facilities, and no buildings other than the *gers*, visitors end up marveling that they've somehow stepped inside a time machine and turned back the dial very, very far.

I dropped back from the group, watching Evan up ahead, holding court again with another of his parabolic tales. A long time later, he was still telling it, everyone was still laughing, and we were only halfway up the same stubbornly steady incline. So vast, so expansive is the Mongolian countryside, that it's impossible for the naked eye to measure distance on a scale of footsteps. Contemplating the last of my coveted chocolate stash that my mom had sent with me to Mongolia, I thought about Evan and the conversation we'd had. No matter which way I looked at it, it came back to me from a distorted angle. Only one thing was clear, though, and that was that I still had the weekend to figure a few things out about him—and myself.

Suddenly, the sky shuddered, groaned, and spit a squall of icy summer rain all over our party. It was time to head back, and not a moment too soon. Like bees threatened from their hive, we evacuated, moving as a tightly knit shadow, swarming determinedly down the craggy hillside, past all those deceptively low ridges that we'd have to save for another day. Back at the mess hall, indulging in tall glasses of cold lager and bowls of hearty mutton stew and pasta, I found Tobie.

After the fruitless steak dinner with the horse researcher back in Ulaanbaatar, he and I had done our own homework on Khustain. It was then that we discovered that none other than Julia Roberts had been involved in the 1999 making of a documentary about the region and its Przewalski horse tenants. Obviously, the story we'd pitched had been upstaged by a Hollywood starlet. Tobie and I would have to bring a different angle to a tale that had already been told, or we'd have to tell another one entirely. We would end up doing neither; instead, a story would find us.

In the meantime though, we'd see for ourselves what all the fuss in Khustain was about. We were determined to try to get a glimpse of these famed horses, called *takhi* in Mongolian. This wouldn't be easy. Like all horses, the *takhi* are shy, but like few horses, they roam freely across a massive national park. Actually, seeing one would be a real treat, but would require a bit of luck and some transportation that we didn't have. The Mongolian man who'd driven us to Khustain had left us behind many hours earlier and taken his keys with him. But—it just so happened—he'd left his van behind.

Tobie and I finished our dinner, and along with the rest of the group, set off on foot. Although the rain had let up, dusk was falling; there wasn't much time to find the Przewalski—until someone in our group came up with the genius idea to, temporarily anyway, steal the driver's van.

"I'll hot-wire it!" the backpacker had shouted in that fearless, bullet-proof sort of way you do when your determination is dogged. He'd said it as if hot-wiring were an everyday task for him, and who knows, maybe it was. So, with impressive ease, he did as he'd promised, and in no time at all, the van's engine was rumbling. We all piled in and kept our eyes peeled. And it's a good thing we did, because the first species we spotted was our driver, and he was furious. But not for very long. Just as I turned around to peer out the dusty back window and see him beating the air with his fists, we were all treated to a magical sight.

There, in a meadow at the base of the valley alongside the dirt path, was a group of endangered Przewalski horses. Side by side they stood, observing us as coolly and carefully as we observed them.

In the 1970s, a small Dutch group formed the Foundation for the Preservation and Protection of the Przewalski Horse. At the time, it was estimated that as few as three hundred of these wild horses were still alive. Worse still, the last time anyone could remember having even *heard* about a Przewalski sighting, only one had supposedly been seen. Of course, this makes for very lonely mating and procreation activity. So, in an effort to salvage the species, now facing extinction in the wild and in captivity, the Dutch foundation bought several barely related male and female horses from zoos, turned down the lights, and let them go at it. It didn't take long for the foals to arrive, and not long after that, in 1992, the foundation began shipping horses back to Mongolia, where hundreds of them roam in a mostly free existence in Khustain National Park.

"Stop!" the driver barked hoarsely behind us. But he didn't give us the dressing-down we deserved; instead, his jaw dropped. *"Takhi,"* he whispered in awe, captivated by what had captivated us.

"Camera?" someone finally suggested. Keeping our eyes trained on the distant horses, we slowly, deftly dug into our pockets and bags to find our cameras. One false move, we knew, would ruin this photo op for good.

Startled by the sounds of zippers and human voices, the horses seemed to confer with each other. Then, as if on cue, they playfully pranced away, gracefully spurning us. Adobe-matte coats and stiff taupe mullet manes didn't budge an inch in the musky breeze. As Julia Roberts put it in her documentary, the *takhi* look like zebras but without the stripes. Effortlessly, the pack glided away, trailed by misty curls of foggy dusk. It was almost as if we were the exhibit in their zoo, rather than the other way around. For a long time, all of us stood stock still in the enveloping darkness.

CHAPTER 15

Another Dream, Another Dreamer

A third Mongolian athlete will be going to the 2008 Beijing Olympics. Pistol shooter Miss Munkhzul has taken fourth place in the world championship of shooting. Over 100 participants from forty countries competed in a shooting event in the Croatian city of Zagreb.

—Lead story, *MM Today* broadcast

This time, with the official driver behind the wheel, instead of a teenaged backpacker, we returned to our *gers* and campsites. The campers spent the evening tending to a sputtering fire, eating dry soup packets mixed with lukewarm water while Evan and Tobie and I were treated to a night of unexpected entertainment.

"Hi, my name is Nara," a young Mongolian woman said in English, smiling at me and holding out her hand. She was short and plump, with chubby cheeks and a pug nose. "Why have you come here to my country?"

I'd been standing in the provisions shop that the *ger* owners ran, looking at pictures of Julia Roberts and her film crew, who'd produced the documentary about the Przewalski horse, hanging on the wall. "She stayed here long time, you know," Nara confided before introducing herself to Tobie and Evan.

"I work at *Mongol Televit*," I said to Nara, using the Mongolian colloquialism for the network. Shaking her hand, I explained that I'd come as an intern and would be in Mongolia for the rest of the summer.

"Thank you for coming to my country," she said, as if I were the one doing Mongolia a favor, rather than the other way around. "I invite you and your friends for special Mongolia drink in my *ger*," she said, gesturing to Evan and Tobie. In return, we purchased a bottle of vodka from the provisions shop and followed Nara to where she was staying.

Just a few doors down from our own *ger*, Nara was bunking with a French woman. Their *ger* was spartan, one of a few reserved for travelers on a longer stay than just a weekend. Ducking inside the tiny doorway, Nara made room for us to sit down. There were just two single beds along the wall and a wooden desk with a couple of matching chairs. A table lamp shone brightly at the back of the *ger,* an obtrusive spotlight in an otherwise cozy evening. Without all the colorful furniture and the third bed, Nara's *ger* seemed quite spacious. She sat down at the desk across from her roommate and motioned for us to sit on the bed.

"I am guiding Valerie," Nara said as she introduced us to the French woman, who was about my age. Tobie, Evan, and I sat together, facing Nara and Valerie. "Valerie has come from France to work with the *takhi* in Khustain." Although it was difficult to hear over the pounding thump of a small but powerful stereo on top of the desk, Valerie told us her story. She had goldilocks blond curls and big blue eyes that seemed more melancholy than bright.

"I came here to track the horses," Valerie said quietly, explaining that there was a volunteer program that allowed foreigners to spend three weeks in the Khustain steppe, recording the movements of *takhi*. From the way she described it, the benefits of the program were a two-way street: the person tracking the horses got a chance to spend several weeks in solitude in the Mongolian countryside, and the administrators of the Khustain *takhi* program got a free researcher who would manually record coordinates of the horses' locations and daily migration patterns.

But still, I was intrigued by the reason Valerie had come all this way to Mongolia. She was thirty-two years old, and, like me, she'd been in the middle of a successful career in the corporate world. Why had she too left all that behind? I asked her, but she didn't look as if she knew the answer anymore.

"Because? I'm not sure," she said in an alluring French accent. "What is expected of me as a woman? It is babies and a husband. I am not sure if this is all I want from life."

Valerie said this in a matter-of-fact way, but she said it with sadness. Even so, I understood just what she meant. Living life in the shadows of other people's expectations is not quite living at all. But still, I wanted to understand specifically why she seemed so unhappy. After all, it scared me to think that someone could follow her dream and get it all wrong.

"So how have you found the experience?" I pressed. If nothing else, I was simply amazed by her tenacity to remain in solitude. Valerie would spend three weeks entirely alone, walking through the steppe in silent contemplation. Her only conversation would be with Nara, who came weekly to check on her and bring any needed supplies.

"It's been the loneliest time of my life," Valerie said simply, almost regrettably. Evan and Tobie were silent, and Nara seemed to sense that her party was fizzling. I'd have to find out more about Valerie later.

"Patricia, have you tried *airag?*" Nara asked, offering me what looked like a saucer of milk.

"What is it?" I asked as I brought the saucer to my nose. The smell was utterly overpowering, like sour-smelling steamed socks.

"You will try it," Nara ordered. "It is a Mongolian favorite. Very, very good," she added as Evan let out a cavalier whoop, suggesting he knew otherwise.

Airag and *arkhi* are two of the most popular alcoholic beverages in Mongolia. Made from fermented mare's milk, the only difference between them is the amount of time spent in fermentation, and the fact that one tastes more like socks than the other. Pumped partially full of the mare's milk, wooden barrels are sealed shut for just a few weeks to produce a vintage as rich or as weak as time allows. Like moonshine in America or table wine in southern Europe, *airag* and *arkhi* are common enough to be found in unmarked bottles. Absolutely everyone in the country drinks it, even my teetotaling Mormon host family.

Tipping the saucer to my lips, I bared my front teeth as a filter to the milk skin that had grown and now stretched over the top of the brew. Flecks of coagulated, lumpy cheese bobbed to the surface and I sipped delicately at the sour, milky mixture that was surprisingly fizzy. It was certainly unique, like a cheese-flavored soda, and I can't say that I loved it. In fact, I knew precisely why I didn't love it.

Years earlier, when I'd lived in Japan, I'd made a culinary commitment to try absolutely everything on every menu I came across. "Eating local" in any country is always an interesting adventure, especially if you grew up in the midwestern United States, knowing seafood only as Mrs. Paul's frozen fish sticks and cheese as the American, orange, plastic-wrapped slices. So eating local in Japan, where seafood is religion, can be a little overwhelming at times.

And so it was one night while on a date with a Japanese-speaking American man. He had treated me to a very posh restaurant, the kind of place that has perfectly dimmed lights, a sushi bar crafted from scrubbed sandstone, and chefs speaking to patrons in hushed tones.

Aside from serving so-called ordinary items such as bowls of sea urchin (exquisite when fresh but tastes like a wet orange sponge if eaten stale), puffer fish sashimi (deadly poisonous if prepared incorrectly), and natto (a surprisingly tasty fermented, gluey soybean mucus that's served over steamed rice), the restaurant offered delicacies considered exotic even for their seasoned Japanese clientele. Leaning forward to speak in a barely audible whisper, the counter chef and my date conversed in Japanese for a long-enough time to suggest that something serious was about to happen.

"Would you like to try a rare delicacy?" my date asked, translating for me what the chef had asked him.

"Absolutely," I said, assuring him that I would love to, as long as he didn't tell me what I was eating before I finished. At that point, my date issued a disclaimer.

"A word of warning," he said. "What they're offering you is something I would never, ever eat."

"Even better!" I said, growing a little hesitant. But still, I was curious, and I refused to walk away from this moment knowing I'd been a culinary coward.

"Thanks," I said enthusiastically as my date nodded to the chef to bring whatever-it-was to me.

Moments later, a small dish of grayish-white chunks arrived. Bland and slightly fishy, it had the look of a bowl of tiny tubular oatmeal. I ate it quickly, making certain to swallow the soft, lumpy substance without lingering too long.

"So, what was it?" I asked after I'd finished.

"Whale sperm," he answered a bit triumphantly.

Unlike the *airag* Nara had offered me, whale sperm was actually tolerable because it tasted like nothing I'd ever tasted before—a bowl of fish oatmeal. Although the texture was definitely peculiar, the flavor itself was completely unfamiliar.

Airag, on the other hand, was completely familiar. It tastes like nail polish remover smells, and smells like bleu cheese tastes. In a word, it was *interesting*. And it wasn't the worst thing I'd ever put in my mouth. That spot has always been reserved for liquid American cheese that squirts out of a canister.

"You like it?" Nara asked, giggling, surveying my reaction carefully.

"Yep," I said graciously, still unsure.

Nara passed the bowl of *airag* to Tobie, and I nodded encouragingly at him.

"It's or-full," Tobie said candidly after he'd sampled it, handing it right back to her.

"Patricia likes it," Nara giggled appreciatively, returning the cup to me.

Actually, not just yet, so I passed the cup to Evan. "This is good music, Nara," I said to her, changing the subject to what the stereo was pumping out.

"You like Mongolian hip-hop?" she asked.

"I definitely do now!" Although I'd never heard Mongolian hip-hop before, there was something very captivating about the jaunty beat and the poignantly clipped tone of the lead singer. He sounded like Eminem, if Eminem were to rap in German or Turkish or any other language with an awful lot of consonants.

"He is Quiza," Nara said. "Top hip-hop artist in Mongolia."

"He's great," I said, and I meant it.

"He's my brother-in-law," Nara said simply. "You would like to meet him?"

It's funny; sometimes, maybe every time, when you throw caution to the wind to follow a dream, you find that fate goes to work for you. Nara's invitation to meet her husband, who was Quiza's manager, and Quiza himself, would completely alter the tempo of the rest of my experience in Mongolia. And not in a way I could have expected.

Catching Tobie's eye, I didn't need to ask what he was thinking, because it was clear we were both thinking exactly the same thing: *feature story.*

"I'd love to," he and I both said simultaneously.

"Good," Nara said, looking as pleased with herself as she was with us.

Valerie had to get up early the next morning to track the horses, so Evan and Tobie and I left her behind with Nara to turn in for the night.

Back outside, the night sky had come to life. It was as if someone had switched on thousands and thousands of night lights, tiny white pinpricks studding an enormous canvas of deep, black curtain, pulled taut over the ends of the horizon. Long, textured strips of diamond-dusted galaxies wrinkled into the curtain's folds. There were more stars than I'd ever seen, and they created the effect of a shadow box, where we all were the subjects of someone else's musings.

With my neck craned backward at a ninety-degree angle, I stood in awe. And so did everyone else. One by one, dressed in pajamas and overcoats, guests were spilling outside and gasping at the wide-open space above them. Together, Evan and Tobie and I stared in silence until finally, Evan spoke.

"Drink at our place?" he said, and Tobie took his cue to head back to his own *ger*, alone. Obviously our recent conversation was on Evan's mind too.

Inside, he lit a fire in the stovepipe and we sat across from each other at the little wooden dining table in the center of the *ger*. Backs to each other, modestly, we'd quickly changed into our pajamas.

"Vodka?" he asked. We'd run out of drinking water, so neither of us had much of a choice.

"Got anything to water that down?" I asked.

"Orange soda," he said with a smile, and mixed our drinks in two makeshift tumblers crafted from two empty water bottles whose tops had been sliced off.

Almost mechanically, we meandered through myriad topics only ever discussed when two people are trying to avoid tackling the obvious. From my experience in banking and his in law school to the obscure subject of the history of North Korea's leadership, we managed to cover pretty much everything. By the time there wasn't much else left to say, we'd had a little bit too much to drink. Of course, it was at this point that the only thing left to discuss was us.

"The thing is," Evan said, "you are just not the marrying kind."

He'd said it abruptly, apropos of nothing at all. For a long time, I was speechless. Evan had made one of those staggering remarks that seems to all but stop time. Worse, he went on. With steepled fingers, he provided proof for this newfound wisdom.

"You are just a fantasy, an adventurer," he began again, suddenly and di-dactically pointing a swaying finger in my direction. "You are the woman men think they want to be with, but in the end, men don't want adventure. Men choose wives and mothers, not fantasies."

Numbly, I stared at him and still said nothing. He could hardly know how prophetic his statement was, at least in my mind.

Months before I'd left for Mongolia, before I'd even quit my banking job, I'd met a man. Not just any man, but a cliché—the kind of guy you warn your friends about. Handsome, successful, and witty, he was engaged. To the wrong woman, of course, as he put it.

"It's complicated," he'd explained to me one night over dinner. He said it as if I didn't already know what that meant. "Give me one year," he begged, promising me that he'd untie the knot he'd already promised another woman that he'd tie with her, permanently. Ironically, we were having dinner at the very restaurant where the fortune-teller worked who would later tell me I'd meet a man named E.

"I'd like to read your tarot cards," the fortune-teller had said that same night, abruptly interrupting our dinner. He was standing impatiently at our table as if he were a waiter with a food order to take.

"Sure," I said. "Pull up a chair."

"No," he'd said. "I must talk to you alone," he'd insisted.

"Forget it, then," I'd said, pointing to the engaged man. "I'm on a date!"

A week later, unable to dismiss the urgency of the fortune-teller's offer, I returned alone to the restaurant to seek him out. Not only did the tarot cards reveal that Evan was supposedly my future husband, but they sig-naled I'd met this engaged man for no other reason than to learn a lesson about myself.

Then, one day, the engaged man said it, preempting what Evan would say just months later: "You are simply a fantasy to me."

Obviously, the fortune-teller had gotten it all wrong about Evan. And so had I. But like Pimples, Evan had hit a nerve. And Evan had been the last person I'd expected to hit such a nerve. After all, I'd been told I'd fall in love with him, which didn't look much like it would happen soon, or ever.

Like Valerie, the French horse tracker, I could not settle for just any life, for just any man who wanted whatever a "wife" was supposed to be. I wanted more, and I wouldn't stop at Evan to try to find it. If it took remaining single for the rest of my life, then so be it. Besides, I hadn't come all this way to Mongolia to meet the man of my dreams. I'd come all this way to fulfill my own dreams. They weren't fantasies, and neither was I.

With that, I went to bed. I said nothing and instead just crawled under the covers. Even if I'd had a retort, I wouldn't have used it. Some moments are best left without an explanation.

What seemed like a very short amount of time later, there was a tap at the door. "Breakfast!" someone announced from behind it. Inside the *ger*, it was dark as night. Fumbling for my clothes, I dressed as quietly as I could. Evan was still asleep, and it was probably best he stay that way. I laced up my boots and opened the creaking wooden door to reveal spectacular sunshine in another day as bright and blue as a robin's egg.

Blinded, I shielded my eyes from the blazing rectangle of light coming from the doorway and headed to the mess hall. Nursing a dull hangover headache in what felt like a rapidly shrinking skull, I set off to find its antidote. There, at the mess hall, I found Valerie finishing her breakfast, and she invited me to join her. Most of our group was there, tucking into plates of eggs and mugs of hot coffee, laughing jovially and reminiscing about the night before. Nara had left earlier that morning to return to her husband and son in Ulaanbaatar, and Valerie was at a table by herself.

"You would like to join me for a walk in the steppe?" she asked. Valerie had to make her rounds with the horses, but I could tag along beforehand. I finished my breakfast, and we set off.

"And what about you?" she asked as we ambled over rocky plains in the rosemary haze of the endless steppe. "What we talked about last night, what do you think about marriage and children and"—she hesitated a moment—"and expectations?"

"I don't think I'm cut out for any of that," I said succinctly as we sat near a stream. I felt strangely relieved as I said it, as if, finally, I'd committed to the real me instead of the person I sometimes thought I should be.

Here and there, dotting the hillside around us, were the remains of animal carcasses, their bones picked and bleached completely clean by predators and the sun. In such a vast and empty setting, they looked like pieces of discarded and overturned furniture scattered across a desolate ranch.

CHAPTER 16

As Bold as Breasts

The Mongolian government has decided to enact financial reform in order to reduce budget expenditures. The finance minister tells us that structural changes will need to be undertaken. A special working group has begun to examine the manner in which these reforms can be initiated.

—Lead story, *MM Today* broadcast

"I am Bold, bold like breasts."

Back in Ulaanbaatar, Nara made good on her promise to introduce Tobie and me to her husband, Bold, the manager of one of Mongolia's hottest hip-hop stars, as well as his brother, Quiza, the hip-hop star himself.

"Breasts?" I repeated, confused. With brooding black eyes in a chiseled face with high cheekbones and a square jaw, Boldoo, nicknamed "Bold," seemed too handsome to have a sense of humor.

"Breasts?" he repeated back to me, an embarrassed shade of pink setting first into his jaw and then climbing into the arched peaks of those cheekbones. "Ha! No!" he quickly retracted. "I am Bold, as bold as *brass*! Not *breasts*!" Laughing self-consciously at his misfired joke, he tripped over his words as he explained, apologizing for the mistake. Bold had a good-natured laugh, the easy kind that you find yourself joining. For the first time since I'd met him, Tobie let out an infectious belly laugh of his own.

Brothers in their mid-twenties, Quiza and Bold had a passion for hip-hop, and American hip-hop in particular. A decade earlier, they'd both been fans of the Wu Tang Clan, Cypress Hill, and Dr. Dre, and Quiza liked to emulate the various groups' styles and moves. On a whim as a teenager, he'd recorded a single song to submit to Mongolia's FM 102.5, a commercial radio station in the capital. The song was an instant hit, and the station played it often. Armed with nods of approval from the general public and the professional DJs, Quiza had earned himself a chance to make it big.

Instead, he went ahead with his family's plan to send him to the Czech Republic to go to school. At the time he was only sixteen years old and the youngest of eight children; his mother had died long ago. On a government clerk's salary, his father had supported the family, but money had been tight and the family's hopes for Quiza had been high. In Prague, he studied agricultural business. Like anyone who's hanging on to an improbable dream, Quiza snubbed his passion and stuck to what he was supposed to be doing, like his homework.

Until he recorded another song.

With the embers of passion stoked all over again, Quiza began toying with the idea of setting up a band. Through the Internet grapevine, he found a fellow Mongolian musician living in the UK and together they formed a group called the Crew. Quiza quit school and moved to London. Facing the cresting wave of his passion, he left in his wake all those expectations that had been set out for him. Shortly thereafter, Quiza's brother, Bold, joined him in London. Together, the brothers worked in restaurants to save enough money to make the music they so loved.

Depending on whom you asked in 2006, take-home pay for your average Mongolian family was anywhere from thirty US dollars a month in the rural areas, to a few hundred dollars a month in the capital. Without any record labels in the country's cottage music industry, and with no outside support from the music industry at large, Bold and Quiza would have faced a bill of five to ten times their combined monthly income back home to produce just one more song, never mind a whole album. Including marketing, the finished product of an album can easily run up a bill of thousands of dollars. It's hard to imagine how any band can make it at all in the country, until you see for yourself the creativity artists employ in order to be employed by their creativity.

Consolidating the savings they'd made in the United Kingdom, Quiza and Bold purchased sound and recording equipment from eBay. Bold returned to Mongolia while Quiza remained in London, writing lyrics for the Crew, gaining traction and increasing confidence.

In late 2005, Quiza moved back home. By this point, he'd written, sung, or coproduced about sixty songs, creating a grassroots fan base. No sooner had he arrived in Ulaanbaatar than a member of Camerton, then Mongolia's hottest boy band, asked Quiza to write lyrics for three songs he was producing. The band member was going solo and wanted to use Quiza's broadening fan base as well as his unique ability to capture the essence of local flavor in his lyrics. Quiza eagerly accepted, and that December he received the Mongolian Grammy for Best R&B and Best Dance lyrics.

Finally, with Bold as manager, the band was able to use the sound and recording equipment they'd bought. And with Bold, Quiza produced his first album, *TAABAR MET,* which was released the following winter. Singing about problems endemically personal to Mongolia and Mongolians—poverty in the *ger* districts, political corruption, and human rights—Quiza's homespun lyrics and literal tone hit the airwaves as a smashing success. Mongolians simply loved him.

By the spring of 2006, a music video featuring Quiza performing his title track made him one of the most recognizable artists in the country. His second album followed soon after. Titled, *HIIMORIIN SAN,* or "Spirit Catcher," it couldn't have been a better or more fitting name for someone who'd staked everything he'd known to follow his dream.

Mongolians love music, and they've loved music for as long as anyone can remember. Whether sending a message in song to a distant lover on the steppe, coaxing an ornery camel (again, in song) to suckle her calf, or announcing sports results at an annual festival, your average Mongolian will go to any length whatsoever to get his message across lyrically. Take, for instance, the practice of throat singing. Called *khöömii* in Mongolian, it's the ancient art of producing two *simultaneous* sounds from deep within the throat. The result is both a whistle *and* a guttural vibration. However, it happens to be quite dangerous.

There are five methods to learning throat singing, one local told me, and four of them will completely destroy your larynx within just a few years. In other words, Mongolians who learn this age-old practice must really be committed to it if they're willing to risk losing their speech.

In fact, throat singing is such a coveted skill that there is currently a massive diplomatic argument brewing over its origin. In a still-simmering dispute, Chinese students learning throat singing from Mongolian master Odsuren Baatar supposedly betrayed their teacher, secretly using a video of what he'd taught them in order to pitch to UNESCO that throat singing had originated in China, which Mongolians insist isn't true.

In a downtown housing block, Bold and Quiza had rented a small apartment and installed a makeshift music studio. They shared their space with the Lemons, a local indie rock band. While Tobie and I waited for Quiza to arrive, Bold pulled up a few chairs and we watched the Lemons practice amid a cacophonic jumble of cymbals, throat-clearing, and high-pitched microphone whines.

I was excited to meet Quiza. Earlier that week, we'd pitched his and Bold's story to Gandima. She was skeptical, and her interest seemed limited to getting us out of her office and off her back. Reluctantly, she agreed to make a final decision after we showed her a sample of the footage we were about to get.

Suddenly, the Lemons stopped playing, and a rounder version of Bold walked in the door. "Hello," the man with the cherubic mouth said softly as he tentatively stuck out his hand. "I am Quiza."

Quiza was twenty-five years old and very shy. Pasty blotches had spread across his smooth face, and he shifted uncomfortably in his seat next to mine in front of the camera. After Tobie signaled that he'd begun rolling, I first asked Quiza about the hip-hop scene and Mongolian hip-hop in particular. But it wasn't just his music that I was interested in. It was his passion. Truth was, I knew little about music, and even less about hip-hop. Finally, I asked the question I'd been waiting to ask.

"As an artist," I said, "what do you do to make your passion happen?"

Quiza didn't answer. In fact, he seemed a little confused, almost timorous, as if he were lost. Throughout the interview so far, he'd struggled to answer my questions. Bold had helped bridge the language barrier when he could and did so again. However, this left me with only a hesitant, somewhat wooden account of what Quiza and his music were all about. That is, until he took to the stage in the little studio apartment where we were filming. It was the only way he could answer the question. Right away, any evidence of nerves vanished completely, and Quiza was immediately transformed.

Closing his eyes, he began to rap. Rocking and tapping to the steady rhythmic beat, Quiza submerged himself in the music. When the song ended, he actually looked surprised, as if someone had just awakened him from a blissful dream. Quiza had performed the title track to *TAABAR MET,* which means "As a Quest." The name couldn't have been more apt, and I noticed in him just the same expression I'd discovered in Anne O'Brien, the pregnant Irish cyclist. Quiza looked *found.* It had been incredible to witness, once again, this transformation.

With nothing more than a demure nod to his small crowd, Quiza stepped down from the stage. Completely impervious to his own glory, he politely thanked Tobie and me and sat down to watch the Lemons resume practicing their riffs.

"You will join us to watch Quiza perform live tonight?" Bold asked as he showed us to the door, explaining that Quiza was scheduled to open for the Lemons at a local music venue. Nara would be there too. It was the first time I'd been invited out by a local Mongolian, and I felt truly honored to be making friends in a place so far from home.

Before meeting Bold and Quiza that night, Tobie and I made our way to the Grand Khan Irish Pub. The manager of the Grand Khan had made sure that his pub was *the* pub to go to if you wanted to watch the 2006 Football World Cup matches. And he'd agreed to let us interview him. Tobie and I figured we should hedge our bets with Gandima. She hadn't seemed particularly interested in our pitch to produce a feature story on Quiza and Mongolian hip-hop, and we'd have to deal with that later. But for now, surely she'd agree to a story on Mongolia's take on World Cup viewing rituals.

That summer, all over Mongolia, from city folk to nomads, local Mongolians were doing everything they could to watch the soccer matches, going as far as hooking up satellite dishes to *gers.* Some of these outposts were so remote that they were dozens of miles from their nearest neighbor, not to mention a reliable food source. But they all made sure they had access to the matches. Fascinated by this creative dedication to a sport that's not exactly part of the country's culture, Tobie and I were sure everyone else would be just as fascinated.

"I'm here at Ulaanbaatar's famous Grand Khan Irish Pub!" I shouted into the mike over the deafening din of revelers. Standing in the lobby of the bar next to the coat check, I was being pushed aside by people trying to get inside to see the match, which was just about to begin. A slow-moving line snaked from the doorway out through the parking lot. On a much smaller scale, it was like what reporting in the midst of the Super Bowl or Olympic mayhem must be like: crowds, bouncers, security, and excitement.

"And we are in for a treat!" I shouted as a security guard shoved me aside.

Earlier that week, Tobie had uncovered the name of the Grand Khan's manager. A jetsetter among the Ulaanbaatar elite, he'd been surprisingly difficult to track down, and we'd spent an entire day trying to locate his private telephone number. When he'd agreed to talk to us for our story, even Gandima had seemed impressed. But once we got to his bar, he was nowhere to be found. Or so we thought.

Standing inside watching the game, *he* told me *he* was nowhere to be found. Of course, the joke was lost on me. It wasn't until I saw him being introduced on camera by another reporter that I finally understood: he'd changed his mind about who was going to interview him. And instead of granting an interview to MNB, he'd decided at the last minute to grant one to TV5.

One of a handful of Mongolian television broadcasters, TV5 was the new kid on the broadcasting block in the country. Funded in part by private investors, the station's goal was to shake up the somewhat staid atmosphere of traditional post-Soviet, government-funded local broadcasting. With cutting-edge technology, the station boasted luminescent new studios, a snazzy Web site with access to online video streaming, and arrestingly handsome reporters to deliver the whole package to you. Where MNB commanded authority from years in the job, TV5 won respect for trying something new and looking good doing it. Grumbling to ourselves, Tobie and I tried to figure out how to get decent enough footage to beat an actual interview.

"They're good," Tobie said as he watched the TV5 production crew. He seemed to imply that he'd rather be there than where he was. Incredibly, he soon would be.

Tobie and I filmed as much as we could and then packed up to head back to the office, just as a Beatles cover band began playing. Sporting an authentic retro bowl cut, a Mongolian man belted out "Sgt. Pepper's Lonely Hearts Club Band" and a cheer went up from the tightly packed crowd. He stopped suddenly midsong. All of the bar's flat-screen television sets, positioned around its perimeter, were tuned in to the World Cup matches, and their volume had been turned all the way up. The Japan-Croatia match was about to begin, and a hush fell over the crowd.

⚏

"Nomads," I began my pitch to Gandima, a little bit theatrically. "Watching"—I paused—"the World Cup!"

Gandima's eyes narrowed.

"Patricia," she began with breathy irritation. Over the last few weeks since I'd arrived in Mongolia, I'd noticed that Gandima's patience wasn't exactly exhaustible. And right this minute, I realized I'd discovered its limit, and I thought I knew why.

"Patricia," she said again, this time with exaggerated patience. "Mongolia is about more than nomads watching television," she added reproachfully, her voice rising in exasperation. Right away, I knew what she was insinuating and where our pitch had gone wrong.

Many of the Mongolians I'd met so far that summer were quick to point out the rapid pace of the capital's evolution since the fall of Communism. At the same time, they seemed reluctant to acknowledge the quaintness of the steppe. Proud of their heritage, they were fiercely protective of it, too, as if protecting a kid brother. Occasionally, foreigners' interest in Mongolia's recent past is regarded a little bit suspiciously, sometimes with outright hostility. Basically, you're guilty of poking fun until you're proven innocent. And proving ourselves innocent to Gandima was just what Tobie and I needed to do to get the go-ahead from her to film World Cup–viewing rituals in the steppe.

"But wait, Gandima, what I meant was . . ." I pleaded, hastily tripping over my words to paint the picture that Tobie and I had envisioned, making sure to leave out the part about how intriguing we'd both found the imagery of an old nomad tinkering with his satellite dish so he could cheer for the Japanese soccer team. Leading her through the thought process behind our concept, I trailed off as I finished, as you do when you've been talking far too long to convince someone who was never going to change her mind anyway.

Sitting quietly at his desk, even Tobie looked on skeptically.

While we waited for her verdict, the seconds seemed to stack themselves on top of each other, and it was clear that Gandima was going to turn us down.

"No," she said finally, explaining that Mongolia cannot be defined exclusively by its nomads and that highlighting their World Cup viewing practices was definitely not news. It wasn't even a feature. Frowning, she stalked off to her office.

A third of Mongolians are herders living and working in the steppe, which provides pasture for their grazing livestock—livestock that happens to outnumber human beings by a margin of no less than sixteen to one (compared to New York City, where people outnumber livestock by approximately eight million to zero). In my mind, no matter what image Mongolians wanted to portray to the outside world, they would be hard-pressed to change their own facts. Besides, many of our viewers were foreigners, tourists who'd come to the country to see the steppe and its nomads. It was a case of then and now, and the fusion of the two seemed as beguiling as any news story I'd seen on the air since I'd arrived.

At the time, I didn't quite realize it, but Tobie was angry. Angry enough, in fact, to quit, land another job at a rival television station, and finish it all off in a shouting match with Gandima. For Tobie, this was unusual. Although we'd spent an entire month working together, I didn't know much about him, other than that he was English, nineteen years old by now, and gifted at whatever he tried his hand at. But what I did know about Tobie was that he was polite to a fault. He had a well-bred, aristocratic air about him; he simply never lost his temper.

That night, Tobie was still smoldering as we made our way to the local pub where Bold had invited us to watch Quiza and the Lemons perform. At some point, and he'd never said when, Tobie had put in a call to Urna to help him find a new job. Because it was Urna's responsibility to make sure all the interns were happy and fulfilled in their summer roles in Mongolia, she would've been his first call. But as it turned out, Tobie's reputation preceded him, and he would hardly need the recommendation of either Urna or the British company for whom she worked.

TV5, the rival television station where Tobie would soon end up, had already heard about Tobie.

Lost in our own thoughts, Tobie and I walked in silence through a warren of streets and gritty back alleys until finally we found Bold and Nara, who were waiting outside to invite us in to watch Quiza. The venue had been difficult to find; it was one of those places you'd only locate with the benefit of explicit directions or luck. Fortunately, we had a bit of both.

"Hello, welcome!" Bold cried warmly, clasping our hands to shake in that intimate way you do when you've known someone a lot longer than we'd all actually known each other. He had an intensity about him, a real philosophical air that made you want to think carefully before answering any of his probing questions.

"Why are you here?" Bold asked after we sat down at a wooden picnic table, his dark and brooding eyes staring intently, not blinking once. Although he was only in his twenties, he seemed to be much older, much wiser.

I had to think a moment, because it was obvious Bold was not one to suffer fools. By his side, Nara sat quietly and smiled.

"Because I believe in taking risks," I said, without elaborating.

"And is Mongolia a risk to you?" he probed.

"Well, yes," I said. "Isn't any new adventure a kind of risk, no matter where it takes place?"

Bold nodded and said nothing more. Tobie was quiet.

"I would like to say welcome to my guests," Quiza said from up on the stage, pointing in our direction. Tobie and I raised our glasses in return and sat back, listening to the performance. That summer, Quiza was able to draw a small yet lively crowd at obscure venues like this one, but it wouldn't be long before he'd be one of the biggest music sensations in the entire country. Both he and his brother, Bold, had pursued their passions, and they were squarely in the middle of making it happen for themselves.

CHAPTER 17

Consonant Omelet

The Asia-Pacific Director of the International Labor Organization visited the Mongolian Prime Minister today. Mr. Gyok Bu Ng told Prime Minister Enkhbold that Mongolia's progress in developing the labor market has been significant.

—Lead story, *MM Today* broadcast

"Have you tasted Mongolian cheese?" Chinzo asked a few days later.

Chinzo and Tobie and I were sitting in the English news office, working on translations for that evening's script. It was the first time any of the anchors had spoken to us, other than to inform me that I should find another place to sit. Without waiting for a response, Chinzo produced from his pants pocket a chip of pale yellow, almost white, hard cheese. Snapping it in two, like a piece of candy, he offered us both halves.

"Go ahead," Chinzo encouraged. "Try it."

Popping the chip into my mouth, I bit into it. It didn't budge, not even a crack.

"Suck on it, like candy," Chinzo suggested, grinning broadly.

Nomads in the countryside make cheese from their twenty-seven million livestock: cows, yaks, goats, sheep, and even camels. After milking the animal, they boil the liquid and stir in yogurt. Once the mixture has curdled, the solids are strained out and pressed between wooden boards.

The pressed cheese is placed on the roof in the sun where it will eventually dry and harden into brittle chips. Depending on the type of cheese being made, and there are many, leftover liquids are used to produce everything from dipping oils to infant bathwater. Unlike aged European cheeses, Mongolian cheeses are relatively young. Usually left to develop over just a period of days, the taste is far milder than their counterparts around the world. Soft, fresh cheese is eaten on its own, while dried, hard cheese is dipped in tea or sucked on like candy.

"Do you like it?" Chinzo asked earnestly. Mongolians are famous for their dairy products. In fact, a common misperception about the country is that people living there are devoted to eating endless quantities of meat. This is only true in the capital, where a lot of mutton dishes are consumed. But in the countryside, the focus is on fresh, organic dairy products. And many of these products, like the cheese I was sampling now, were made fresh daily by the matron of the house.

"I do like it," I said, and I really did. Once the chip had begun to melt in my mouth, it revealed an almost nutty flavor, like Manchego crossed with Gruyère.

"I am very happy to hear this," Chinzo said with enthusiasm. "I will bring you more!"

With that, he dashed out of our office to retrieve the rest of his stash.

"I brought you a soft cheese this time," Chinzo shouted from some-where down the hallway. He sounded breathless with excitement, and I tried to imagine myself feeling so strongly about American cheese that I'd inflict its nearly dozen ingredients and preservatives and food color-ings on a foreign guest. Chinzo bounded back into the office. In his out-stretched palm was a cube of what looked like a firmer version of Brie.

"Try this!" he said, plucking a black, wiry hair from its center.

"Oh, sorry! Animal coat," he apologized, laughing, before handing it over.

It tasted just as it appeared it would taste, like Brie, only far milder. And it was definitely firmer, almost chewy.

"This is really good," I said to Chinzo, passing to Tobie the remainder of what I hadn't finished.

"I'm glad you like it," Chinzo said proudly, just as Gandima suddenly appeared in our doorway.

"Patricia, Chinzo?" she said. "Come with me."

"Patricia, you will help Chinzo read the voice overs for tonight's news," Gandima announced as she led us down the corridor to the recording studio.

Voiceovers! This was quite a promotion. Not only did it mean more responsibility for me; it meant I was becoming an integral part of the English news team. As we headed toward the studio, I tried to take this all in stride—Gandima had a way of granting promotions without any fanfare whatsoever. If she needed someone to report, read voice overs, or even teach English, well, that's just what she'd tell you to do.

Like most television stations, MNB produced a story, a "package," with just one reporter. The reporter would go out into the field with a producer, shoot the story, and return to the station to edit it with the help of the editing team. Of course, that same reporter's voice would be used for the voiceover. But when it came to MNB's English news, things were completely different.

Only one of the Mongolian reporters spoke fluent English, fluent enough to perform voice over reads, anyway. That reporter was Gandima, and she was too senior and too busy to spend her time reading copy into a microphone. So the task was left to the English news anchors, like Chinzo, who were not necessarily reporters at all, but well-educated and well-spoken Mongolians with fluency in English.

Gandima opened the door and led us inside the glass-walled studio. A tiny, wizened old man, no more than five feet tall, waited for us, holding out a microphone. Several of the editors and technicians were also there, arms folded across their chests, waiting to begin. I got the feeling that this wasn't really a promotion for me but an audition.

Silently, I practiced in my head just what I'd need to do. As I'd learned from Magee Hickey, performing a voice over wasn't as simple as reading deadpan from a piece of paper into a microphone. Rather, it's more like getting into character for a part in a film. In fact, because you must exaggerate your voice so much, it's like getting into character for a part in a cartoon film.

"Patricia," Gandima said, "you go first," and she handed me a sheet of copy. The old man nodded and put the mike in my hands.

"Speak into the mike and start," Gandima instructed. The story was a familiar one; Chinzo and I had just written it. This helped a lot. But reading translated copy from Mongolian scripts is like eating a consonant omelet without a glass of water, and I was nervous. Dipping my voice into a theatrical, cartoonish baritone, I began.

"'Locals in the Nailakh district bleakly joke that the hardest thing to find here is a job,'" I said, shifting awkwardly from one foot to the other, trying to exaggerate the silky and resonant lilt that I'd watched Magee decant effortlessly from her vocal chords. To me, Magee had sounded more like she was confiding in someone, rather than reading from a sheet of paper, so I tried to do just the same.

"Patricia, stop," Gandima said, and I trailed off midsentence. "Now start again, and read much more slowly." Arms folded across her chest, she was standing on the other side of the studio with the rest of the crew.

"Okay." I gulped and began again, reading from the report on faltering economic prospects for a nearby province. "'Locals in the Nailakh district ...'"

"Slower," Gandima said sharply.

Taking a deep breath, I cleared my throat and licked my teeth, which were so dry they felt like postage stamps sticking backward to my gums.

"'Locals in the Nailakh district bleakly joke that the hardest thing to find here is a job. An area housewife tells us she prays every day for her husband and grown children, who are illegally working in the now-closed mine ...'"

Quickly, I swallowed and continued.

"'... With neither prior experience in mining nor knowledge of safety regulations, she worries about the dangers her family will face while illegally working. In order to address the situation, the local government is working on a project that they hope will increase the employment numbers. Nailakh is the beneficiary of New Village Movement, a Korean Aid Project.'"

"Very good," Gandima said after I'd finished. She still had her arms folded across her chest, and so did the rest of the crew.

"Chinzo, begin," she ordered, and turned to me.

"So, does that mean ...," I began, wondering if my audition had resulted in a promotion.

"Yes," Gandima said. "From now on, you and Chinzo will read voice overs for the news."

"And," she went on, as Chinzo read from the scripts. "You can help Chinzo with his English pronunciation."

"Okay," I said, vowing right then and there to do just the opposite. Not only was Chinzo a proud man, the sort of guy who didn't want the American female intern telling him how to correct his pronunciation, but things between us had just gotten off, albeit belatedly, to a good start.

"Listen," Gandima said, pointing in his direction. "He says 'Parliament' without the 'r,' like 'poll lament,' right?"

"True," I conceded.

"Work on this with him, yes?" she said.

"Yes, of course," I said, hoping I wouldn't need to follow through.

"Now about your Quiza pitch," Gandima began ominously, and I waited nervously for her to continue.

"The answer is no," she said, after she'd collected Tobie. With us in tow, she filed into her office.

After Tobie and I had met Quiza and Bold, we'd offered to produce a story on them for MNB. In fact, we hadn't so much offered as we'd promised. In our excitement, it had never occurred to us that Gandima wouldn't agree to our pitch. So, without even waiting for her approval, we'd filmed the brothers, interviewed them, and written most of their story. This was a problem. In Mongolia, loyalty is earned, not granted, and we were going to have to let the brothers down.

" . . . not newsworthy . . ." Gandima went on.

" . . . responsibility to the three-quarters of the Mongolian population that watches this station . . ."

" . . . commitment to journalism . . ."

"This television station is not an advertisement for a rock band," she concluded finally.

"Hip-hop," Tobie pointed out under his breath, just loud enough that I could hear the bristle in his retort. Without another word, she rose from her desk and ended our meeting.

Back in the English news office, Tobie was unusually quiet, and I could tell he was fuming. He'd become close to the brothers, Bold in particular.

For Tobie especially, it wasn't just a case of striking out with Gandima on another pitch; it was a case of breaking a promise to the brothers.

Fed up, Tobie quit. But he was too angry to even bother to tell Gandima that.

Through Urna, Tobie had made contact with network management at TV5, and she'd brokered a deal for him to meet the station's director. The director took one look at Tobie's hardware and editing software and hired him on the spot to create animation graphics. Incredibly, he'd landed a production role with an office and a high-speed Internet connection.

This put me in a bind. Without Tobie as my cameraman and producer, I had no one to shoot video with. I didn't have a broadcast-quality video camera of my own, so I would no longer be able to report. And although I'd just been promoted by Gandima to work with Chinzo on reading voice overs, what I really wanted to do was report on camera. I decided to make the same phone call to Urna that Tobie had made. But instead of quitting my job working at MNB, I planned to work a second job with Tobie at TV5.

"I have a job for you," Urna said after I called her and explained the situation. I could hear crackling and crunching in the background; it sounded as if she were interrupting a noisy lunch of fried food.

"Hello?" I said into the receiver.

"Yes, Patricia," she said only after she'd finished chewing.

"About the job you mentioned? What is it?" Urna was unpredictable, not the sort of staunch ally you need when seeking a favor, and although I wanted to remain on her good side, my patience was wearing thin again.

"I can get work for you in a textile factory."

"A . . . what?"

"When do you want to start?"

"I don't," I said. The muffled sound of Urna chomping away at her lunch filtered again through the receiver. I let her return to it and hung up the phone, vowing to take matters into my own hands. It never occurred to me, at least not right then, that Gandima would mind if I worked a second job. After all, I would fulfill my responsibilities to her in the afternoons, as I'd always done. In the mornings, I would go meet Tobie, as I'd always done, but this time for a different television station.

CHAPTER 18

Time Travel

The special working group has been tasked with finding the most effective manner by which to reduce expenses, not limited to simply reducing the workforce. Government officials as senior as vice-premiers, as well as ministerial secretaries, have begun the research required to make the proper changes.

—Voiceover, *MM Today* broadcast

Evan had an idea, and even I was listening. After our trip to Khustain, the one where I'd been informed I wasn't the marrying kind, he and I had still seen each other socially. It was impossible not to. We ran in the same circles, and expat circles in Ulaanbaatar are predictably small. And actually, I did enjoy his erudite and witty company; everyone did. You simply can't ignore the life of the party. Besides, Evan's idea was *that* good.

Through the grapevine, he'd heard about a unique tour company called Ger-to-Ger. Unusual in its concept, Ger-to-Ger promised "epic" adventures into the vast Mongolian grassland steppe, complete with cultural home stays, where guests camp just outside the family's *ger*.

This really interested me. Mongolia's relationship with the steppe is its ongoing relationship with the past. Tradition is handed down to the next generation as a matter of necessity. Things are done just the way they were done hundreds of years ago, and we'd soon see this for ourselves. For me, this excursion to the nomadic countryside could serve as none other than a trip back in time.

And taking a trip back in time in Mongolia meant understanding the country's founder and hero, Genghis Khan. Before I'd even left New York, I'd made a commitment to myself to learn everything I could about this man, this legend, whose success story is perhaps history's most spectacular and also most improbable. How on earth someone could rise from poverty so desperate that he was eating vermin for breakfast to ruling no less than *a third* of the world, absolutely captivated me. And there was no better way to get to know the legend of Genghis Khan than to visit his stomping grounds, which was just what Evan had suggested we do. Thus, a few days later, we departed on our second adventure into the steppe.

"Where is the autobus?" each of us took turns begging in Mongolian. At dawn, Evan, along with his young American colleague Jason, and I met in an empty parking lot on the southern edge of the capital. We thought we were near the bus stop, but our sleepy taxi driver seemed to have misunderstood "bus stop" for "desolate parking lot."

"Autobus?" Frantic, we were just about to miss the bus to Terelj, a village about fifty miles northeast of the capital. All of us had taken a few days off work and, through Ger-to-Ger, arranged to spend a long weekend riding horseback through the Mongol steppe, stopping and staying at a series of nomads' *gers*. Rather than the nomads catering to us, we'd cater to them: milking sheep, making clothing, and helping to prepare meals.

"Autobus? Autobus?" we asked again and again, of anyone who might listen. The bus to Terelj was due to leave in less than ten minutes, and we were no closer to finding the station or someone who could point us in the right direction.

Suddenly, a middle-aged man leaned out of his car window as he slowly drove past us. "Autobus?" he asked as he motioned for us to get in his car. Quickly piling our bags into his trunk, we didn't have any time to spare. The bus was scheduled to depart any moment.

"Autobus Terelj?" Evan asked an agent smoking outside the station, after the driver had dropped us off at a new location.

"*Bish,*" the man said simply, after taking a bored drag of his cigarette. "No."

"But can you tell us where to find the bus?" Evan tried again, this time in Russian.

"*Bish,*" the man responded, flicking his cigarette to the ground to stamp it out. Shrugging his shoulders, he walked off. Obviously, this was maddening, and without a bit of luck, we were going to miss the bus. And this was just when luck intervened. Somehow, that's what always happens when you're taking a road trip in a foreign country. Without any other ideas but to leave the bus station where the bus didn't seem to be, we did just that. And once we walked out of the station, we found the bus. There, at the main road, a crush of people stood waiting beneath a sign that read TERELJ in Cyrillic. Without a moment to spare, we'd made it. Relieved and breathless, we boarded.

"Well, let's see the goods," I demanded of Evan and Jason. The day before we'd left, we'd each shopped at our local supermarket for essential provisions: chocolate, sausages, and a bottle of whiskey. After Evan and Jason had demonstrated their prizes, I triumphantly displayed mine: a bottle of bootlegged Chinese whiskey. At the counter as I'd waited for the cashier to tabulate my bill, I noticed the Johnny Walker whiskey that I was paying full retail price for was not exactly Johnny Walker. Nor was it Red Label. Upon closer inspection, I saw that the label read, "Johnny Worker," and beneath it, instead of "Red Label," it actually read, "Red *Labial.*"

"Want to buy an egg?" a young boy asked me as he made room for himself on the seat next to me. Black hair bleached blond, he looked like an Asian version of Eminem. Balancing the cardboard racks of eggs on his lap, he slowly and carefully tipped himself forward and began slapping a pretty girl sitting in the seat in front of us. She turned around to shout at him, and he resumed his egg sales pitch to me.

"You speak English?" a heavily made-up woman asked me as she squeezed past the egg seller. Slowly and laboriously, she lowered her generous backside into the small space between me and the boy, making room for three of us on the bench.

I nodded.

Ignoring the chaos the boy was creating, she peered at me from behind tinted glasses. "Do you want to buy a horse?" she asked.

"Do I want to buy a horse?" I repeated back to her.

"Yes, a horse," she said, as if this were an obvious question to ask. Patiently, the woman waited for me to respond.

"Thank you," I said to the woman. "But I don't have anywhere to put a horse."

"I see," she said, and turned her attention to the man seated in front of her.

The bus was still idling and more passengers were squeezing aboard: schoolchildren, nomads, businessmen, businesswomen, and locals carrying more crates of eggs. Sandwiched tightly between Eminem and the horse seller on my left and a steamy window on my right, I unlatched the lock and pushed on the window until I began to sweat, but it was sealed tight. Finally, bursting at its seams with passengers, our bus departed.

"This is the part of the trip we can look forward to forgetting," I heard Evan mutter from the seat behind me.

Settling in for the long ride ahead, I read about Genghis Khan.

Genghis Khan was born in a pretty unremarkable period in world history. The Holy Roman Empire was bearing the weight of squabbles between its government and the clergy. A man named Albert the Bear inherited from a royal friend a little village that is now the city of Berlin. A new London Bridge was under construction, after the first one had fallen down, and the one after that, and the one after that. Japan was in the height of the samurai era, and the Chinese were busy peddling Zen Buddhism to anyone who might listen. The Khmer Empire in Cambodia was thriving at Angkor, not yet the site of the extraordinary and bewitching ruins that it is today. In other words, little could anyone have imagined back then the fate that was about to befall them, brought on by a most unlikely and incredible success story.

Born to a mother who'd been kidnapped by a nomad hunter, Genghis Khan grew up a destitute vagrant. He and his brothers hunted rats and marmots for food, the latter a smarmy little animal that carries the bubonic plague and is still occasionally eaten in Mongolia today. Named Temuujin after an important enemy his father had captured, Genghis Khan's father took him shopping for a wife of his own when he was just thirteen years old. Genghis took a liking to a ten-year-old girl at a nearby village, and the young couple's marriage was agreed upon and arranged by the children's fathers. But before they could marry, Genghis's own father was poisoned to death by enemies he'd foolishly sat down to dinner with, which would put those pending wedding plans on hold for a very long time and, in the end, would change world history.

Suddenly, Genghis Khan's mother became a single parent of five young children. Her own relatives were of no help to her; they'd cut her off the minute her husband died. Without a support network, the entire family struggled. They lived in squalor, and her sons constantly squabbled, competing with each other for attention—and lunch.

One afternoon, Genghis Khan went fishing at a nearby river, and he caught a trout. No sooner than he had, his half brother took it from him. Rushing home to tell on him, Genghis made a strong case to his mother, Hoelun, adding that this was not the first time his lunch had been taken by the same half brother.

But Hoelun had no patience for the endless squabbling, and she scolded Genghis for starting trouble, which would end up being something of a pivotal moment for the boy. According to Jeremiah Curtin in his *The Mongols: A History*, she demanded to know why the brothers were fighting with each other, when they'd already been deserted by their entire extended family. "We have no friends," she said, according to Curtin, "why not agree and gain strength against enemies?"

His mother had a point, but young Genghis didn't think so. Dissatisfied with the fact she hadn't sided with him, Genghis found his bow and arrow, hunted down his half brother, and executed him.

Now the family was in a real pickle.

As told in his account of *The Secret History of the Mongols*, author Jack Weatherford describes the epic fit that Genghis's mother threw when she found out Genghis had murdered his half brother. "She compares her sons to animals," Weatherford writes, quoting the original text, that Genghis in particular was "like an attacking panther, like a lion without control, like a monster swallowing its prey alive." Worse still, her rant goes on to say something no mother should say to her own child: "Now, you have no companion other than your own shadow."

I shudder to think. It must be the only thing worse to hear from your mother than the dreaded, "I'm disappointed in you."

Because Genghis had killed a family member, he was regarded as a traitor. In the Mongolian steppe, where neighbors have nothing to rely upon but each other, disloyalty is as loathed and feared as a plague. Ostracized, the family was forced to flee their home to a place where they could start fresh. Unfortunately though, the neighboring clans weren't finished with Genghis Khan. They wanted justice for the murder committed on their land. Finally, they captured him, put him in prison, and enslaved him. Despised and alone, the family was worse off than they'd ever been, which is hard to imagine when you know they'd been eating rats.

Then one day, years later, Genghis escaped.

By now, he was well into his teens and had little hope of finding his long-lost bride, the girl his father had arranged for him to marry, but he made that his first order of business anyway. A single teenager herself, she would have been considered an old maid if she hadn't already found someone else to marry.

Despite the odds, Genghis found Borte, who was still single, and he married her. Together, they set up a home and had several children. But they didn't live happily ever after, because Borte was about to be kidnapped by the very same clan that had lost Genghis's mother to kidnapping years before! The clan wanted revenge, and stealing Borte would settle the old score, once and for all.

Because it was so common in Mongolia to claim a bride by kidnapping her, losing your daughter, sister, or even wife in this manner hardly would have upset the figurative oxcart. A husband would simply find a replacement, probably by kidnapping her, too. Rarely would anybody go to war over what amounted to a minute detail in a family's genealogy. But Genghis Khan was different. And once again, his unusual response to usual events would be the making of him. As author and historian Jack Weatherford put it, Genghis Khan "had to choose his own destiny."

And that's just what he was about to do.

Now, suddenly, somewhere between Ulaanbaatar and our destination, the driver stopped the bus and made everyone get off. We'd reached a small bridge that was too small for the bus to cross. Taking our cue from the other passengers, we gathered our belongings, disembarked, and crossed the bridge. With that, the driver put the bus into reverse and drove off. With nothing to do but wait until the situation righted itself, we all rested in the warm summer sun in a meadow of petite yellow flowers. While Jason and Evan chatted, I read on.

Unusually, Genghis decided to hunt his wife's hunters. Rather than simply kidnap another bride to act as mother to his children, which would have been customary, he searched for long-lost Borte, just as he'd done as a young boy. This was a risky endeavor, one that could've ended badly, in an altercation or even war with neighboring clans.

But it didn't end badly. In fact, depending on whose account you read of their reunion, it was either the moonlight during the search party's raid, or Borte's anguished cries that clued in Genghis that he'd finally found her. More than just a fabulously romantic love story, the rescue mission would be a game-changer for Genghis Khan, his clan, all their neighbors, and, eventually, the world itself.

Because Genghis Khan's brazen courage gave him something of a reputation, he began to quickly amass power, as well as loyalty, from other clans. With his enemies, he went to war. Time and again, he won. He wasn't even thirty years old when he was proclaimed *Chinggis Khan*, or "universal king." With the help of well-placed gifts, savvy women, a blood brother, and loyal relatives, Genghis Khan had managed to unite all of Mongolia's disparate clans and factions, forming the powerful Mongol Empire. For the next several centuries, he and his sons and their descendants would conquer and rule lands as far-flung as Asia, Europe, Siberia, and the Middle East.

Genghis Khan's legacy has been written by many historians, with tales of rape, slaughter, cruelty, terror, destruction, and bloodlust—exact words I've taken just from the dust jackets of several history books. For centuries, he was regarded as a "Mongol warlord who ravaged Asia and led his barbaric hordes" (*Genghis Khan: The Conqueror, Emperor of All Men* by Harold Lamb). Of course, that was true, but only in part. The other side of the story, told in fascinating detail, has been written by Jack Weatherford, who gave us a *New York Times* best-selling glimpse into what Genghis gave back to society.

And that list is long.

According to Weatherford, after employing an army that could fit into a football stadium (American football or rest-of-the-world soccer, take your pick) to conquer more than twice what any other leader has ever conquered in all of history, Genghis Khan offered his new subjects lower taxes and religious freedom, and he abolished torture, refused to hold hostages, and liberally redistributed the booty he and his army had earned during their conquests.

Frankly, he sounded like a visionary to me, a cross between the best of Barack Obama and Winston Churchill, minus, of course, the parts about pouring molten silver into his enemies' eyes or boiling them alive and using their empty skulls as drinking goblets.

Genghis Khan also even established free trade zones along the Silk Route, created an international postal system, and offered diplomatic immunity to emissaries from regions he was warring with. For someone who loves adventure travel, it's these last three things that really get to me.

Just imagine—it's the year 1175 or so, and you're dreaming of a vacation. Well, you're not dreaming for long, because there's nowhere to go, not that you've heard of anyway. As Weatherford puts it, when Genghis Khan was born in 1162, "no one in China had heard of Europe, and no one in Europe had heard of China." And to think, just a single generation later, millions of people were learning about new continents *and* creating diplomatic links. And actually getting mail!

In 1227, when he was in his sixties, Genghis Khan died. And his story doesn't stop there. Whether he died after falling off a horse (the most widely accepted theory) or during sex (the salacious, but not implausible rumor, given his fecundity), it's his funeral that may be most memorable. In order to keep Genghis Khan's death a secret from his devout followers, his heirs murdered anyone who witnessed the funeral procession. Then, they buried him in such a secret location that, to this day, no one knows where it is.

With a life, and even a death, this fascinating, I found myself in awe of this titillating eight-centuries-old legend of a poor boy turned world conqueror. Once again, I thought about the nature of determination itself, especially in a country that seemed to be defined by just that. Closing my book, I joined Evan and Jason at a nearby stream, and we nibbled on the sausages and chocolates we'd packed while we waited for something to happen. The first bus had dropped us off over an hour ago, and we weren't sure what was supposed to happen next.

Not long after, a second bus arrived, appearing out of nowhere, and we followed our fellow passengers back onboard.

"Is this the bus to Terelj?" I asked an old nomad, just to make sure.

Dressed traditionally in a *deel*, his colorful silken robe was tied with a sash and he wore a pair of pointy leather boots and a fedora. The nomad offered me a wide single-toothed smile, his face rearranging itself into ancient creases.

"*Teem, teem,*" he said gently. "Yes, yes." Looking at me for a long time, he tilted his head in that curious way that old people do, wordlessly reassuring me that everything was going to be just fine.

A few hours later, the bus stopped again. This time, everyone got out and dispersed. Turning off the ignition, the bus driver looked at me and then at Evan and Jason, shrugged his shoulders, and walked off. We were the only ones left. Although we seemed to have arrived, we weren't sure of it—it wasn't as if the driver had parked at a destination or in a lot. He'd simply gotten out of his vehicle at the end of a dirt road and walked away.

"Any idea where we are?" I asked my companions.

"Maybe we've reached Terelj?" Jason said.

Gathering our overnight packs, we sat down on the edge of the path and tried to drum up a solution. The village around us was quiet, ribbons of smoke rising from the afternoon cooking fires inside the *gers* and tiny cement cabins. After waiting just long enough to start worrying, we heard thunder. And it wasn't from a brewing rainstorm.

"*Saiiiiin baiiiin uuuuuuu!*" a man called out from the distance as the thunder grew louder. "Helloooooooo!" A small stampede of five horses stopped at our feet in a cloud of dust. The Ger-to-Ger tour company had arranged a guide for us, and the man and his entourage had just arrived.

"*Sain bain uu,*" he repeated, hopping off his horse in a single sweeping motion. He wore a conical purple felt cap that looked more like a crown, and it bobbed on his head as he lifted our packs onto the horses' backs.

"You can ride," he announced to me, more a statement than a question. He pointed at the horse.

"Well, not really," I protested as he ignored my objections and lifted me onto one of the horses. There's an old Mongolian saying that "The way you mount the horse determines the ride," and I was about to find out just what this meant. After Evan and Jason followed suit, the man in the purple hat briefly pranced on his horse in front of us, demonstrating how to best handle our transportation. And just like that, our horseback adventure into the Mongolian steppe began.

"*Choo, choo,*" the man shouted at my horse. (*Choo* means "go"; there isn't exactly a word for "stop.")

Kicking his own horse's side and shouting some more *choo*s, our guide galloped forward. Then, circling back, he waited for us to follow his lead.

A recommendation from adventurer and author Graham Taylor in the 2005 edition of *The Lonely Planet* guidebook warns that, "Mongolian horses come in two varieties—quiet and terrible." Taylor goes on to strongly suggest avoiding sitting in a Mongolian saddle for long periods of time: "Only a masochist on a short horse-trip should consider using a Mongolian wooden saddle."

Now, on a long horse trip, Evan and Jason and I were about to appreciate precisely what Graham Taylor meant, and then some.

Adjusting myself to get comfortable in my wood-hard seat, I rearranged the two halves of my bottom to cushion my tailbone. Leaning forward into what looked like a tiny tree trunk at the nose of the saddle, I whispered another *choo* as softly as I could. I didn't want to appear *too* encouraging. Suddenly, my horse took off, and Evan's and Jason's horses followed suit. We were headed to the guide's home, where we'd spend the night camping in the steppe alongside his family's *ger* compound.

At a stream, the guide stopped in front of us and held up his hand. Tugging on my mare's reins, I brought her to a quick stop, although not a controlled one. She bucked as if she'd run into an imaginary wall and turned her head halfway to glare at me for halting her. Pointing at me, the stream, and the other side, the guide encouraged me to begin crossing. It was hard work. The water was deep, fast, and cold.

Tucking my knees to my chest, I tried to balance on the ridge of my horse's back, rather than sit on her, so I could avoid getting wet. It wasn't long before I shifted gears, committing instead to simply hanging on to her bridle.

Carefully negotiating the stream's rocky bed, my horse inched forward until she'd gained purchase on the muddy banks, then took off again. Drinking in the dense smell of impending rain, I bent over on her, jockey-style, and dared her to go just a little faster. Suddenly, I'd hit my stride.

"*Choo!*" I screamed into the panorama of endless fields of green, kicking my horse as hard as I could. Obeying me, she bolted. And then, suddenly, she stumbled into a marmot hole, catching her front hoof in the shallow recess in the rocky steppe. Bending her front legs, she pitched forward until she was on her knees and had begun to roll, headfirst.

Time slows down when things go wrong, and as the seconds leisurely ticked and tocked, I had a good, hard look at our predicament and tried to figure out what to do. I could either hop off of her and hope for the best or stick with her and hope for the best. I decided to stay put, gluing myself once again to her back.

Just in time, before she would have doubled over on top of me, she suddenly righted herself, hoisting up to a standing position. Shaking off the tumble like a pro, the mare performed a little trotting dance. Sucking air through my teeth, I steeled myself as she sped off once again. I didn't wonder for long why she appeared so eager to return home; once we got there we were introduced to a well-endowed stallion awaiting her return.

Finally, we arrived. Our guide pointed to his family's *ger* and then to the open steppe, miming that we must set up our tent before nightfall, which was quickly approaching. A gentle, fragrant rain was falling, and beneath the slate sky, we quickly erected our accommodation.

"My family," the man in the conical purple hat called out from across the steppe. It wasn't clear what his name was, and I'm not sure if it was because I'd forgotten it, it was hopelessly complicated, or he'd never told us. Anyway, he was beckoning us toward himself and the gathering clan who'd set up a picnic site outside the *ger*. We'd been invited to dinner.

Set in the middle of the open prairie, with no neighbors as far as the eye could see, the family's *ger* looked just like the one Evan and I had stayed in weeks earlier at Khustain. In fact, *gers* all over Mongolia look much the same: round, white structures with slightly pointed domes and soft felt exteriors, held together and constructed with wooden latticework. If it weren't for the painted wooden front doors, they'd look like caps belonging to giant bottles of contact lens solution.

Just outside the *ger*, under a darkening and suddenly clear evening sky, thick rugs had been laid in the damp grass. A dozen or so of our guide's family were sitting on the rugs, slurping bowls of noodle soup. Watching us, they grinned politely. An old woman ladled hot, salted milk into three bowls and passed one to each of us. In return, Evan offered the family bars of chocolate. After cooking packets of ramen over their open fire, we sat beneath a canopy of starlight that twinkled across the deep indigo of the night sky. The steppe's utter silence and its vast beauty were mesmerizing. After awhile, and without a common language between us, not even Russian, we all turned in for bed.

At dawn, the guide banged on the flap door of our tent. Thin rays of light as fine as gossamer were peeking inside. Although it was early, we'd overslept, the three of us talking late into the night, taking turns sipping from the bottle of sour, yeasty, cloudy Johnny Worker Red Labial. With a long day of riding ahead of us, there was no time to waste, so we quickly ate a breakfast of dried milk curds, clotted cream, and mugs of steaming salted milk tea. Which, by the way, is not a breakfast to have if you're in a hurry. Although its high caloric content and heavy fat keep a nomad's hunger at bay for the better part of a day of hard riding, it's not the sort of meal that goes down swiftly. Soon, we were back on our horses and on our way.

Many hours later, we were still on our way. My knees were creaking with every rhythmic bounce of my horse, and my feet had been cramped and twisted in stirrups for four long hours. Four hours, it happens, is precisely one hour too long to spend riding anything short of a Land Cruiser. The iridescent beauty of the steppe had worn off long ago, and I was grumpy. I was so uncomfortable in my wooden saddle that I'd even begun to find the fields of buttercups infuriating.

"How much longer?" I groaned to no one in particular.

"You think you're in pain?" Jason asked, pointing at his groin.

"Is it far?" I asked the guide, who was riding patiently alongside us. Jabbing his finger out into the distance, he pointed at a tiny white dot. Resting on the edge of the quivering horizon, the little white dot was the *ger* we were looking for. With renewed vigor, we kicked our horses into gear and rode hard for the last hour.

Finally, we arrived at our second night's accommodation and shakily dismounted our horses. Unpacking again, we pitched our tent in a field of fragrant herbs dotted with equally fragrant dried dung. After a refreshing hike in the still heat over smooth mountain ridges, Evan, Jason, and I met our new hosts and helped them prepare dinner. Our guide with the purple conical hat was leaving us behind to return to his home, and I could hardly imagine riding another five hours. He mounted his horse for the long journey and waved good-bye, his purple conical hat bobbing and bouncing as he rode off into the endless distance.

Set in the middle of another empty meadow, with only a pen of sheep for neighbors, our hosts' *ger* looked just like the others. However, eager to introduce us to her home, the matron of the house invited us inside and instructed us to sit on an orange wooden daybed at the rear wall of the tiny round house. She looked to be in her midtwenties and was married to a herder. They had just one daughter.

"Baisaltan," said the woman shyly, introducing us to her little girl. Baisaltan's mother didn't offer us her name, only her daughter's, and she put us to work right away, teaching us the art of milking a sheep.

"*Kho-ni,*" Baisaltan said, "sheep," trailing behind her mother. Baisaltan was about two years old, and she was completely devoted to a lollipop that she'd been alternating between licking and sticking to her cheek. Suddenly, emphatically, she removed the lollipop from her face and, using it as a pointer, she punched the air in front of her. "*Kho-ni!*" she exclaimed. "Sheep!"

"*Khoni!*" I dutifully repeated back to her, and Baisaltan nodded her approval. Her mother was crouched down behind the sheep, demonstrating how to milk it. She pulled and tugged until a steady stream of thin, white cream tinkled into a tin bucket. Offering me the udder, she urged me to try. Relentlessly, I yanked and squeezed on the animal's long, wet, hairy nipple while she brayed like a donkey. But nothing came out, not a single drop. Surely this sort of thing should come naturally to humans, especially women. Then again, I thought, maybe the sheep had emptied herself of milk. So I handed the nipple back to Baisaltan's mother, who looked at me quizzically and finished milking the sheep, who had plenty more to offer the tin bucket.

I retreated to where Baisaltan stood, just outside of the livestock pen. She'd stuck her lollipop back to her cheek and crouched down in the grass. I thought she was playing, so I joined her. But then, making a face of pure consternation, Baisaltan grunted heavily and defecated on the ground beneath her. Smiling satisfactorily, she stood up, removed her lollipop from her cheek, and went to work on finishing it.

Carrying a bowl of fresh, warm milk out of the pen, Baisaltan's mother directed us back inside her *ger,* where we sat at a small wooden table. Over a wood-burning stove in the center of the room, she began to prepare supper. But before we could eat, she seemed to be saying that we'd have to dress properly. From a chest of drawers, nestled between two daybeds lining the rear wall, she produced three *deels,* or traditional Mongolian robes worn by nomads, and laid them side by side on the dinner table. While the rice and mutton steamed, she made a paste from flour and water and used the paste to gingerly affix decorative patterns to the robes. Once she'd finished, she beamed with pride as each of us dressed in the elaborate homemade costumes. Now, dinner could be served, and not a moment too soon. After a long day of riding, hiking, and milking, mutton and rice had never tasted so splendid.

That night, we turned in early. Although Evan and I had a chance to talk about all the things we seemed to have left unsaid, we didn't bother. And we never would. Sometimes things are better left just the way they are. Besides, the next morning, we faced another long journey across the steppe to meet our next host, this time an old herder woman. More than anything, we all needed a good night's sleep.

"You, sit," Baisaltan's mother said to each of us at dawn, pointing at our transportation.

Silently, I thanked the heavens and universe above that it was not, in fact, a horse. This time, we'd be traveling in style on a wooden oxcart driven by Baisaltan's father, who smiled sheepishly at us but did not offer his name. Eagerly climbing aboard to join us for the drive, his wife and Baisaltan clambered into the front seat.

Jason sat on top of our luggage, and Evan and I sat in the rear of the cart facing backward toward the steppe rolling slowly and methodically behind us, our legs dangling over the edge. Baisaltan sat quietly on her father's lap, eating a fresh lollipop and occasionally nodding off. The repeated *thwack* of the whip on the ox's backside kept time, chiming the moments like an old grandfather clock chimes the hour.

Suddenly, Baisaltan screamed. She had tumbled from her father's lap and slipped into the space between the front seat and the cart behind it. Leaping from his seat as if he'd practiced a lifetime for this very moment, her father yanked her from the ground just before the oxcart's wheel rolled over her. After being whisked to safety, Baisaltan threw a halfhearted tantrum, which amounted to little more than a scared whimper. Then, sticking her lollipop back to her cheek, she rested her head in her father's lap and descended once again into heavy-lidded afternoon slumber.

Half a day later, we arrived at our new campsite. Baisaltan and her parents bade us good-bye and set out immediately for home.

"*Sain bain uu!*" our final hostess cried, welcoming us to her compound, where we'd spend our last night in the steppe. Her campsite looked just like all the others: one lone *ger*, some livestock, a horse or two, and vast and empty fields surrounding all of it. The only difference was that she lived near a stream. And she was completely alone.

"Tsetsge!" she exclaimed, pointing to herself and carefully sounding out her name phonetically. A cherubic, rotund old woman, Tsetsge extended her warmth at arm's length, as if she were hesitating to do so. There seemed to be a deep sadness about her, the kind that you can't quite put a finger on, but you're sure is there just the same.

"Yogurt!" she then commanded, as if the word itself were a verb, and we began setting up our tent for lunch. First though, I looked wistfully at the stream, wishing for nothing more than a bath.

With our camp set up halfway between Tsetsge's *ger* and a rushing, cold stream, we took turns stripping down to our underwear and jumping in. I went first, and as quickly as I got in, I got out. The stream water was frigid, as cold as melting snow. Negotiating slippery rocks and a fast-moving current, I tiptoed out and lay down on the dirt beach of the riverbank, delighting in the exquisite sensation of feeling clean again, even though none of us had thought to bring any soap. I tingled all over with that vague burning feeling that comes from contact with numbing cold.

Then, while Evan and Jason bathed, I went for a walk alone in the steppe.

When you follow a dream, one that is long on substance but short on detail, you suddenly realize one day that you've reached your own intersection. Looking left and then right, you know you're free to meander, but of course you won't. You've given up too much, and a glance behind serves as a reminder of just how much. Ticking items off a list you've kept for all the years you've dreamed of a different future—possessions, *things*, experiences you'll miss out on once you've left your comfortable life behind—you finally realize that the one sure thing you're *not* missing is regret. With that small but certain comfort come hope and conviction, and you eventually continue to move forward, whatever the price.

Following the snaking path of the cold stream I'd just bathed in, I walked as far away from Evan and Jason as I could. Feeling peacefully detached, I pressed deeper into the forest that edged our camp. Tucking into a grassy, tree-covered hamlet, I knelt down. A breeze tickled the leaves, and the weakened sun danced on the path in front of me.

"What am I doing here?" I said aloud to the air. The first time, I asked the question calmly. But after awhile, I began shouting, *"What have I done to my life?"* After all, I was alone in the open steppe. At least, I sure hoped so.

The rhetorical questions I'd posed were answered with empty echoes, and I knelt quietly for a long time underneath the canopy of trees. Finally, I spoke aloud again, this time provoking a response that I wasn't sure I wanted.

"God, universe," I ventured with some trepidation for the plea I was about to utter, "please take from me what you must in order to make my dream come true." No matter what the destination, whether I became a foreign correspondent or something else entirely, I committed, out loud, right then and there, to the journey. I would keep moving forward. It was time to cross my own intersection.

With that, I opened my knapsack and took out a sealed plastic bag. Inside the bag was a tiny square cut from a security blanket that I'd kept for a very long time. To me, it symbolized the last vestige of my former life. On my hands and knees, I cleared an area of leaves and began to dig a hole in the soft earth. In the little grave I'd dug, I deposited the square of blanket and buried it, addressing God and the expanse of the universe one more time.

"God," I said, this time nearly pleading. "This is my offering to you." Crying from a combination of fear and relief and hope, I walked back to camp. The sky had grown heavy and was now colored a deep shade of purple.

"Are your animals fattening up nicely?" Evan was saying to Tsetsge in Mongolian, asking what every Mongolian guidebook says is supposed to be a common question when you meet someone new. Sitting in the shade beneath a flap outside our tent, he and Jason were making lunch. Tsetsge sat beside them; she'd brought bowls of homemade yogurt for each of us. In her fifties and widowed, she was the matriarch of a nomad family that had left her long ago. Her husband was dead, and her adult son lived too far away to visit often. She lived alone in the steppe, without any neighbors for miles and miles around. Without even a television, her only contact with the outside world was a radio. I found Tsetsge's complete isolation quite sobering.

"Teem," Tsetsge said, laughing gently, in answer to Evan's question, "Yes." She went on to explain to him just how fat they were, but none of us could understand much of what she was saying. Immediately after meeting someone in the steppe, it is considered obligatory for a guest to ask after the nomad's family and his herd. Usually, the guest follows his queries about whether the animals are fattening up successfully with a command to hold off the dogs, which are trained to attack to protect the homestead. Guard dogs in the Mongolian steppe are particularly vicious in their pursuit of any intruders, even invited ones.

Beckoning us to her *ger*, Tsetsge showed us an old black-and-white photo of her husband. He'd stared point-blank at the camera when the picture was taken, as if he'd been too surprised to smile. The effect was unnerving, seeing a snapshot of a moment in a life that's already ended. With only the commonality of blunt words like "death" and "gone," we changed the subject to the hot mutton soup she offered us.

Suddenly, the *ger* door slammed shut. Tsetsge pushed it back open, revealing behind her a sky black as midnight and a gale-force wind that appeared to be releasing our tent from its stakes.

The three of us leaped to our feet and tried to dash out into the storm, but the howling wind was so strong we could barely stand. Despite being laden with three sleeping bags, overnight packs, and food and water, the tent was succumbing. Raindrops were pelting the ground with such vehemence, the puddles looked as if they were boiling. Using our body weight in a last-ditch attempt to salvage the tent, we barked orders at each other to hold up this end or that end, zip this shut or that open. While Jason and I labored and bent over double, pasting ourselves to whichever end of the tent seemed most likely to pitch forward, Evan tried to secure the tent's stakes.

But it was too late. One by one, they uprooted themselves from the wet earth and our tent slowly fell on top of us while we scrambled out unzipped windows. End over end, it rolled away. But there wasn't any time for regret. The roaring storm was growing stronger, and we had to get inside.

Running and pushing headlong into the wind, we banged on Tsetsge's *ger* door, looking for shelter. Ushering us inside, she showed me to a sagging metal orphanage-issue bed frame topped with a thin mattress, while Evan and Jason were relegated to sleeping on the floor. Across her small one-room home, she sat awake in a chair, watching over us for the rest of the night.

The next morning, we rose early. The sky was a brilliant sapphire, a shade of blue so resplendent that the storm the night before hardly seemed possible. The only evidence of it was our possessions strewn all across the field surrounding Tsetsge's *ger*. We spent hours collecting what we could before we returned by horseback to the village of Terelj and the bus stop where we'd eventually make our way back home to Ulaanbaatar.

In Terelj, a pair of whiskered old nomads invited us into their home for one last lunch, a fitting finale to a truly epic tour of Genghis Khan's steppe. Extending their right arms, touching their right elbows with their left hands in the traditional manner communicating hospitality, they politely offered us a bowl of *airag* to share. They made sure we drained every last drop, and once we did, the elder nomad lifted a knife from its sheath at his hip. Grabbing the hilt, he whisked the knife out with an impressive flourish and held it high above his head. Chunks of meat hung in a circle from hooks on the ceiling's rafters. From this edible chandelier, the old nomad cut a few slices and offered them to us.

"Eat!" he commanded in English, grinning playfully. It wasn't long before we'd had our fill. Once we did, we hoisted our packs onto our backs and boarded the bus bound for our homes in the capital.

CHAPTER 19

Price Tag

The working group will make their proposal to the government in August or September. This will enable the government to begin considering introducing changes to the relevant laws. The entire process should aid in Parliament's decision-making. This will, of course, depend upon the resolution and political will of those in government responsible for this initiative

—Interview, Finance Minister N. Bayartsaikhan, *MM Today* broadcast

"Guch naim!" **declared the taxi** driver, "Thirty-eight degrees!"

"Teem!" I excitedly agreed, before adding, *"Ikh khaluun!"* "Very hot!"

The week in the steppe with Evan and Jason felt as if it had happened a lifetime ago. Now in a taxi on my way to an interview at TV5, I had just experienced the simple euphoria of successfully communicating with a Mongolian cab driver. A word here, a phrase there—this brand of rapture is a traveler's drug. It's a sporadic experience, however—one minute you're rejoicing over finally understanding a simple how-do-you-do; the next you're despairing of your incompetence in asking if someone's sheep are fattening up nicely.

Exchanging our views on the weather, which was still cooking the capital into torpid submission, the taxi driver told me just how hot it was: thirty-eight degrees Celsius, over a hundred degrees Fahrenheit. On my way to meet with Tobie's new boss at TV5, I was doing my best not to overheat in my excitement at having finally and simply understood a conversation in Mongolian. With tissues tucked underneath my moist armpits, I sat as still as possible, suppressing my instinct to jump into the front seat and to embrace the first person I'd successfully communicated with.

"Go straight for a long time and then stop just after the second red building," I went on in Mongolian, directing him with precision that surprised both of us.

There was a certain cachet about TV5. Young, dynamic, and outfitted with lots of new technology, it was *edgy*. When reporting in the field, correspondents and producers wore fancy navy-blue nylon jackets with the "TV5 Mongolia" moniker boldly emblazoned on the breast. Everyone, even the secretary, dressed sharply and bore the handsome good looks of real pros.

But more important than all that, TV5 was a member of Asiavision, a compilation of Asian broadcasters. Each day, member stations from Bhutan to Turkey fed portions of their broadcast to a central hub in Malaysia, which parcels together and spits out foreign news for local audiences.

In other words, viewers in Bhutan could watch select stories from Turkish news, Mongolian news, or any of the other member stations' broadcasts. Mongolia's only member of Asiavision, TV5 was offering Tobie, and maybe me, the chance to air our stories in more than seventeen countries. It was an incredible opportunity. So incredible, in fact, that I never really stopped to think about the consequences of working for two stations at once.

"Come," Tem said as he led me to his office. The manager of TV5, Tem, was tall and dapper and had that self-possessed air required to wear sharp-edged German eyeglasses. His persona seemed a perfect fit for the station.

As I followed him down a brightly lit wood-paneled corridor, he paused for a moment to point out Tobie's office space. In it were three computers, and Tobie was already making use of at least two of them, shuttling between one and then the other to upload video files from his computer to the TV5 network.

"The computers are yours to use," Tem said, as if he'd read my mind. If his intention was to go to work on my practical side alone, he was doing a

fine job of it. The office I'd shared with Tobie at MNB had just one computer, it was short a desk, and its Internet didn't work.

"And the Internet connection is high-speed," he added. "We will talk in
my office," Tem promised after he'd shown me around.

We sat down in his office, and for exactly one minute, he told me about
the job I was interviewing for. It was as if he'd already made an offer, I'd
already accepted, and this meeting was just a formality.

"You and Tobie will have your own talk show. You'll interview subjects
in English, and we'll air it."

"Our own *talk show?*"

"Yes, of course." He said "of course" as if this was a foregone conclusion,
and I'd simply missed a beat.

"You should get to work, then," Tem said, and I did as I was told, although
I was definitely going to have to make it up as I went along. A talk show?
On air? Who would we interview? And how? Although I was really out of
my depth this time, I was too excited to care. Surely I could figure it out
along the way. Besides, back in the steppe, I'd made a commitment that it
was time to cross my own intersection. And once again, it was now or never.

"Our own talk show?" I said to Tobie, still in disbelief, once I'd returned
to what was now our office.

"Yeah, good move to come work here, I think," he said as he organized a spaghetti pile of computer wires. From the looks of it, Tobie hadn't
thought twice about his decision to switch stations.

Looking at him quizzically but getting no reaction, I sat down at my
desk and unpacked. If there had been a better idea about what to do with
my morning, I didn't know what it was. Since I worked only late afternoons and evenings at Mongolia TV, it wouldn't be hard for me to do both
jobs. Sure, the workload would be a lot to manage, but I hadn't come all the
way to Mongolia to relax. I'd come all this way to find a new career, to discover and pursue my passion, and suddenly it seemed as if it had found me.

"A talk show. With our own interviews," I said, still amazed by our
good fortune.

"Yup."

"Like, on television?"

"Yup."

"High-speed Internet access?"

"The best part," he said, resuming his organizing.

"But what about Gandima?" I said finally.

"What *about* Gandima?" Tobie said in such a matter-of-fact way that I felt silly for even asking. "If we air our segments on Asiavision, they won't air here in Mongolia. They'll air in . . . Bhutan."

He was right. In our corner, Tobie and I had a technicality, one that we would use to absolutely no avail when Gandima found out what we'd been doing behind her back. And what we were doing behind her back was starting up, theoretically anyway, a talk show that Tobie would produce and I would host while still working for Gandima at the state-owned television station. Perhaps this should've given us more pause than it did. Not to mention the fact that Tobie had not yet even informed Gandima of his decision to quit MNB.

Pamela Slutz, I said suddenly to myself. My hesitation had stuck around for only as long as it had taken me to get online, where I'd found the name of the American ambassador to Mongolia, who'd lived all over Asia, participated in nuke talks with the old USSR, and had helped set up Ulaanbaatar's first shelter for abused women. Landing an interview with Ambassador Slutz would be ideal for our talk show, and the very best part about it might be the timing.

In just a few weeks, Naadam would begin. Every summer, Mongolia throws itself a massive party steeped in ancient traditions. Called Naadam, meaning "festival" or "games," it is a carnival of Olympic sporting events, theatrical dance, knucklebone fortune-telling, and copious amounts of sliced sheep meat and vodka. And the Naadam of that summer was particularly important. Celebrating the eight hundredth anniversary of the founding of the Mongol Republic by Genghis Khan, the Mongolian prime minister had invited dignitaries and royalty from around the world to attend the opening ceremony.

Surely Pamela Slutz, who by then had been in Mongolia for several years, would lend our debut talk show the credibility it would need. And, if we managed to get her on air, we'd have a shot at getting other high-profile guests on air. Prince Andrew had also been invited to Naadam, and he'd surely be hanging in the same circle as Ambassador Slutz.

Right away, I marched to Tem's office to get his approval for the interview request we'd have to put through the American Embassy.

"Of course," Tem said without any hesitation. Just as I was about to get up, he stopped me. "There's just one thing," Tem went on. He wore an expression that suggested there might very well be a catch to the job that Tobie and I had just landed.

"Sure, anything," I said.

"I understand you come from the banking world in New York City?" he asked. Tem spoke in flawless, crisp English with a hint of a British accent.

"Yes, that's right," I said evenly, wondering what on earth my banking background could lend to a talk show.

"A portion of TV5 is privately funded," Tem began to explain. When he said, "funded," I understood right away where this was headed. Rumor had it that Tem wasn't just running TV5, but that he was also the finance director for a venture capital holding company that happened to have TV5 in its portfolio. He explained that a contact of his was hoping to build Mongolia's first five-star hotel, then got right to the point.

"We need about a million dollars to make this happen." Here Tem paused and my mental cogs went to work. "Do you think you can find someone on Wall Street to invest?"

"Possibly," I said carefully, imagining how I might pitch to an old hedge fund client why he should be interested in building deluxe accommodation in the Mongolian steppe.

"Oh, and the Slutz interview?" Tem said. "Just type it up on official letterhead, and I'll sign it right away."

The thing is, I thought as I walked back to our office, this was all getting a bit complicated. Not only had I taken a second job behind Gandima's back, but I'd just agreed to host a talk show that seemed to have one large and rather expensive string attached.

"Well," Tobie said when I'd returned to our office. "What did Tem say?"

"He gave us the green light to interview the ambassador," I said. There didn't seem to be any point in telling Tobie the rest. Instead, I e-mailed a few contacts about Tem's investment offer. After all, it couldn't hurt to try to broker a deal for him, but it certainly could help my budding career in television.

CHAPTER 20

Betting The Ranch

*For the first time since Mongolia became a market economy, budget income
will decline in the coming fiscal year. If we do not make appropriate changes
in reducing budget expenditures, the new tax law will yield no positive results. So, we have decided to begin work to reduce expenditures.*

—Interview, Finance Minister N. Bayartsaikhan, *MM Today* broadcast

I'd heard it was Evan's last week in the country, but I had more important
things to think about. After all, I had a new job and an old job, and the old
job didn't know about the new job. It felt as if I were cheating on myself,
with myself.

Hello Mongolia!, the name Tem had chosen for our talk show, was getting under way. Although I hadn't heard back from any of my clients
about investing in Tem's project, Tobie and I had been busy. While we
waited for the American Embassy to respond to our request for an interview with Ambassador Slutz, Tobie and I decided to produce a feature on
food. Mongolian food is something of a mystery to the outside world, and
TV5's partnership with Asiavision would give us the opportunity to tell
seventeen member countries just what a typical Mongolian lunch was all
about. Provided, of course, that a local restaurant manager would allow us
to interview him and his staff.

So far, things were really looking up. Tem had hired a translator and driver to assist us in the interview process. And even though neither of them had shown up, Tem had loved our pitch, which was the most important thing.

Tobie and I hailed a cab and made it downtown just as lunch hour was beginning. Traffic had slowed to a crawl in the choking haze of the high noon sun, and the restaurants lining Peace Avenue were packed. We agreed the best way to approach our unannounced interview would be to find the busiest restaurant, which usually has the very best food, and wing it. It would take a few trial runs, surely, but eventually we'd get it done.

"*Sain bain uu!*" I said to a restaurant manager, who'd rushed to the door as soon as he'd seen Tobie's camera. "We are from TV5 and—" I stopped talking when he shut the door in my face.

"*Bish!*" the next manager said, catching us before we'd even managed to get anywhere near the front door.

"*Bish!*" another said, crossing his hands in front of his face in an X.

Did these managers suspect we were from the Mongolian Health Department? Tobie and I were getting nowhere, and obviously we needed a different strategy. Sometimes the best thing to do in situations where you haven't exactly been invited is to pretend the opposite. And that's just what we did next.

"*Sain bain uu!*" I said, greeting another restaurant manager with an especially effusive hello. "We are here for a TV5 interview."

At the mention of TV5, he seemed excited. At the mention of an interview, he seemed bewildered—exactly what Tobie and I had been hoping for. Spying our TV5 identification badges, the manager shrugged his shoulders as if he should've been expecting us all along, smoothed his tousled hair, and led us into the steaming heat of his restaurant's chaotic kitchen. After he barked some orders at his cooks, one of them dutifully made her way toward us, wiping her hands on her apron as she did.

Tobie switched on the camera and started filming. While he panned the kitchen and food preparation, I memorized the new words I'd need to interview the chef standing beside me.

"You, cook, food, what?" I began.

"Eh?"

"Food, you, cook, what?" I said. Holding my Mongolian pronunciation dictionary at arm's length, just outside the camera's shot, I snuck a glance at it and tried again.

"You, *buuz*, cook?" I asked, using the Mongolian word for "dumpling."

"*Bish*," she said, puzzled. Tobie was still filming; I really needed to get to the point!

"*Buuz?*" I said finally, resorting to the one word I was sure we could communicate.

"*Buuz!*" she shouted, and cracked a wide grin. Pointing from a cook rolling out long sheaths of dough to another lifting the enormous round tin lid of a steam bath, the dumpling chef launched into a lengthy explanation as I nodded vigorously. With a jumble of consonants, she finished and looked at me expectantly.

"And *that*, everyone, is how Mongolian *buuz* dumplings are prepared," I said, smiling into the camera.

"Maybe we can use those shots as B-roll," Tobie said politely. "Best we get an interview with an English speaker from now on."

There was one perfect place to do just that. Not only was there a restaurant inside an actual *ger*, right in the middle of downtown city life, but it served up a wide variety of dishes, and the staff did so in English. Mongolian cuisine offered up some pretty unusual items, and Tobie and I knew we could either labor over a stew of boiled organs for viewers, or we could showcase our absolute favorite dish, deep-fried meat pancakes. We chose the pancakes and decided to start filming with me drinking a bowl of salt-milk tea, a staple in homes from deep in the country to the heart of the capital.

"You made a face," Tobie said. "Do it again."

Unfortunately, I hate milk and always have. This has nothing to do with Mongolia and everything to do with the stale-breath aftertaste milk leaves behind. I've never willingly drunk it, not even as a baby, but I was determined to do so now—even if it was warm and salted.

"And *this*," I gestured excitedly to the camera, "is salt-milk tea, famous in Tibet and here in Mongolia, made from hot water, salt, and milk!" With that, I took the tiniest sip I could from the steaming bowl in front of me and smiled cheerfully.

"Good enough," Tobie said as the rest of our food order arrived. We'd ordered a cornucopia of our favorite Mongolian foods: deep-fried salty meat pancakes, roasted mutton, and pickled purple cabbage. We weren't just working—we were feasting. Relishing the savory succulence, Tobie and I filmed and interviewed staff while diving greedily into our lunch.

As we walked out of the restaurant, we finally broached the subject of what we might say to Gandima. Tobie still hadn't officially quit, although he hadn't even stopped by MNB in more than a week, and I had been working both jobs without mentioning any of this to Gandima.

Although we were *technically* free agents, and we *technically* hadn't done anything wrong by agreeing to work for TV5, we were *absolutely* moonlighting for Gandima's competitor. It wasn't right. Besides, I certainly didn't want to be betting the ranch on a technicality.

"We're going to get caught," I said finally to Tobie, knowing that Gandima was never going to see our side of it, which barely made sense even to us.

That afternoon, with just an hour to spare before we had to be at work at MNB, Tobie and I decided to film one last interview. It would be our undoing. The just-one-more usually is. More specifically, it would be an orange microphone that would be our undoing.

The head brewmaster and his deputy greeted us warmly at the entrance to the Chinggis Khan Brewery. Named after Genghis Khan in the English transliteration of his name, the brewery was the only one in the country to officially carry the namesake of the country's hero and founder. After the Soviets left, naming a product or an establishment after Genghis Khan became something of a hit. Pretty much everything had the Genghis Khan stamp, from streets to a brewery to vodka and chocolate brands to, supposedly anyway, toilet paper—until Parliament put its foot down and banned such a reference.

An old expat, Guenther Lengefeld was an unlikely brewmaster. Face scrubbed red-raw and clothing ironed to perfection, he seemed like an earnest man, maybe somebody's doting grandfather. Years earlier, passionate about the process of making good lager, Guenther had left his life in Germany to travel to Ulaanbaatar to oversee beer production at Chinggis Khan Brewery. Aside from occasional visits back home, he had left pretty much everything behind in order to pursue his dream . . . to make beer.

Tobie and I were staring in silence at Guenther and Babbu, Guenther's Mongolian deputy. Chattering at us in a combination of German and Mongolian, it was clear something that had been lost in translation, because we barely had a common language between the four of us.

"I studied German back at school," Tobie said apprehensively. "I could try to translate into English what Guenther is saying in German while I'm filming."

"And," Babbu added, "I could help by translating the Mongolian words into English."

By now, Tobie and I had grown accustomed to rolling with some pretty unusual punches while filming. Guenther and I looked at each other, shrugged our shoulders, and got started.

Presenting us with white smocks, shoe covers, and plastic shower caps, Guenther and Babbu instructed us to put them on before entering the sterile environment of the brewery. Grinning with infectious pride, Guenther barely waited for the red "on" light to flash on Tobie's camera before telling us about how he makes Mongolia's most famous brew.

"The hops," Guenther said in German.

"Grain? Hops? I think?" Tobie translated.

" . . . do not come from Mongolia," Guenther went on, offering me a crunchy hop to taste.

Suddenly Guenther's eyes shone wet as he choked back a swell of pride. This wasn't the first time this had happened while I was asking someone about a subject he was passionate about. First, it had been Anne and Jonny O'Brien, the Irish cyclists. Then it was Bold, Quiza's manager, and Quiza himself. It was the same even with Valerie, the melancholy French horse tracker. Each of them had been simply captivated. With Guenther and the rest, I'd begun to notice an unmistakable pattern of bald, exposed emotion, the look of someone so magnetically drawn to whatever it was they were doing in life that they simply couldn't hold back their own raw reaction.

Guenther went on and nearly wept as he did so.

"The water," Guenther added, pausing for Tobie to translate.

"The water . . . ," Tobie said.

"Is what makes Chinggis beer the finest in the country. It is from the Tuul, very cold."

The Tuul splits Ulaanbaatar in two, carving a frigid path between its northern and southern halves. It's a stream so cold and so fast that, even at a depth of just a few inches, it's almost impossible to cross on foot. Attempting to walk across it is like trying to tiptoe across the raging path of a fully released fire hydrant.

While Guenther displayed an impressive array of dials, switches, levers, and cranks, I repeated back to him what Tobie told me he'd said.

"So, it's all in the water then?"

Guenther looked at me blankly, so Babbu jumped in, explaining in Mongolian. They both looked at me and shrugged their shoulders, so Tobie tried again to bridge the divide.

"Yes, water!" Guenther suddenly shouted in English. "Come!" he ordered, leading the three of us into the pub next door. Tipping back the handle of the tap, he poured four steins of lager.

Mongolians aren't exactly beer drinkers; they overwhelmingly prefer their dairy cocktails. In fact, the average German drinks 160 times the single liter of beer that a Mongolian will consume in an entire year's time. However, the Chinggis brand is beginning to grow on the locals, and for good reason—the brewery manages to take the very best from both Mongolia and Germany. It's brewed according to German purity laws, but the water is local Mongolian, and the finished product is piped straight to the tap in the adjacent Chinggis pub.

"A gift for you," Guenther proclaimed as he passed out our beers.

"Guenther, thank you," I said, infused with the emotion of his passion for what he'd come all this way to do. Inspired, I'd begun to notice a pattern; first, in the Irish cyclists, then in Quiza and Bold, and now in Guenther. Every one of them had been simply transformed when describing their dream or their work. It was like a light switch had been flipped on, right behind their eyes.

"No," he said, proud eyes shining brightly. "Thank you."

"Cheers, Guenther," I said, raising my glass to meet his.

CHAPTER 21

NO

Previously, we were handling our local business in Japan by setting up a coop-eration committee. Representing the Institute of Economics in Japan, I came to Mongolia. It is my assessment that we need a special body that will be able to promote trade and commercial relations between our two countries.

—Voiceover, *MM Today* broadcast

"Uh-oh," Tobie said after we'd left the brewery. "Gandima's been calling me."

"What do you mean 'been calling'?"

"I mean, about a dozen times."

"Uh-oh," I said.

Our number was up. Digging into my bag for my own cell phone, I learned that our suspicions were correct. Gandima had been calling me, too. There could be only one reason for the sense of urgency—we'd been caught working for TV5.

"Where have you two been?" she demanded angrily after we'd arrived together at the station. The ride there had seemed interminable, like the wait for a stay of execution that you're not going to get. Eyes blazing, Gandima was as angry as you might expect; she'd been lied to and avoided, and now we would pay for it.

"Are you two working for another station?" she demanded without preamble.

Squirming, I made a split decision to gamble on our technicality. "Not exactly," I said.

That was it. Her eyes flashing with rage, Gandima exploded.

"The orange microphone!" she said. "I saw you holding it, Patricia! That is TV5's microphone! Are you or are you not working for them?"

She was right. The orange microphone was undeniably TV5's, and I'd been holding it, talking into it, with Tobie's camera in my face, right in front of Guenther's brewery. Gandima's case was airtight.

"I drove *right by* you two," she spat, and I winced. How could we have been so reckless? On one hand, we were unpaid interns, and we were simply seeking more and better opportunities. But on the other hand, and Gandima would point this out right away, it was all a matter of loyalty.

Right away, I came down with that queasy feeling you always get when you're caught completely in the wrong, when there is absolutely no good reason for your behavior and no good way to explain your way out of it.

"Do you understand the word 'loyalty'?" Gandima said, drawing out that last word for maximum impact. If it was meant to be a verbal slap, it succeeded.

"I've already told Enkhtuya what you've done," she added, quietly now, the resignation in her voice audible.

"Gandima," I said, treading carefully, "I'm sorry." Unfortunately, I didn't stop there.

"The thing is," I began, launching into an explanation of the technicality upon which Tobie and I had based our fabrication. I was about to learn that sometimes an apology is best left without the "but."

"No," she said, cutting me off. "*The thing is,*" she said, mocking me, "the entire station is disappointed in you. Here in Mongolia, it's a matter of loyalty."

"And you, Tobie," she said, turning her attention to him, "you owe the station for your trip to Roaring Hooves. What you have done is illegal."

Gandima's office was a tinderbox, and we'd all thrown in a match.

Unmoved, still resolute, Tobie stared stony-faced at Gandima. "If I've done something illegal, then let's take this to court."

The room went quiet, and with that, Gandima stood up and left. Tobie and I looked at each other and said nothing. A moment later, she returned, and Tobie walked out. For good.

"You," she said, staring hard at me after Tobie left. "You must not appear on air at TV5."

Right away, I promised her I wouldn't. And I meant it. When your dependability, your very word, is being called into question, you make things right. And if it took losing my chance to have my own talk show at TV5 to make things right, then that's just the sacrifice I'd make.

"And if you plan to stay working here, you must apologize to every single person at the station, starting with Enkhtuya."

"Of course," I said, contritely. I felt terrible, and right away, I vowed to right my wrong.

Head hung low, I marched myself straight into Enkhtuya's office. *"Uchlarai,"* I said to her. Head down, eyes squeezed shut to seal away the tears, I made the best of what little Mongolian I knew for a situation as complicated as the one I'd created. "Excuse me," I offered, sparing us all a long explanation in English.

"Uchlarai," I said to the cameraman. The height of a young teenager, he was as short as he was wiry and strong. Unsmiling eyes set in a withered and deeply lined face, he looked at me for a long time, like he was sizing up my sincerity before accepting my apology. Tipping his chin forward, he was still bearing down on me with only vaguely softening resentment. But then, ever so subtly, he nodded.

And it was much the same with everyone else at the station too. My apology tentatively accepted, it was time for me to really make things right.

Still though, there was the problem of what to do next. And incredibly, it was Gandima who offered the solution—the same solution Tobie and I had concocted in the first place. I could go on working for TV5 as long as the stories that Tobie and I produced would air only internationally and didn't appear on air locally in Mongolia. I could also continue working for Gandima at MNB, correcting scripts and reading voice overs. The only snag was that Tobie and I would no longer work together for her. At that moment, though, it hardly seemed to matter. Besides, her falling-out with Tobie was about to become permanent. Gandima and Tobie would never speak again.

After I'd spoken individually to everyone I knew at the station, apologizing to each of them, I left for the day. It was the middle of summer, a dry, warm evening, and I walked into town.

Up ahead, I spotted Evan walking along Peace Avenue. It was his last night in the country, and there would be a farewell dinner for him later at one of the local restaurants.

"I'm leaving," he said, and we both knew that this meant more than getting on a plane.

Concentrating as hard as I could on my toe and the circles it was drawing in the dirt, I inhaled the choking smell of dusty concrete deeply. Neither one of us spoke. Although I'd had plenty of occasions to remind myself why this was never going to work anyway, I couldn't help but wonder what would have happened *if.* Meeting Evan at all had seemed like destiny. And letting go of a fantasy always takes a little bit longer than you want it to.

"I know," I said, still looking at my feet. There were plenty of things we'd left unsaid, but it was better this way. Lingering only harbors regrets.

So, with that, we said good-bye. The next time I'd run into Evan, he'd be engaged to the girlfriend he told me about.

CHAPTER 22

YES

The Institute conducts research studies on economic and trade relations in East Asia. We do hope that the matters discussed at this meeting will yield positive results for intense development of these ties between Mongolia and Japan. This will set a precedent for other East Asian nations seeking to foster prosperous cooperation and collaboration."

—Voiceover, *MM Today* broadcast

"Come," Gandima commanded sternly, and I followed her back to her office. It had only been a few days since I'd apologized to her and everyone else at MNB. Since then, I'd kept my head down and worked hard on script translations. At TV5, I'd followed Gandima's orders and confirmed with Tem that *Hello Mongolia!* would be broadcast only internationally, not locally in Mongolia.

In the meantime, no one at MNB had spoken to me. Until now. I held my breath and waited for her to speak.

"You will do a screen test," she said as soon as we sat down.

"A screen test?"

"A screen test."

"But isn't that . . . ?"

"Yes, for the anchor role."

"For the *anchor* role?"

"Yes, for the *anchor* role," Gandima repeated, a smile playing on her lips.

"But, why?" I was dumbfounded. Delightfully dumbfounded, but dumbfounded nevertheless.

"Because we might need you to anchor," she said simply.

"But what about . . . ?" I began.

"What happened last week?" she asked.

"Yes."

"That matter, it is finished," she said, waving her hand as if to dismiss it entirely. "You said you were sorry, didn't you? To everyone?"

"Yes, I did," I said.

"Then that is done." Gandima spoke with finality and then changed the subject.

"Tomorrow," she said, tapping her pen against the only bare spot on her cluttered desk. "Tomorrow is your screen test." Rising halfway from her seat, Gandima concluded our meeting with another wave of her hand. It would be up to me to figure out how to prepare for a shot at anchoring the national Mongolian news, but I knew what my first order of business would be. I would need to buy a suit.

Right away, I headed to the *Ikh Delghuur*, the State Department Store, and made for the women's department. There were about a dozen suits on display, all of them black, and I tried on each of them. Inside the tag of one of the pantsuits read the instructions, "Cry Clean Only," and I knew I'd found the one. What had been lost in translation would be my lucky charm.

The next morning, I woke just after dawn. I had a lot of work to do. Auditioning for the anchor role and actually landing it were two very different things. Somewhere in between success and failure was a long-overdue face scrub.

I'd taken the day off work at TV5, and I put my time to good use. Scrubbing my face until it was raw and glowing, I daubed the new layer of pink skin with a thin coat of foundation, followed by concealer, blush, bronzer, and loose powder. I was going for the natural look, the one where you spend a lot of time applying cosmetics that are supposed to have the effect of looking as if you hadn't spent a lot of time applying cosmetics. Slipping into my "Cry Clean Only" suit, I was more ready than I'd ever been.

Once at the station, I waited, and I'd do so for many hours. For Mongolians, the concept of punctuality is a somewhat fluid one, but this would work in my favor. While I paced the halls, calming my nerves, I reminded myself why I was here at all. I was here to follow a dream. Whatever happened next, well, it would all be part of the story I was creating for myself. My determination was absolute. I simply had to do my best.

Finally, Gandima arrived.

"Let's go," she said as she collected me from the hallway and led me downstairs to the studio.

"Are you ready?" Gandima asked, all business.

"Of course," I said.

The studio was crowded; it seemed like the entire station had come for the show. Seasoned anchors, editors, and cameramen lined the walls. A stunning young Mongolian woman who looked more like Lucy Liu than Lucy Liu did, was there as well.

"Who is she?" I whispered to Gandima, pointing to the nubile vixen tossing her silky mane back and forth as if she were auditioning for a shampoo commercial.

"Your competition," Gandima said before she walked off to arrange the teleprompter.

"Hi," I said to the girl. "Are you here for what I'm here for?"

"Yes," her mother said, answering for her. "I'm her mother. She's twenty-two. And you are?"

"Her competition," I said, squaring off in kind.

Tilting her chin up ever so slightly and cocking her head, the girl's mother regarded me warily. "I see," she said as she helped her daughter brush more luster into her pin-straight hair.

"Patricia?" Gandima called out from the front of the studio. "You will test first."

I hadn't expected that, and I had been eating a banana, something I would soon regret. There's an old wives' tale, or at least some advice repeatedly issued by my mother, which postulates that a banana has the power to calm a nervous stomach. This isn't true, unless the old wives' tale meant looking at a banana instead of actually ingesting it. Not only do bananas do nothing of the calming kind, they also turn to a sticky paste in an already dry mouth, making someone about to audition feel as if they've sipped a glass of glue and then inhaled a puff of talcum powder.

"Sure," I said, swallowing energetically. "May I have a glass of water?"

"No," Gandima said, directing me to the large angled desk at the front of the studio. "Sit down, read from the teleprompter, and be yourself."

Noisily, I licked my lips and sat down. I had only one shot here, and I was determined to make it happen.

Fashioned out of an old overhead projector, the kind you might see at work in a primary school, the teleprompter possessed the charm of being entirely makeshift. An assistant fed sheets of script beneath its mirrored reflector. At an angle, the words appeared on a small screen a few feet in front of me.

"Can you see the words okay? Because if you need to wear glasses, you will be disqualified."

"No, no, they're fine—it's fine," I assured Gandima, and began reading, cocking my head to match the angle on the projector. Peppered with Mongolian names and places like "Jargalsaikhan," "Enkhbayar," and "Arkhangai," the script was a land mine of consonants. But I was nothing if not ready for just that. After all, I'd spent a summer writing stories just like this one.

"Next," Gandima said abruptly after I'd finished.

As I stepped out from behind the anchor desk and the spotlights, the photogenic vixen approached. "Good luck," I whispered, completely insincerely.

For every Mongolian word that I'd been confronted with, she faced down the same battle with the English words, and there were many more of them. From "prime minister" to "initiative," the gorgeous girl butchered the entire English news script, save the Mongolian words it was peppered with. Right in front of us all, Gandima and the station manager deliberated. Back and forth, they negotiated. The girl, her mother, and I made a point of looking anywhere but at each other. Finally, and without any fanfare, Gandima made the announcement.

"Za, okay, Patricia, the anchor role is yours."

Without another word, Gandima left the studio. One by one, so did everyone else, and I stood alone, silently beating the air with my fists.

CHAPTER 23

A Mormon Picnic

We are preparing for the possibility of setting up an industrial park, and we are looking forward to the joint implementation of other projects in the fields of geology and mining. This should attract more Japanese investors to Mongolia. We hope this will make more efficient the current investments as well as other areas of mutual interest.

—Interview, Director Japan Institute of Economics, *MM Today* broadcast

"Where's the toilet paper?" I called out to Meg from the bathroom the next morning.

"Where's the freezer?" she responded from the kitchen.

After performing my morning ablutions with my hand, I found Meg in the kitchen, looking for stuff that wasn't there. The freezer was gone. And the fridge had been emptied, save half a dozen or so large, raw bones and one cucumber. The water filter was gone too.

"The futons are missing," Meg called out from the living room. "And most of the other furniture too."

Had we been robbed? We pondered this as we sat down at the bare kitchen table, drumming our fingers in contemplation. Usually Batma left breakfast for us every morning, a bowl of brown bread and jam, with maybe a single fried egg apiece. The bowl and the jam were gone, and there was no sign of either the eggs or Batma. The apartment was quiet. Where was the family?

We needed drinking water, so I boiled a pot of tap water while Meg and I munched on the lone cucumber that had been left behind.

Days later, the phone rang. Surprised that it had rung at all, Meg and I both jumped.

"*Sain bain uu?*" I said uncertainly into the telephone receiver. The last time the host family's landline had rung, they'd been living in the apartment. And that had been awhile ago.

"Hello, is that Patricia?" a voice said in heavily accented English.

"Yes, but who is this?"

"This is the uncle, and I would like to invite you," he said.

Invite me? Where?

"The family is in the countryside. They will come for you and for Meg Saturday morning," he said.

"But wait, are they living there?" I asked, a bit annoyed. Batma and Badaa had made an agreement with the British company to provide food and a home for Meg and me. In return, we'd paid the British company, and the British company had paid the family. Although we'd been provided with a home, we hadn't seen any food in weeks. And strangely, every time we went grocery shopping, the food we'd bought would disappear soon after, along with the freezer, the toilet paper, and, eventually, even the welcome mat. It soon became clear that the family's visits back home were for the sole purpose of appropriating our groceries—but never our beer! Which may have had something to do with the fact that the family was Mormon.

"When will they be back in Ulaanbaatar?" I asked.

"I don't know, maybe September," the uncle said, and hung up.

September? "But it's only *July*," I said into the dead receiver.

Saturday morning, right on schedule, the family returned to the apartment. Hoisting a heavy and unwieldy sack through the front door, Badaa deposited it on the kitchen floor. Without an explanation of where they'd been, the family began to quickly pack up the last of the bones in the refrigerator. After the apartment was emptied of absolutely everything, even the television and pots and pans, they unwrapped the sack that was still lying in the middle of the floor. Skinned, it was difficult to tell what it was, but it looked as if it had been a goat.

With a cleaver, Batma hacked at the carcass until she had divided it into quarters and separated its limbs from its body. Gathering the animal's remains, she loosely retied the sack and made her way back out the front door.

Shrugging our shoulders in disbelief, Meg and I did as we were told and packed overnight bags. It was the weekend, and we were both off from work. Although I'd landed the anchor title, I hadn't yet had an opportunity to fill the role. Following Batma and Badaa outside to their car, we put our sleeping mats and quilts in the trunk. On top of them, Badaa emptied the raw contents of the sack of goat.

"*Za*, okay, let's go," Batma said. Sometimes the very best thing about traveling is having no idea why you're doing what you're doing, especially when you don't even know *where* you're going to be doing it.

Seven of us piled into their red Chevy sedan. The old grandmother, now in her traditional gold-and-green silk *deel*, the same one she'd worn that first day I'd seen her in the apartment courtyard, glowered at me and squeezed onto my lap. Batma and Badaa's two children squeezed onto Meg's.

Before our road trip officially got under way, Badaa stopped the car outside the headquarters of the Mongolian Mormon mission in Ulaanbaatar. We'd known he was an important man at the church, but we didn't know he was part of the top brass. The whole family got out of the car—and that's when we realized what this weekend trip was all about. We were headed into the countryside for a picnic with the Mongolian Mormon Church and their American missionary hosts.

Now this was going to be interesting. Already, Sister Baker, one of the missionaries from Utah, had made a point of officiously introducing herself to us and her boss, Loren, whom she told me was the American head of the Mormon mission in Mongolia. He'd appreciatively nodded when he'd met us, assuming, as he put it, that we were his two newest Mormon "investigators" in the country. As far as decorum was concerned, we were skating on thin ice.

"Did Batma give you a Mormon Bible?" Meg whispered to me in the car, after Sister Baker had left to board one of the buses.

"No," I said, pondering Batma's choice of Meg over me for salvation.

Just then, the family returned to the car and we were off, trailed by several yellow school buses full of church members. About a half hour into our drive, Badaa stopped the car. On the side of an especially desolate and deserted part of the road, sitting in a lawn chair, was a leathery old man. Beside him was an enormous barrel with a tin lid, and hanging from the barrel was a little saucepot.

"Two," Badaa grunted, handing him a pair of empty two-liter plastic water bottles, as well as a fistful of small *tugrug* notes.

Slowly, as if he were creaking inside, the old man removed the tin lid, stood, and bent into the barrel, dipping the saucepot deep inside. Little by little, in shifts, he raised himself back up again, and ladled the cloudy white mixture he'd collected in the saucepot into Badaa's water bottles. It was *airag*, the fermented mare's milk I'd sampled for the first time weeks earlier with Evan and Tobie.

Not long afterward, we arrived. Badaa parked the car in the shade of a grove of trees, and the buses followed suit. One by one, we clambered out. The grandmother hoisted herself off my lap, looked around at her fellow Mongolian Mormons, and scowled deeply. Like a lot of old people, she had an almost theatrical way of silently voicing her displeasure, although it was anyone's guess what was bothering her.

In the cool shadow beneath the canopy of trees, the women set out blankets and thick, heavy rugs to sit on. There were dozens of children, who immediately scattered, racing to the top of a nearby hillock and then back down again. The Mongolian men gathered and built a fire.

Meg and I stood on the edge of all this, wondering how we should participate. Just then, Loren, the American head of the Mormon mission, ambled over. He was tall, had a shock of thick white hair, and appeared to be permanently sunburned.

"Afternoon, young ladies," he said affably, even a little curiously. "Anyone looking after you here in Mongolia? I mean, it's not always safe in this country, you know. Perhaps I can offer you the services of two male escorts from the church?"

Beside me, I could feel Meg bristle. I would've bristled too, if it hadn't been for the fact that he'd referred to both of us as "young."

"So, what do you say?" Loren pressed.

Meg was cautiously quiet, so I spoke up. It was unusual to see her lose her cool, and it made me uneasy.

"Well, we've done okay so far," I said evenly. "But thank you anyway."

"Now, Patricia," Loren went on. "I understand you work for the television station in the capital, is that right?"

Loren sure did know a lot about me; I don't know why he was looking for more "investigators," as he'd mistakenly referred to Meg and me earlier. After all, he seemed to be doing a pretty good job himself of investigating.

"That's right, I do," I said.

"Have you considered working for a Christian station?" Loren asked.

I admitted I hadn't, although I had heard of such a TV station back in Ulaanbaatar.

"They hire their staff based exclusively on acceptance of Christ as the savior," Loren went on, referring to the station back in the capital.

I was at a loss for words; I didn't want to insult my hosts, especially the Mongolian ones, but I didn't exactly want to engage the head of the Mormon Mongolian mission on my job prospects. Obviously my employment situation was complicated enough already without adding Jesus or Joseph Smith into the picture. Anyway, Loren didn't seem to notice my discomfort and went on. In fact, he went on for quite some time, telling me and still-silent Meg in great detail about the Mormon Church's activities in Mongolia, including their donation of wheelchairs to every single *aimag*, or province, in the country. He also talked about their positive impact on maternal mortality, and the evils of the World Bank in impoverishing underdeveloped countries.

"You know what?" Loren said suddenly. "You should tell Mongolia TV to do a story on the good work the Mormon Church is doing here," he said.

I didn't have the heart to tell him that his pitch would have to get in line behind a host of others that were still awaiting Gandima's approval. Fortunately, I wouldn't have to. Just in the nick of time, Batma arrived.

"Patricia, Meg," she said, beaming. "You must drink the *airag* now."

Extending her right arm, left hand poised politely at her right elbow, Batma offered me a saucer of *airag*.

"Thank you!" Meg and I both declared gratefully, accepting the *airag* and sipping leisurely. Eventually, Loren left.

Across the meadow, Badaa and the other Mongolian men had hauled the goat carcass from the trunk of the car, and were clipping it into serving-sized pieces. They were about to make a meal of grave historical significance, and I pulled up a seat ringside. There is nothing more exciting than watching history resurface, many centuries later, especially when the history might lend a clue as to how Genghis Khan himself used to cook. In Mongolia, there are many legends, and even recipes are part of local lore.

Eight hundred years ago, when Genghis Khan and the Mongol horde roamed the steppe, the constant threat of conflict made it foolish to use fire to prepare dinner. Fire caused smoke, and smoke alerted enemies. In order to avoid sending these smoke warning signals to enemies, the troops would only build fires when they felt they were roaming through areas of relative safety. When in need of food during the rest of their expedition, even in areas deemed dangerous, they figured out a way to make use of the fire, even after it was put out.

After depositing large stones into the flames, they'd leave them to heat. While they waited, someone had the unenviable task of stripping a goat of its head and scooping out its internal organs through its open neck. Then, into the hollowed-out carcass went the red-hot rocks, and while the animal cooked itself from inside out, the fire was extinguished. Whole and mostly intact, the bloated creature must have looked like its own piece of carry-on luggage, and it surely traveled well. Called *boodog*, this recipe invites you to also experiment with marmot.

Without the threat of imminent war, this cooking method has changed somewhat over the centuries. For starters, Badaa was preparing *khorkhog*, pronounced "whore hog," a riff on what surely is the more ancient *boodog*. He was neither preparing it in secret nor was he risking serving us a marmot infected with the plague. The only downside, of course, was that I wouldn't get to see him burn the fur off of a goat; one of the technological developments adopted in *boodog* cooking is the use of a blowtorch to singe off the animal's fur.

Removing dozens of stones from the heat of the fire, Badaa stuffed them and the meat hunks into tall tin milk canisters. He shut the lids tight and we all waited patiently for a very long time. About two hours later, Badaa unsealed the containers, tipping the contents of bones, cooked goat, and stones onto a cutting board. While he carved the meat into bite-sized pieces, Batma distributed the hot, greasy rocks.

"Watch," Batma said to me, rubbing one of the stones between her hands, onto her face, and over her arms and legs.

"You take," she said, putting the hot, greasy rock into my outstretched palms, encouraging me to do what she'd done. "Good for skin," she explained. Not only is this practice supposedly good for keeping a youthful face, but Mongolians also believe that cooking stones transmit energy to the human body. Whatever the case, the smell of hot meat was making my mouth water energetically.

Just then, Loren called everyone to prayer. Gathering in a loose circle around the smoldering fire, the Mormons and Americans prayed first in Mongolian, led by Badaa, and then in English. Not invited to join them, Meg and I stood a short distance from the group and bowed our heads.

"*Makh*," Batma said after they'd finished praying, and handed me a paper plate with three pieces of steaming hot goat on it. Consummate hosts, the Mongolians had served their guests first. And they'd also served us the largest portion.

"Eat, eat," Batma said before serving the others. Tender and salty, the *khorkhog* tasted like a slow-cooked and succulent brisket. After everyone had finished eating, we rested on quilts the Mongolian women had laid out in the steppe, gazing up at the late afternoon sky.

"Yellow horse," Batma said in Mongolian. She'd suddenly begun collecting our belongings and packing them into the trunk of the car. Pointing off in the distance, she repeated herself, and Meg and I simply shrugged and did as she instructed. We got back into the car and drove for a short time to a low, shallow valley. In it were nestled hundreds of tiny cabins. It looked like a small town made up of farmyard barns painted almost exclusively in bright, primary colors.

"Yellow horse," she said a second time, pointing at the village of *Shar Mori*. The family owned a summer home here in the little vacation town of Yellow Horse.

We unpacked our overnight bags, and Batma set up a tent in the front yard. Next to the tent was the freezer that she and Badaa had transported from the apartment in Ulaanbaatar. And beside it was most of the living room furniture that had been missing all summer. While Meg and the children kicked a soccer ball around, the grandmother sat on the front porch and stoically glared straight ahead. On a rug Batma laid out for me, I lay down and watched the dimming light of early evening fade into dusk.

"Batma, where is the bathroom?" I asked.

"*Za, za,*" she responded, putting her shoes back on.

Walking down a dusty road as dusk deepened into night, we shared the comfortable quiet of familiarity. Pointing at a wooden shed a few blocks from the cabin, Batma directed me to the community outhouse. While she waited for me, I could hear her talking and laughing with neighbors in that sociable way you do in the still heat of a summer night. I couldn't help but wonder where all my friends and family were at that moment. What was Netta doing, and Meghan, and my brothers and parents? What had their summers in New York and Ohio been like? Suddenly, I was overcome with nostalgia and homesickness, and I took far longer than I needed to in the outhouse, pulling myself together. Outside, Batma just waited patiently, chatting with her neighbors.

Back at the cabin, the grandmother was gone. Dipping below the horizon, the sun had also left for the day, and the air was growing chilly. Out of the trunk, Batma retrieved our sleeping mats and blankets. Spreading out two beds for us inside the tent, she instructed Meg and me to lie down and wait for her. A few minutes later, she was back, clutching a small guitar.

Mongolians are real romantics. Considering the country is one of the least populated in the world, it isn't difficult to imagine that a lot of relationships start out as long-distance love affairs. With an average of one person living in a space of four square kilometers in one of the least densely populated countries on Earth, Mongolians spend a lot of time pining, and their music certainly reflects this.

Batma began to strum, and then she sang. Slowly, almost sadly, she drew out the notes and the syllables, enunciating at every turn a lullaby about the sweet sorrow of loss. I drifted off to sleep. Hours later I woke up, and she was still there.

CHAPTER 24

Anniversary Crashers

Locals in the Nailakh district bleakly joke that the hardest thing to find here is a job. An area housewife tells us that she prays every day for her husband and grown children, who are illegally working in the now-closed mine.

—Voiceover, MM Today broadcast

"Tem, please, *please* call me back," I said, leaving a message on my TV5 boss's voice mail. "It's urgent."

Back at home in the capital, Meg and I had returned to our routine. Sometimes the family was there; sometimes they weren't. Ulaanbaatar was buzzing with excitement. It was the weekend before Naadam, the country's most famous festival.

For weeks, Tobie and I had been strategizing a plan to get into the Opening Ceremony, but so far, we weren't having much luck. Tickets, just ordinary ones, had sold out long ago. Even *counterfeit* tickets had sold out when the counterfeiters had run out of paper. As for press passes, which is what Tobie and I were after, they, too, were long gone. Journalists from all over the world were flying to Mongolia for this summer's annual Naadam, marking the eight-hundredth anniversary of the founding of the Mongol Republic.

Because Tem had offered Tobie and me a shot at producing our own talk show, we thought we were a shoo-in for press passes. After all, a talk show debuting around the same time as the historic anniversary of Naadam could not have been better timed. But, none of our big interview requests, like the American ambassador, had panned out yet.

Tem had begun to avoid us in the hallways and wasn't returning our telephone calls. He seemed to have lost interest in me, in particular, and I wondered if this was because I hadn't been able to deliver the money he'd been hoping for. None of my old clients had ever responded to the e-mail I'd sent about the investment potential.

Weeks earlier, before things had thawed with Tem, while Tobie and I had been waiting for Ambassador Slutz's office to respond, we pitched a backup story to him in the hopes of making our case that we belonged with the press corps at Naadam. Pitching a feature on the cultural and historical significance of the festival seemed a no-brainer. The TV5 piece would air only internationally, thereby abiding by Gandima's and MNB's requirement that I not appear on air locally in Mongolia. Much to our delight, Tem seemed to love our pitch and immediately agreed to grant us press passes to cover the event.

But, he'd added, he'd only issue us the passes on one condition. With that, he had listed several conditions. Ticking off a list of a dozen administrative tasks that are approximately 100 percent impossible to complete quickly in an ex-Communist bureaucracy, Tem seemed to be stalling. But he was no match for our determination.

Working with the tenacity of two people who need tickets to the most exciting event in Central Asia since the breakup of the Soviet Union, Tobie and I were dogged in our attempts to accomplish every near-impossible task on Tem's list. Begging secretaries to forward paperwork, forwarding paperwork ourselves to carefully copied Cyrillic-script addresses, clandestinely offering a few bribes—and finally, our application was complete. Even Tem had seemed surprised. Somewhat begrudgingly, he agreed to meet us the next morning to issue our passes. It would be just in time; the Naadam celebrations began at noon the next day.

As it turned out, we'd never hear from Tem again about Naadam, and I'd never hear from him again at all.

In the meantime, Tobie and I were suspicious of Tem's begrudging reaction. Our hunch was that he didn't have any passes for us. And if he didn't have any passes, Tobie and I would miss out on this once-in-a-lifetime event. And so, we did what anyone would do who was hoping to gain entry into a historic event in a foreign country: we forged our own press passes. After all, desperate times call for desperate measures.

Swearing each other to secrecy, Tobie and I divided up our responsibilities. I would source glossy photocopy paper, colored markers, plastic sleeves for the finished product, and scissors to cut perfectly sized passport photos to paste onto them. Tobie would be responsible for actually creating the passes from scratch. He'd happened to see a few of them lying around the newsroom at TV5, and he'd covertly photographed them to use as a guide. Everything we bought had to be an identical match for the actual passes, or we'd risk getting caught.

I spent all day hunting down the items on my shopping list, and Tobie spent all night using Photoshop to carefully craft the homemade badges. By the next morning, we had minted our final product by glue-sticking our photos onto the forgeries. They were perfect.

And that morning, just as we'd suspected, Tem never arrived at the station. In fact, no one else did either, except the receptionist. Everyone from TV5 was attending Naadam. But, as it would turn out, the receptionist was just the person we needed. On her desk were two official TV5-logoed jackets. Nothing would better complement our counterfeit passes than authentic clothing.

"May I have two, please?" I said to the receptionist, as Tobie and I left the station for the opening ceremony. She was on her cell phone, texting, and had a habit of not looking up from it, ever.

"Bish," she said without looking up. "No."

I tried again. "Please?"

"Bish."

"Yes?"

"Bish!"

The clock was ticking its countdown toward the noon start of Naadam. It was now thirty minutes before the ceremony, and between it and us was a lot of traffic.

One last time, I pleaded with her. "Please, *please*," I said.

And for some reason, she relented. Still without looking up, she shoved the jackets at us and went back to her cell phone.

"Thank you! Thank you!" we cried as we dashed out the door and into a taxi.

"Sükhbaatar Square!" we instructed the taxi driver.

"Bish," he said.

In Mongolia, it goes without saying that the locals are sticklers for pronunciation. This may be due to the fact that, at least to my ears, words and phrases with very different meanings sound exactly like each other. For instance, "I'm hungry," sounds just like "Currently I'm drinking a glass of water." When one made a request of a local, a language lesson would *always* come first and the request second, regardless of the urgency of the situation. Most of the time, this was incredibly useful, but on the inaugural day of Naadam, it was anything but.

Once more, *"Bish."*

"Sokh-bodder?" I tried one more time.

"Za," he said, "Okay." With that, we sat in traffic for exactly twenty-eight minutes.

Finally, just as the prime minister was beginning his welcome speech, Tobie and I arrived. A brass band trumpeted off in the distance, and the crowd roared. Thousands of tourists lined the perimeter of Sükhbaatar Square. At the center of this throng, diplomats, royalty, and government officials stood on a large dais in front of a statue of Genghis Khan. Security was tight; police and even the military ringed the edges of the square.

Up ahead, though, was the foreign press corps, just the place that Tobie and I wanted to be in order to film. Weighing our options, we realized we had only two. Either we could play it safe and watch from the sidelines, or we could try to get past security. Without further hesitation, we took one look at each other and made a run for it—right toward the prime minister and his government entourage, the enormous statue of Genghis Khan, and the press corps.

"Stop!" a guard yelled in English, and we froze in our tracks. Pointing down, rather than at us, he didn't take issue with where we were heading, but what we were standing on—the red carpet. Absolutely everyone seemed to be watching us. And there was only one thing to do—make another run for it. So that's what we did, running as fast as we could until we reached the press corps.

The BBC, AFP, and Reuters were all there, along with many other foreign news outlets and their correspondents. And so was TV5, with Tem and his crew of reporters and producers. Tobie and I knew he'd spotted us; the surprise was evident on his face from across the crowd of journalists. But we did like any jilted party would do and pretended otherwise, and so did he.

Just then, a trumpet sounded off in the distance and the prime minister concluded his welcome remarks. Thundering past the eastern edge of Sükhbaatar Square, auburn horses stomped past, marching in time to a deafening drumbeat. Their manes had been brushed silky and lustrous, and they came with fierce cavalrymen on their backs. Decorated in overcoats of resplendent gold, rich red, and peacock blue, the riding warriors wore pointed metal helmets and heavy combat boots. There was no mistaking the analogy; this was meant to be the return of Genghis Khan's formidable cavalry, after an eight-century absence.

Heading south from the edge of the square, the cavalry marched, leading the crowds in a parade to the national stadium where the eighthundredth anniversary Naadam games were about to begin.

Centuries ago, the Mongol army enlisted soon-to-be-departed souls to fight in battles. Shearing a length of hair from his finest stallion, a warrior would attach the horsehair just beneath the tip of the spear. Holding this *sulde*, or "spirit banner," upright while charging into battle, the warrior believed that, when he died, his spirit would be able to continue on, living inside the banner. Propped upright outside his family's *ger*, or carried into battle by another soldier, the swish and sway of the breeze was believed to bring eternal life to the warrior's spirit.

Now, leading the procession at the helm, one of the soldiers held upright an enormous horsehair spirit banner. At the very front and center of the phalanx, it symbolized the soul of Genghis Khan himself. In fact, after his death in the thirteenth century, Genghis Khan's *sulde* had been hidden in a protective place. When the Soviets came knocking in the 1930s, they wanted to know where it was, so that they could successfully destroy any notion of reverence for the Mongolian past.

Fortunately, it had been hidden so well, just like Genghis Khan's grave itself, that the Soviets couldn't find it. Unfortunately, his *sulde* had been hidden so well that no one else has ever found it again either, including the Mongolians. But that wasn't going to stop them from trying today, and they'd obviously masterfully re-created the original to mark this historic anniversary.

The cavalry rumbled past and filed into the national stadium. Sonorously and deeply, drums thumped, tinny cymbals clapped, and the air was electrified and full of reverberating sound. Tobie and I followed the procession until we reached the stadium, where we found ourselves in a real mess.

Up ahead, a riot had broken out. The stadium was filled to capacity, and those who'd been duped into buying counterfeit tickets had been refused entry. In fact, Tobie and I had actually been given tickets. The British company had paid for them, but when Tem had told us we'd been approved for press passes, we'd given them away. There was only one way to get in, and that would be to use our forged passes. We hadn't done so yet; this would be our first attempt. The guards who'd stopped us on the red carpet hadn't even bothered to check them. But it was now or never.

Around the perimeter of the stadium was a private entrance reserved exclusively for dignitaries and royalty—as in the Prince Andrew sort of royalty. Tobie and I made our way there. Although we knew we wouldn't get in, we wanted to test drive our press passes. The glue stick I'd used had come unstuck, and we'd already had to perform emergency repair work.

Passes dangling from our necks, donning our official TV5 jackets, camera gear in hand, Tobie and I approached the private entrance. Flashing our badges, we waited for a response from the guard standing sentry.

"*Bish,*" he said, dismissing us with a wave of his hand. "Journalist people, over there!" the guard ordered, pointing to the entrance reserved for the press.

It had worked! Tobie and I were official. At least the guard thought so.

At the press entrance, we faced a tougher challenge. The guard on duty was not just a guard but some sort of highly decorated soldier. He had enough pins on his collar and brocade on his epaulets to suggest he was part of Mongolia's top brass. Upon closer inspection, we saw that his lapel was prominently sporting actual gold stars, several of them.

Tobie and I handed over our passes to the soldier. Unlike his colleague, he took a long time inspecting them and removed mine from its plastic sleeve. Looking at me, puzzled, he began to peel my passport photo away from the pass itself. Quickly and without thinking, I snatched it from him and told Tobie to turn on the camera. With the mike at my mouth, I pretended to chatter into it, as if we were about to go live.

"Welcome to Naadam!" I shouted into the camera as Tobie filmed, picking his way backward through the doorway and scooting past the decorated soldier, who couldn't seem to decide if he should interrupt a live news broadcast to make an arrest.

And then, suddenly, we were inside. The soldier didn't follow. The opening ceremony was just beginning. The drums and cymbals had stopped, and a *morin-khuur* horsehair fiddle was whining a solemn welcome to Mongolia's most important guests of honor, a man and woman dressed as Genghis Khan and his long-lost bride, Borte. Tobie and I silently tucked into the anonymity of the press box and looked around to spot none other than Britain's Prince Andrew sitting just behind us.

Circling the pitch on a track ringing the field, Genghis and Borte led the last of the procession, which was making its way around the stadium to close the ceremony. Decorated horses curtsied to the crowd and pranced past; costumed children performed traditional dances. Enormous skin drums boomed and resonated. At the end of this magnificent parade, Genghis and Borte waved regally to the crowd. He was sporting an elaborate handlebar moustache, she a luxurious fur *deel* and matching hat.

As the opening ceremony ended after only a half hour or so, the press corps was invited onto the field to film and photograph. There, Tobie and I shot video of the ornate spectacle and interviewed dignitaries and guests, one of whom had flown from as far as Canada to attend Naadam. All of them had come to watch the ancient sporting events that Naadam is known for. These would begin the following day and last an entire week.

After we finished filming and interviewing, Tobie and I collected Meg, who'd also attended Naadam, and headed for lunch at a local Turkish restaurant.

"I'll have the 'Meat Covered With Garbage,'" I said to the waitress. It was the restaurant's most popular dish and my favorite, not least because of its misspelling of cabbage; it happened to be absolutely delicious—a casserole of savory meats and tender vegetables. While we waited for our food to arrive, we drank cold beer and smoked a hookah pipe stuffed with Kuwaiti apple tobacco.

"Are you free this afternoon?" the restaurant owner said, stopping by our table. "Because I'd like you to interview someone, someone important, someone from my country."

Several times a week, every single week that summer, Meg and Tobie and I visited the Turkish restaurant. Not only was the food tasty, but the owner had become a friend. That day, he'd even reserved a private room for us in his restaurant. This was quite a courtesy to extend, considering how many Turkish dignitaries had come to Mongolia for Naadam; they were all dressed in dark suits and darker glasses and sat in the main dining room, eating their own plates of mouthwatering Meat Covered with Garbage.

How the restaurant owner had arranged to have Tobie and I interview the Deputy Speaker of the Turkish National Assembly was a complete mystery to us, but we were both very eager to put a more formal spin onto our interviews. So far, we'd been filming the lives of regular people on irregular paths: the German brewmaster, the Mongolian hip-hop brothers, the Irish cyclists. But this interview would be altogether different. This was what real journalism was made of.

After lunch, Tobie and I headed to the Turkish embassy. We were led through security into a plush drawing room. Half a dozen men in those dark suits sat on striped satin sofas, sipping thick espresso and chain-smoking cigarettes. While Tobie set up the shot, the deputy speaker's assistant approached me and introduced himself.

"There are some rules," he said right away. There would be no questions about politics; the interview was to be conducted solely on the speaker's impressions of the Naadam festivities. "And," he added, "the interview must take place in Turkish."

"You know I don't speak any Turkish, don't you?" I said. "Not a single word."

"Oh," he said. "Then I suppose I will have to translate."

Now somewhat anxious, I sat stiffly on one of the satin sofas while I waited for Mr. Deputy Speaker to arrive. Across the room, the men in suits continued to drink their coffee, smoke, and stare in my direction with that penetrating gaze all diplomats seem to possess. In turn, I smiled and then busied myself with finding anywhere else to look. Finally, Sadik Yakut arrived.

After butchering the pronunciation of his name so many times that he took my notebook to spell out his name phonetically for me, we began the interview. Through his assistant, I dutifully asked Mr. Yakut how he was enjoying Naadam and what he thought of this momentous year's celebrations compared to other years. Hoping to circumvent the assistant's warning to refrain from asking about politics, I inched toward a compromise. After all, if this was going to be my first shot at being a foreign correspondent, I'd better make the most of it.

TIKA, the Turkish International Cooperation and Development Agency, delivers aid in the form of educational, social, and cultural projects in developing countries. Mongolia is a beneficiary of these projects. That year, in 2006, Turkey provided assistance in support of youth theater, the Mongolian National Library, and a symposium on the history of Mongolia. This last project interested me because the Turks and the Mongols don't exactly have a polite history with each other.

In the middle of the thirteenth century, after Genghis Khan had died, his children and grandchildren (aside from Ogodei, the wayward party animal) didn't waste any time annexing more land and people. In 1243, they knocked on the doors of the Seljuks in Anatolia, what is now Turkey. Although the Mongolians were outnumbered, they roundly defeated their adversaries, the Seljuk state crumbled, and its people became vassals of the mighty Mongol Empire.

Right around this time, Mongolian warriors had come up with some rather creative ways to kill their enemies, such as stomping them to death or stuffing their mouths with dirt and rocks until they choked. It seemed inconceivable to me that the Turks, even many centuries later, were providing any sort of aid to descendants of warriors who may or may not have stuffed dirt and rocks down their ancestors' throats. That seemed like the kind of grudge one would be sure to hold on to. In any case, I found it fascinating that the Turks would be willing to shed light on a part of history that had all but emasculated a significant part of their heritage.

"So, Mr. Deputy Speaker," I imagined myself saying, "what do you say to worldwide claims that the Mongol horde, *just eight centuries ago*, routed your own people?"

In a 2001 interview on the BBC's *Hardtalk* program, host Tim Sebastian sat down with the wife of former Yugoslav president, Slobodan Milosevic. His legendary tough line of questioning caught Mira Markovic off-guard, and the interview supposedly ended abruptly when Markovic insisted she would "only answer the questions I want to answer." And this was after she touched up her hair *while* being asked about claims of genocide. Sebastian's style has always seemed to me to be investigative journalism at its best, and for a moment, I thought I'd try out a few of those same tactics on the genteel Turkish deputy speaker.

But unfortunately for me, he wasn't hiding anything, not that I'd have figured it out if he had been. I couldn't understand a single thing the deputy speaker was saying, I could barely understand what his assistant was translating, and the men in the dark suits were still staring me down. So I politely asked about Naadam and wrapped up the interview. Afterward, the men in suits offered us coffee and baklava.

CHAPTER 25

Fashion Means Forward

The closure of the Nailakh coal mine has resulted in an increase in unemployment in this district. Because the local government coffers are now unable to turn a profit, the central government has begun to implement a plan that will direct foreign investment to the region.

— Lead story, **MM Today** broadcast

After the Naadam Opening Ceremony, its actual sporting games were being hosted all around Ulaanbaatar and the surrounding countryside. Over the course of a week, contestants would compete until a winner was declared in each event.

While Olympic athletes compete in dozens of sporting events, Mongolian Naadam athletes compete in just three: wrestling, archery, and horseback riding, and a distant fourth if you count flicking dried knucklebones at a target. The first three, the "three manly sports" as they're called, date back to a sort of warrior boot camp, when combat training was necessary for survival. Centuries earlier in the steppe, as competitions grew out of these training sessions, local festivals began to sprout up, matching one neighborhood's best athlete against another's. This went on every third year for about three hundred years, until the 1921 revolution when someone decided they'd better make this age-old tradition an official party. From then on, every July, to mark the anniversary of the 1921 revolution, the national Naadam festivities take place in Ulaanbaatar, and athletes from all over the country come to compete. As one local magazine described the event, "If you do not have a good time, you are just not trying!"

Each of the three sports has its quirks, to say the least.

The national pastime, wrestling, is by far the most popular. Dressed in tight blue underpants, tiny red jackets that cover only their forearms and the small of their backs (instead of sleeveless shirts, think shirtless sleeves), knee-high go-go boots, and a rather phallic-looking cap, competitors are *not* put into weight categories. This can make for pretty good viewing when a scrawny David is up against a Goliath beefy enough to register on the Richter scale. The first wrestler to simply touch the ground with anything other than his hands and feet loses the match, and winners are awarded with an animal title after performing an "eagle dance" (which looks something like a cross between ballet and sumo) in a ritual honoring the horsehair *sulde* spirit banners.

Both men and women compete in the archery events, and if any of the legends are true, Mongolian archers are some of the most superhuman shooters on the planet. From hitting targets as far off as 1,760 feet (536 meters), to hitting moving targets *twice* in midair, to splitting arrows in a single shot, lore has it in Mongolia that this is where the ancient bow and arrow was perfected. Made from nylon, sheep guts, bones, and fish glue, the entire contraption is enormous—and elegant. If the stencil outline of a viola could be a weapon, this would be it.

Although the archers no longer take aim at people, they do take aim at a target the size of a golf ball up to a hundred yards off in the distance. Oddly, for a sport requiring so much upper-body dexterity, competitors dress as if it were winter, tied up tight in long-sleeved silken *deels*. As each archer shoots forty times wrapped in his elaborately decorative straitjacket, judges actually sing out the results.

But legends and popularity aside, probably the most thrilling of the three Naadam sports is horseback riding. Frankly, any sport that allows a five-year-old to compete on a national level is going to be thrilling entertainment, especially when these miniature jockeys aren't wearing helmets. Or shoes. And there is no racetrack—just the wide-open steppe and speeds of up to fifty miles per hour. Hundreds of horses race across seventeen miles of hard riding; then, upon arrival at the finish, often drop dead from exhaustion. The lucky ones simply survive, and the luckiest horse of all is proclaimed the winner by sprinkling a cup of fermented mare's milk *airag* over his head.

Strangely, although Tem hadn't spoken to us since the incident with the press passes, he'd provided Tobie and me with a car and driver so that we could attend and cover the horse racing event out in the countryside. The morning of the race, Tobie and I met just before dawn in TV5's parking lot. It was cold, and we waited for an hour as we began to wonder if our driver would show at all.

Just as the sun was cracking its yolk over the horizon, two journalists emerged from TV5's studios. Before they slipped into their waiting SUV, we called out to them, hoping to hitch a ride. We knew they were headed to the same race, and it was getting late. Tobie and I worried we'd miss the start. Wordlessly, they ignored us and sped off.

Finally, an old Russian Lada van rolled into the parking lot. Still half-asleep, the driver leaned over to the passenger door, grumbling about the early hour, and motioned for us to get inside.

"Where is Naadam?" he began shouting into the empty stillness of the morning. At every stop light and every intersection he did this, shouting to anyone who was awake, and these people numbered exactly two: Tobie and me. Eventually, he found someone who showed us how to get where we were going.

"North!" the passerby had shouted, and we were on our way. Crouching on metal benches bolted to the walls, Tobie and I hung on tightly while the driver sped deftly over dirt roads and jagged bumps, negotiating catnaps along the way. It didn't take long for us to figure out that the ceiling was carpeted not for its aesthetic appeal, but to prevent head injuries.

Finally, we made it. Tumbling and jostling as we crested the lip of a low hill, we saw spread out before us a carnival. Smoke from cooking fires rose out of white tents dotting the valley. A large banner that read Finish had been erected alongside a huge wooden platform and sets of bleachers packed with nomads. Parking in a field of swishing grass and meat-roasting stalls, we gathered our equipment and hurried off to where the young jockeys would soon arrive—at the finish line.

Just as we presented our press passes to the guard, we heard it before we saw it, the unmistakable thunder of approaching hooves. Tobie set up the shot just as they emerged. Rounding a bend in the valley to our left, a black SUV led the pack, purring softly ahead, an enormous TV5 flag fluttering and flapping in the breeze from the rear tinted window it was affixed to. A camera had been hoisted from the back seat and latched onto the frame of the open window. Just behind the TV5 crew, a herd of tiny jockeys on horseback stampeded through the steppe and into the base of the valley to the finish line.

"Quick, get ready to roll!" Tobie said, turning on the camera and panning the fields around us from our vantage point atop the media riser.

"I'm at Mongolian Naadam!" I shouted into the mike. "Where boys as young as *four* ride horseback through the steppe, right to the finish!" Just as I finished, so did the jockeys. Cap askew, the first boy crossed the finish line with one hand on his horse and the other hand on his head, clasping his cap. Nomads lined the edge of the cordoned-off finish line, and all of them excitedly whooped as if it were their own son who'd won.

Sliding off his horse, the boy adjusted his hat one more time. He looked like he was trying pretty hard to keep his emotions in check, but he wasn't doing a very good job of it. Pulling down the corners of his smile into cool glowering ambivalence, he couldn't have been much more than eight years old. Later that afternoon, in front of a huge crowd and in a very traditional ceremony, he'd be proclaimed *"Tumny Ekh,"* or "Leader of the Ten Thousand." He and his horse would be so revered that, as the *Mongolia Expat* magazine described it, his "sweat [will be] treated as liquid gold and flung about like champagne, and a life of stud awaits the lucky horse." Lucky boy, luckier horse!

"Come on, I'm starved," Tobie said. "Let's go find some *khooshur!*" There's nothing quite like a platter of meat pancakes to round out a day of adventure. Drinking in the sunshine and bottles of cold orange soda, we sat at a meat-roaster's stall. With a bird's-eye view of the countryside, I could see a completely uninterrupted horizon, something I've never caught sight of anywhere else in the world.

"You are a journalist?" an old Israeli photojournalist asked me, after introducing himself. Older, distinguished, and with a camera slung from his neck, he had that weathered look of an aged artist who has spent a lifetime on the road.

"I guess I am," I acknowledged, and proceeded to tell him the abridged version of how and why I'd come to Mongolia.

"One day," he said. "One day you will return here. Mongolia will get under your skin, and you will come back to find out how that happened."

And just as mysteriously as he'd shown up, the Israeli photojournalist left.

CHAPTER 26

Chance of a Lifetime

*The Asian Cultural Prize of Fukuoka, which has been awarded internation-
ally since 1990, was once awarded to another Mongolian, Mrs. Norovbanzad,
a famous singer. Asians awarded this prize have achieved extraordinary success in the fields of science, culture, or art. Japanese Secretary-General Ya-
maguchi Ishimora presided over the award ceremony, where Mr. Bira was
awarded along with a Japanese and a Pakistani.*

—Voiceover, *MM Today* broadcast

For the rest of the week, Tobie and I wove in and out of Naadam events. We
ate a lot of mutton dishes, sampled *airag* and *arkhi*, and watched knucklebone dice competition under the eaves of hawker stalls. Even though
the festival was winding down, the entire capital was still in party mode.
It was like a weeklong Christmas in July; no one went to work and shops
and restaurants only opened for business if they felt up to it.

But by the time the week had ended, absolutely everyone was worn-
out. The organizers seemed especially exhausted. Likewise, Naadam's
finale was so muted and understated that it seemed no one, not even the
officials in charge, could take one more minute of partying. After one last
interminably long wrestling session that wore on for the better part of an
entire day, the prime minister finally took to a dais and bid everyone farewell. The closing ceremony was so brief, I double-checked my schedule to
make sure it had actually taken place.

Tobie and I had plenty of footage and interviews to produce a piece on

Naadam, the story we'd pitched to Tem for international broadcast, but I never heard from him again, and it certainly wasn't for lack of trying. And although our office was right down the hall from his, I never even once saw him again. So, one day, I gave up on Tem and TV5 and packed up my desk to resume full-time work for Gandima at Mongolia National Broadcaster.

Tobie stayed on at TV5 until he left Mongolia later that summer. He even produced a music video for Bold and Quiza, featuring one of Quiza's best songs from his chart-topping album.

"Chinzo has food poisoning," Gandima said to me one morning. "And you need to comb your hair."

"Huh?" I said, looking up from the scripts I was correcting. What did Chinzo's food poisoning have to do with unruly hair?

"He called in sick," she said, a playful smile curling her lips.

"I'm sorry to hear that?" I said, unclear what my response was supposed to be.

"And he can't anchor the news tonight."

"And?" I prodded, suddenly knowing what it was she was about to say. Of course, I'd only landed the anchor role in theory, and Gandima had made it very clear to me that I'd only ever anchor in a pinch. But with Chinzo sick and the other anchors unavailable, Gandima was finally in the pinch I'd been waiting for.

"And," Gandima said, obviously enjoying herself as she drew out the conclusion, "tonight you will anchor the Mongolian news."

"Really?" I said, so many times that she interrupted me.

"You need to hurry. We don't have much time before we go to air. Do you have a suit at home?"

Did I? Did I ever! Freshly pressed and hanging in the closet was my "Cry Clean Only" suit, waiting for just such an opportunity. Racing home, I collected the suit, a comb, and makeup and raced right back to the station to put myself together.

"You look old," Gandima said, surveying me after I'd finished. "But it'll have to do. This time, anyway."

Had she said "this time"?

Gandima led me downstairs to the same studio where I'd auditioned, and I recited my lines from a sheet of paper. As usual, there were a lot of land mines embedded in the script, endless combinations of consonants in words like "Gobi Gurvan Saikhan" and "Nambarin Enkhbayar."

"You know," Gandima said as she grabbed my elbow. "Mongolia National TV has never allowed anyone to take over the anchor chair so quickly. Not a foreigner, and certainly not a woman." She smiled at me conspiratorially but emphatically and led me into the studio.

Enkhtuya, Gandima's boss was there waiting. Beside her, in a row, stood most of the station's production staff. I only recognized a few of the editors; the rest of the faces were new. Clearly, I had an audience.

"Sain bain uu," I said, nodding at them. "Hello."

No one spoke; the studio was completely silent. I was so nervous I felt as if I were standing on gelatinous, boneless legs.

One by one, the spotlights flickered on and blazed, and I was shown to my seat in the anchor's chair. Affixing a mike to the lapel of my jacket and smoothing my hair, Gandima whispered in my ear. "You'll be fine," she said.

Steeling myself, I sat ramrod straight and glued my hands to the desk in front of me to keep them from shaking.

The leathery old cameraman, the one I'd apologized to just a few weeks earlier, tinkered with his equipment. While he adjusted the angle of the lens and the height of the tripod, I reminded myself of some very good advice a friend had given me many years ago.

"The body's reaction to fear is the same as its reaction to excitement," my friend had said, and I'd never forgotten it. There was no doubt that I was feeling fear: fear that I'd make an idiot of myself in front of millions of people, fear that I'd disappoint Gandima and Enkhtuya—again.

But I was also feeling more excited and alive than I'd ever felt in my life. After all, this was *the* opportunity, at least so far, of my lifetime. And it never would've happened if I hadn't left behind what I thought I was *supposed* to be doing with my life.

Suddenly, and without any adieu at all, someone called out the Mongolian equivalent of "Action!" and I welcomed viewers to the evening news.

"Good evening. I'm Patricia Sexton for the *MM Today* English News Broadcast of the Mongolia National Public Broadcaster," I began, reading from the teleprompter, and then opened with our top story. "The emblematic torch of world peace is currently in Mongolia. After traveling nearly six-hundred-kilometers from Bayandchandmani *soum* in Tov Province, the torch has arrived in Ulaanbaatar."

While I paused to catch my breath before introducing the second story, I stole a glance at Gandima, and she nodded, urging me to go on.

"A local art gallery will present an exhibition centered around ancient household items and personal effects. In honor of the eight-hundredth anniversary of the Great Mongol State, the Mongolian Life Exhibition will display artifacts from as early as the seventh century BC as well as more recent pieces from the nineteenth and twentieth centuries."

I went on, continuing with a story about yaks in Bayankhongor *aimag*. And then, licking my lips, I sneaked a swallow. I was about to need it.

"A five-meter statue of Demul will be erected in Manlai *soum* of Omnogov *aimag*, . . ." I read, careful to enunciate each and every last consonant. "The sculptor of this statue hopes to immortalize the legend of the famous wrestler as well as inspire young wrestling athletes."

And, then, as suddenly as it had begun, it was over.

"For *MM Today*, I'm Patricia Sexton. We'll be back on Friday. Thanks for watching," I said. The cameraman sliced at the air, gesturing that we'd finished. Gandima clapped, and then the producers, editors, and even Enkhtuya followed suit.

"Good job, Patricia," Gandima said as she removed my mike. "Very good."

I was elated. And not just because I'd managed to tiptoe around all those missing vowels. I was elated because I was actually and finally *here*, because it had taken me so long to believe that a risk was worth taking, and now I knew for sure—the risk was worth taking.

That evening, as the sun sank behind the monolithic apartment blocks, I walked home. On the way, I bought a sack of peaches from a street vendor. A pearl moon illuminated the twinkling, cloudless twilight. Together, Meg and I tucked onto the couch in Batma's living room and watched the broadcast. And there it was, right on the screen in bold typeface: "Patricia Sexton, Anchor."

CHAPTER 27

Mongolian Heimlich

We'll be back on Friday. Thanks and good night.

—*MM Today* Broadcast

"Pa-tricia!" Batma called out as she opened the apartment door. Judging by her empty satchels, she'd returned from the countryside to restock. "You are *hut-lugch!*" she said with a big smile.

"*Hut-lugch?*" I asked, rummaging through my Mongolian-English dictionary for a translation.

Placing her hands out in front of her chest, as if they were resting on a flat surface, she bobbed her head and moved her mouth silently.

"Oh! Is *hut-lugch* 'anchor'?" I asked.

"*Teem!*" she said, "Yes!" her familiar smile crinkling the corners of her eyes. "Nervous," she added, miming my rigid hands pasted to the anchor desk. Bobbing her head, just as I'd done, Batma began to laugh hysterically.

"Good!" she proclaimed—finally—and walked off still giggling.

It was our thirtieth consecutive day without hot water. And I was definitely counting. Often, and in most places, the absence of hot water means the presence of lukewarm water. Not so in Mongolia, where streams of recently melted ice run in the country's streams and from their taps.

"Batma, is the hot water coming back now?" we'd always ask, on the few occasions when we'd run into her during one of her trips into the capital from the family's summer home at Yellow Horse in the countryside.

"Not today," she'd say with nearly limitless patience, until that day when her patience wore a little thin. "Not until the summer is over," she said with finality, and we never asked again.

"Want to go to the theater?" Meg asked later that afternoon. It was a great idea, the perfect way to spend a lazy summer evening. But there was just one problem—we'd have to bathe. This was a prospect neither of us relished. Meg and I drew straws and I lost, so I went first.

Marveling once again just how cold "cold" could be, I knelt on all fours in the family's bathtub. Clenching my teeth, I reversed backward into the faucet. With a lathered hand already prepared, I quickly soaped and rinsed. Taking a deep breath and holding it, I turned forward and squatted upright in front of the thin stream of frigid water. Lathering once more, I washed my armpits, rinsing my hands first and then using those corpse-cold and bluish hands to wipe away the soap, rather than wash it away. Standing, to avoid at all costs any excess water dribbling down my chest, I bent quickly to scrub my face. Over the last thirty days, this was a technique I'd perfected, and I'd made sure to clean only the most important parts. For logistical reasons of goose bumps and ice cream headaches, shaving and showering were simply out of the question—even if Meg and I were going to spend an evening at the theater.

Theater began here in Mongolia back in 1922, a year after the Communist revolution. An ambitious youth league began to put on European-style plays, a combination of local folklore with a Soviet bent. Although their productions were amateur, they grew in popularity. A decade later, the group went pro and set up a drama company as well as an opera and ballet company. They did so with the help of the Russians, which surprised me to no end, until I read that the drama company had started out staging revolutionary plays, one of which Meg and I were about to see.

On our way downtown, I insisted, somewhat regrettably, that we get a bite to eat beforehand. Sitting at an outdoor picnic table in the sun at a German restaurant, I ordered cold tea and a platter of coleslaw.

"You know," Meg said after I'd ordered. "I think the platter of slaw is for an entire table; I don't think it's an individual portion."

It had been a long time since I'd had an entire plate of roughage, and I wasn't about to get hung up on details. Throwing caution to the wind, I ate every last shred of the three enormous mounds of beet, cabbage, and carrot slaws—but in just a few hours, I'd meet them all again on their way back up. The slaw dressing had spoiled and I was about to come down with an unforgettable, whirlwind case of food poisoning.

"Meg, I'm suddenly exhausted," I gasped as we walked the few short blocks from the restaurant to the opera house. Feeling as if I were wading through wet cement, my every motion required effort. Chalking it up to heat and fatigue, I displayed my ticket to the usher and located our seats. We were going to see *Three Fateful Hills*, a local production. At least, I thought that was what we were seeing, and someone had told us that's what we'd be seeing, but the translations we'd been given ranged anywhere from "Almond Hill of Sorrows" to "Among Three Hills of Sorrow" to "Three Fateful Lives."

No one we asked could seem to agree who had authored the production, but we'd overheard whispers of a certain Mr. Natsagdorj, Mongolia's most famous playwright. But by this point, I was so confused and disoriented, I wasn't even sure if we were seeing a ballet, an opera, or a play. Clutching my midsection, I swallowed deeply and shut my eyes tight.

Just then an announcement over the loudspeaker caused two waves of commotion, first, after it was made in Mongolian, then, after it was made in English. The orchestra that had been scheduled to accompany the performance was unavailable that evening; a recording would replace it. Everyone in the audience seemed miffed, but as I grew foggier and drowsier, I hardly cared.

It took awhile for the sound engineers to adjust the volume for the building's acoustics, and while they did, I fell fast asleep. Midway through the first half, I woke up to the granular sound of scratching and shrill high notes, and at first I thought it was coming from my stomach. Instead, it seemed the engineers had employed the use of an old gramophone to replace the live orchestra.

A few feet away, the usher's cell phone rang persistently. Staring angrily at its screen while it continued to ring, she ignored it. All around us, there was a lot of noise and a lot of disturbance.

"Meg, I don't know how much you're enjoying this, but I feel terrible. Maybe I'm just hungry?" Growling and burbling, my stomach was sending a message that I was completely misinterpreting.

At intermission, we left.

"How about the 'spicy fried lamp'?" I suggested to Meg as we sat down at a nearby Chinese restaurant. Of course "lamp" meant "lamb," and we ordered a plate of it to share. Spicy, greasy, and savory, we ate every bit. Afterward, the clawing in my stomach grew worse.

"Maybe you need something cold, like ice cream," Meg suggested.

"Now *that* is a great idea," I said. "Let's get a brownie sundae at the American restaurant." Explaining away the newer, more urgent pain as a reaction to the spicy lamb we'd eaten, I ordered a brownie sundae and two spoons.

But then, suddenly, I knew. We needed to get home, now. Quickly, we paid for our ice cream and raced out of the restaurant and into a taxi, whose driver proceeded to extort our vulnerability for seven times the regular fare.

"Batma," I gasped as we flung open the front door of the apartment. "Sick!"

She'd been chatting with friends and knitting, but immediately flew into action. Just as quickly, her friends left, Meg was sent to her room, and I was escorted into the bathroom and onto my knees. While I clutched the rim of the toilet, my head hanging inside, choking for breath between purges so violent that they made a rushing sound coming out of my mouth, Batma went to work in the kitchen.

Boiling rice just long enough to soften it, she stirred in a spoonful of salt until it dissolved. Back in the bathroom, she strained the solids out and force-fed me a mug of the scalding, starchy mixture. Squatting behind me, she kneaded the muscles of my back and stomach, pushing aggressively upward on my guts, in the Mongolian version of the Heimlich.

Again and again, I retched. I could taste and feel the "spicy fried lamp" coming back up, and it felt like I was vomiting the lamp's broken glass. Tears streamed down my face; I was scared. I'd never been this sick. Again and again, Batma forced the salted rice water down my throat. Gagging as I swallowed, the excess dribbled out of my mouth and onto my clothes.

Hours later, it was nearly dawn and we'd repeated the drinking-vomiting ritual until I was hollow and flaccid. Spent, with dried and caked rivulets of mascara staining my cheeks and pooling around my chin, I crawled, limp, to the bedroom. Wrapping a warm *deel* around me, Batma helped me into bed, tucking me beneath an extra set of blankets.

"Patricia, *za?*" she asked. "Okay?"

"*Za,*" I mumbled.

"Patricia, *za?*" she persisted.

I opened my eyes and she was holding a needle in front of my face. It was so long and its diameter so thick that there could have been an eye on the dull end of it, like the ones she'd been knitting with the night before.

"What are you planning to do with that?" I asked her, now fully awake.

"Awk you pon sure," she said slowly, smiling gently.

"What?"

Producing the sterile package from which the needle came, proving it was neither used, nor for knitting, she repeated herself. "Awk you pon sure?"

"Acupuncture?" I said.

"*Teem!*" she said, "Yes!"

I could have refused, but I certainly didn't. Batma had just spent hours healing me; she'd all but saved my life. And it certainly didn't hurt that she'd gone out of her way to show me that the needle was fresh. Holding up the little sword, Batma grabbed my hand and one by one, poked a hole in all ten fingertips. I bled onto the *deel* and the blankets and agony lingered awhile longer.

Just a few hours later, I woke up. I felt fine. Yes, I was weak and considerably lighter, but fine. In the bathroom, I peered closely at myself in the mirror. My eyes were bloodshot and my face was a chalky shade of gray. But I was *cured*.

Still stunned, I tried to thank Batma, but she looked at me as if nothing extraordinary had taken place. Trying to explain to her that food poisoning usually takes days to cure, and that most of the western world pops a lot of pills to keep everything in, rather than the Mongolian way of forcing everything out, I gave up and hugged her instead.

Bewildered, she laughed at me and left for work, and miraculously, I did the same.

Over the next few weeks, I anchored the news several more times. And not because Chinzo had a chronic case of food poisoning either, but because Gandima and Enkhtuya had decided to give me a real shot at the role. In fact, the anchor chair wasn't even where Chinzo wanted to be. One afternoon, while we were preparing the English scripts for that night's broadcast, he confided in me that he, too, had a dream. And his dream had nothing to do with journalism. Chinzo wanted to work for the Foreign Ministry, Mongolia's version of the US State Department. As it turns out, he was really only moonlighting as Mongolia TV's English anchor in order to make ends meet. In that moment, it seemed to me that, no matter where I turned, everyone I was coming in contact with had a burning desire to take their own leaps of faith. I hoped one day Chinzo would do just that, and I told him so just as he left for the day.

"Maybe I will," he said, looking at me intently as he gathered his belongings.

"You are single?" Otgon, one of the four editors at the station, asked as I presented her with our completed scripts. Otgon appeared to be in her early thirties. She wore tinted eyeglasses, which lent her a mysterious air. Quiet and petite, she didn't often have much to say, but when she did, her dry sense of humor managed to transcend languages and cultures.

I nodded.

"I am too," she said with a sigh. "Mongolian men are, how do you say, *hetzu?*"

"*Hetzu!*" I shouted triumphantly. *Hetzu,* the very first word that Batma had taught me earlier that summer, had become indispensable. Someone would try to explain a Mongolian word that was new to me, and I'd try to repeat it back to them. Shrugging our shoulders when the going got too tough, we'd invariably splutter a couple of *hetzu's* to curse our inability to communicate. It means "difficult."

"You think Mongolian dating is *hetzu*?" I asked Otgon. "You're lucky you don't have Match.com," I said, and then spent the next ten minutes trying to explain the concept of Internet dating to her. That night, our broadcast reported on perhaps the most *hetzu* of all Mongolian men, at least as far as serial philandering went.

According to a 2003 article in *National Geographic*, "Genghis Khan a Prolific Lover, DNA Data Implies," Genghis and his offspring were so successful impregnating women that as many as *sixteen million* males living today can trace their ancestry directly to him and his lineage. That's like replacing the entire population of New York City with Genghis Khan's descendants—twice. Even an accounting professor in Florida once claimed to share an ancestor with him. Mention this fact to any Mongolian and you'll get a reaction, every time, of unabashed pride. And so it was with our evening report, which was, literally, a nod toward Genghis Khan's fecundity in the sack.

Earlier that day, President Enkhbayar had taken the time to invite some of those expatriate descendants on a road trip from Ulaanbaatar to Kharkhorum to establish a center for Mongolians of international descent. In other words, this proposed cultural center we were reporting on was a celebration of sexual prowess—and that wasn't even the lead story! We'd also report on a corruption scandal, which had surprised me, considering how young a democracy Mongolia was (and still is).

Best of all though, the script that evening was peppered with more consonants than a Finnish phone book: Tsetserleg, Jarkgalsaikhan, Enkhbayar, Kharkhorum, and Arkhangai, to name but a few.

Before we went to air, I put on a traditional Mongolian jacket. It was a faded sky blue, the color of a winter day, and hemmed at the cuffs and edges with boxy black diagonals.

"A study done on laws pertaining to nature reserves has revealed *inefficiency* and *corruption*," I read from the teleprompter, wishing right then and there that I wasn't leaving Mongolia in just a few weeks. But my days were numbered. I'd signed up for a summer internship, and by this time it was August; summer was nearly over.

"Mongolian expats from around the world have gathered today to meet President Enkhbayar," I read as we switched to a voice over I'd worked on with Chinzo. "An estimated eight million Mongolian descendants are living in a dozen countries around the world. Over a hundred representatives of Mongolian expatriate citizenship will arrive today in Ulaanbaatar, and then continue on to Kharkhorum, Mongolia's ancient capital city, where the delegation plans to establish a center for international Mongolian nationalities."

The broadcast closed with a warning about the degradation of Mongolian forests, and I signed off. Although it wouldn't be long before I left the country, I had one more adventure to embark upon, and that adventure would begin the next morning. I wasn't finished with Mongolia just yet, and Mongolia wasn't finished with me.

CHAPTER 28

The Gobi

The vice director of Parliament presented Dr. Tara Tritara Karn with the anniversary award. Today at her home, Parliament member Gandi received the Thai doctors as guests in order to express her gratitude for their efforts.

—Voiceover, *MM Today* broadcast

From the moment I'd arrived in Mongolia, I'd been fascinated with the Gobi Desert. It's hard not to be. Although one of the harshest, driest, most inhospitable places on Earth, it's actually populated, and the few people living there happen to be some of the most hospitable you'll ever meet.

Covering half a million square miles, the Gobi is the largest desert in Asia and one of the largest on Earth. Ten times the size of the American Mojave, it's just a tenth the size of the world's biggest desert: Antarctica.

Fifty million years ago, a little island we now call India collided with the Asian continent. The collision caused buckling, like two fenders in a slow-motion car crash, and this buckling of the earth's crust eventually created the world's tallest mountains—the Himalayas. In turn, those Himalayan peaks created what's called a "rain shadow," which is what happens to a region when a mountain range blocks off the path of rainstorms. And of course, because the Himalayas are so enormous, they've created a huge rain shadow, which has resulted in the large desert region; that is the Gobi.

Through a small tour company in Ulaanbaatar, Tobie, Meg, and I had pooled our funds and arranged to be driven from the capital into the Gobi. For seven days, we'd be transported nearly one thousand miles in the scorching summer heat to embark upon one of the most spectacular adventures of our lives.

It was dawn on a Saturday morning in August, one of my last in Mongolia, and I dressed quickly. In the kitchen, I boiled a pot of eggs, double-checked the contents of my backpack, and knocked on Meg's door. It was unlike her to oversleep.

"Meg? Are you ready?" I whispered, and she emerged. Her face was drawn and gray, and she looked as if she'd been up all night.

"Food poisoning," Meg said, and I understood: she actually *had* been up all night. But Meg wasn't one to cower in the face of adversity, and she certainly wouldn't do so now, not before our last adventure together. "Let's go," she said, hoisting her pack onto her back. Feebly, she limped out the front door, stoically refusing my offer to carry her bag for her.

Outside, in a lot across the main road, we met our driver. Mongolian drivers, at least the kind who transport you on epic journeys such as this one, don't simply transfer you from one destination to the next like some sort of livery cab chauffeur. On the contrary, they are tour guides, cooks, mechanics, language teachers, and sometimes even would-be therapists. They're responsible for the health of their vehicle over incredibly rugged terrain, as well as the health and well-being of the travelers. Although it's possible to fly to the Gobi, rather than drive, we'd paid for the longer version of the adventure, which was also the cheapest.

"*Sain bain uuuuu!*" our driver called out, waving us toward him. Stout, stubby, and bespectacled, he had a head of thick gray hair and wore pulled-up knee-high socks and short pants, his generous waistband hiked up in the style of a Japanese tourist.

"I am Dergui!" he said, energetically pumping our hands. Then, Tobie arrived, and Dergui helped us all deposit our packs into the open hatch of the trunk.

"We go!" he declared after we'd settled into the van.

"Food shop," Dergui explained as he sped down the empty streets of Ulaanbaatar. "Buy food." He held up a finger to underscore his point, and

I marveled at the size of it—it looked like a toe! In fact, his entire hand was so chubby it looked as if he were holding a fistful of stumps. At any rate, the message was clear: we would need provisions before we headed south.

Still ashen and weak, Meg stayed in the van with Dergui while Tobie and I shopped.

Impatient to get on the road, we did so haphazardly: packets of Ramen noodles, bars of chocolate, bricks of cheese, a bag of walnuts, one tube of salami, green apples, and a box of iced lemon cookies. Tobie and I paid for our groceries and returned to the van, where Dergui inspected our wares. With one glance at our eclectic assortment of items, he raised a bushy eyebrow, shouted a little bit, and gestured wildly. Who knew what he was saying, but we were ready to go, so we got into the van and shut the door. Finally, Dergui shrugged his shoulders and followed suit.

"Glvi!" Dergui said, punching his sausage-like fingers in the direction we were headed. The word "Gobi" actually means "desert," and the Mongolians pronounce it with a gulp, like "glove" without the "o."

Because the Gobi is so dry, so vast, and so inhospitable to its guests, it doesn't have many residents. One of the least populated places on our planet, there's only *half* a person for each square kilometer. In other words, if you and your spouse and two kids are willing to put up with the whole living-in-a-desert-thing, you can have yourself a five-mile backyard without any neighbors.

And precisely because the Gobi is so dry, so vast, and so inhospitable, Dergui wasn't just stating the obvious by pointing in the direction we were heading and announcing "Gobi." He was gently warning us.

"Clothes?" Dergui asked, turning around from his seat in the front to check that each of us had packed appropriately.

"Yes," we each confirmed. Tobie and I may not have purchased the most nutritional food for a week on the road, but we all knew better than to pack inappropriately. Even Meg had diligently done so after a night on her knees, getting her stomach pumped by Batma.

Temperatures in Mongolia are the world's most extreme. But what makes the Gobi unique is how normal its extremes are. On any given day, the thermostat can fluctuate by an *average* of fifty-five degrees. After spending the day sweating in the dead heat of summer, you could end up wondering if you'd tucked in on a winter night.

Dergui made an abrupt turn, drove southwest for a time, and then hesitated at a fork in the road. Studying the sky, he squinted, studied it some more, and then hung a left, putting the van into all-terrain mode. He never once used a map during our trip; the sun and his wristwatch would be his guides. Rolling and bumping along, fields of bright yellow flowers whizzed past, looking like a faint and careless brushstroke on a bare canvas. Wispy cotton clouds off in the distance masked the sun in gauze.

Hours later, Dergui drove up a hillside and parked. "Lunch," he mimed silently, pushing one of his ten thumbs into his mouth. Tobie and I spread a sheet along the lip of the gently rolling hill and set up a picnic. Meg finally appeared from the nap she'd been taking in the van's backseat. Color had returned to her face, and she was ready to eat again. While we lunched, nibbling on apples and cheese and the boiled eggs I'd brought from home, Dergui introduced us to our first artifact.

"*Ovoo,*" he said, pointing.

Off in the distance, on the peak of a nearby hillside, a pile of stones was stacked into a pyramid. At its base were discarded mementos: a wheelchair, a pair of crutches, even a burned-out car. At its top, a flagpole had been fashioned out of a tree branch and stuck into a mound of rocks. Rippling in the wind from the flagpole's top was a tattered blue cloth, a pendant to the offerings beneath it.

Ovoos pay homage to the spirits, and by now we already knew what to do when we saw one. Each of us, including Dergui, collected three stones. Circling the makeshift pyramid slowly, three times, we tossed our stones on top of the pile, paying our respects to those who had come before us. Mindful of the resident spirits, and of Dergui making his own offering, we did so somberly. Visiting an *ovoo* on an epic adventure into the heart of the Gobi, it was almost impossible to imagine returning to New York City, but that's just where I'd soon be. Silently, I offered a prayer up to the heavens that my journey wouldn't end here, that this wasn't the last of it.

Piling back into the van, we made our way deeper into desolation, toward one of the most spectacular sites Mongolia has to offer. We were headed for the famous Flaming Cliffs of Bayanzag, a town nicknamed by none other than one of history's most famous explorers. More than anything else, this was what we'd come to see. Little did we know that this was just the beginning, and that we'd experience far more than we'd ever bargained for.

In the 1920s, American explorer Roy Chapman Andrews paid a visit to Mongolia in search of nothing short of the origin of man. Into the Gobi he and his party traveled, stopping awestruck at a town featuring something of an inside-out, upside-down Grand Canyon. Aptly named the "Flaming Cliffs," the town's massive curtains of bright red bluffs cut into the desert landscape with such authority, it appeared as if a roaring fire had overtaken stage curtains but left the stage intact.

For Bayanzag, this nickname was something of an improvement; the word *bayanzag* is simply a description for the bush that populates the region. With tiny, dusty leaves of a gray pallor, the *bayanzag* looks as if it died of thirst a long time ago, and it might as well have done so—it's actually facing extinction because it's been overused as a fuel source.

Anyway, after Andrews and his team stopped, they dug. Although they didn't stumble upon the origin of man, they did stumble upon the world's first modern-day discovery of dinosaur eggs. And they didn't stop at just petrified eggs. Andrews, who is rumored to be the inspiration for the Indiana Jones character, discovered the fossilized remains of an actual dinosaur. This was not just any dinosaur, but the infamous Velociraptor, a sort of savage, feathered kangaroo that used its fingernails to dig its enemies to pieces. Of course, this was quite a find for the fossil world, and the Velociraptor ended up on none other than the silver screen—playing a leading role in *Jurassic Park*. Interestingly, the renown for the town of Bayanzag wouldn't stop at Hollywood.

Some fifty years later, in 1971, a team of Polish and Mongolian archaeologists returned to Bayanzag and unearthed a fossil so spectacular that it's a national treasure of Mongolia and has been on loan to the American Museum of Natural History in New York. Beneath the sand, the scientists found *two* dinosaurs—right in the middle of a fight to the death. Their match ended prematurely when a sand dune suddenly collapsed on top of both of them, preserving the moment and capturing an actual snapshot of what had happened some eighty million years ago.

Now, standing in the still air facing these historic flaming red cliffs, I absorbed the oncoming dusk. Silence radiated in my ears like a synthesizer droning on one note in perpetuity. I could hardly believe I was in this place, where so few had gone before, where explorers and adventurers had journeyed to fulfill their own dreams and had walked away with much more than they'd ever even thought to ask for. Behind me, a couple of weathered old locals stood beside a lunch table of fossils, calling out into the quiet, inserting commas of noise into the tranquility, offering us the chance to buy supposedly authentic dinosaur eggs.

Signaling that it was time to go, Dergui collected us and drove off, looking for a place to set up camp for the night. Without any fanfare other than sticking his head out the window to check if we were on someone's property, he pulled over to the side of the road, opened the hatch, and pointed at our camping gear. After spending a lot of time negotiating poles, sheets of nylon, little metal parts, and stubborn zippers, we erected our home and set about igniting a gas fire to boil a dinner of ramen noodles.

While we ate, it grew dark, as if someone had been slowly stretching a film of black elastic from the indigo eastern horizon to the rusted western horizon. Once the last slivered edge of light had been sealed off, we sat underneath the expanse of sky, studded with white pinpricks. No one said a word.

⬧

As expansive as the Gobi night is dark, so is the dawn of the Gobi morning. There is no middle ground between night and day; it's as if a main light switch somewhere in the heavens has been turned on, illuminating everything at once.

Amid the clamor of pots and pans early the next morning, Dergui began to make breakfast. Meg and I crawled out of our tent to see Tobie sleeping half-inside, half-outside his own tent. He was so tall that he didn't quite fit, his legs dangling outside the door flap like the wicked witch under Dorothy's tornado-flung house in the *Wizard of Oz*.

"Eat big!" Dergui instructed, using his hands to mime. The water on the makeshift gas stove hissed and boiled, and we made instant coffee and reheated leftover ramen noodles from dinner the night before. We had a long drive ahead of us and made sure to follow Dergui's orders to "eat big." Later that afternoon, we'd get a chance to see something that no one should ever have to personally witness but everyone ought to see. After breakfast, we set off once more, deeper south still, for the haunting emptiness of Barlim Khiid monastery, now a monument to that terrible epoch last century when the world seemed intent on destroying itself.

Like most of the rest of the world in the 1930s, Mongolia was in bad shape. A power struggle a decade earlier had resulted in the formation of a Communist government that would closely align itself with the leadership of Stalin's Soviet Union. Hardly an ideal role model, Stalin made it clear who was boss by eliminating pretty much anyone who disagreed with him. Referred to as the Great Purge, this official policy of mass elimination began in the Soviet Union and eventually made its way south to Mongolia. Topping the list of enemies were none other than the country's monks.

To get the purge under way in Mongolia, Stalin met with Prime Minister Genden and pressured him to begin eliminating these enemies. Genden wanted no part of this, so he refused. Legend has it that this Mongolian prime minister had a set of balls, but we're talking about facing down *Stalin*. Stalin could, say, order Genden's execution if he didn't do as he was told—which is exactly what would happen—but not just yet.

One evening in 1935, at a particularly liquid function at the Mongolian embassy in Moscow, "the two men clashed, literally," as Michael Kohn writes in the *Lonely Planet*. "Stalin kicked Genden's walking stick; Genden slapped Stalin and broke Stalin's trademark pipe." If you're wondering if you read that right, I wondered the very same thing. A drunk prime minister gets into a girl-fight with his boss, who happens to be the world's most feared despot?

The obvious happened next. Prime Minister Genden was put under house arrest back in Ulaanbaatar and eventually ordered to return to Moscow, where he was executed in November 1937. But the madness doesn't quite stop there. To add insult to injury, Genden was posthumously declared a "nonperson" by the government. What this means in theory is unclear; what it meant in practice was that no good would come of anyone who even so much as mentioned this nonperson's name. In fact, this lasted decades after Genden's death— until the 1990s, when his daughter established a museum in his honor in Ulaanbaatar after the Soviets left.

Genden's successor was eager to begin where his predecessor had left off. New Prime Minister Choibalsan hoped to climb the career ladder and readily agreed to begin the purges that Stalin had ordered. A "more willing puppet," as *Lonely Planet's* Kohn describes him, Choibalsan was both ambitious and ruthless, the most effective kind of sycophant. Incredibly, this *former monk* ordered the execution deaths of tens of thousands of monks, all in the name of Mongolian independence, which is terribly ironic when you consider that this independence itself was based on Mongolia's leader taking orders from another nation.

In fact, Choibalsan got so worked up over any threat to Mongolian independence that he actually slapped a fellow regional leader for suggesting Mongolia team up with the Soviet Union. Anyway, playing the country's hand with the dexterity of a poker champion, Prime Minister Choibalsan used the purge of the monks to keep the Soviets on Mongolia's side but at a comfortable distance, which would turn out to be crucial.

In fact, because Mongolia was able to retain some semblance of autonomy, which had been all but impossible to achieve for other nations caught in Stalin's snare, Choibalsan's memory is respected, if not revered, in many circles in the country today. Incredibly, a province is named after him, and statues have been erected in his honor. When questioned about their feelings for the man and his legacy of genocide in their own country, Mongolians will shake their heads, acknowledging the dark period in their history, and then shrug their shoulders, as if to say, "Everything has its price."

⁂

Barlim Khiid, where we were headed, is a kind of living monument to these deaths. One of those many monasteries to have been "purged" during the Soviet era, nearly all of its monks were executed or forced to flee, and the buildings were torn down or burned. Eerily, all of that destruction was left pretty much intact, as if someone had been pressing a pause button since 1938. Since then, a few monks have returned to the site of Barlim Khiid to set up a museum in the midst of its ruins, a tribute to that terrible moment in time.

Dergui rolled to a stop in the dust, got out of the van, and motioned for us to follow him toward the entrance. Walking with his head bowed, hands clasped behind his back, he said nothing. At the entrance, while he paced, Tobie and Meg and I each paid a dollar to a lone guard sitting in a security booth perched on this edge of nowhere. Gaping at this scene of abandoned chaos, we silently dispersed to have a look around on our own.

It was sunny, hot, and dusty, and I meandered in stifling heat through the crumbling buildings, my footsteps crunching and echoing in the booming silence. Ducking into a low stone doorway, I was surprised to find pots and pans hanging on a wall amid the rubble. It was as if those young monks had been midway through preparing a meal and would return any moment to finish what they'd started. An enormous dried bird lay on its side in the corner of the kitchen.

I was moved by the sense of hopelessness and grief; it was overwhelming. Unlike museums with plate-glass displays and scrubbed and polished floors, the ruins at Barlim Khiid weren't detached from someone else's yesterday. They actually were someone else's yesterday, the despair of their interrupted lives and hopes and dreams. In the sepulchral quiet, I'd peered into a window on someone's very last moment.

Off in the distance, I spotted Meg sitting alone, knees tucked up underneath her chin. Climbing a narrow staircase, I sat on what was left of a wall. Looking out over a snaking river that splices the complex into two defunct monasteries, I eventually wandered back to the van, where Dergui was still pacing. Tobie and then Meg returned. In silence, we left.

For the next few days, we drove and camped and drove some more. Bumping along at a crawl in the oppressive heat, we were deep in the depths of the Gobi. The roads weren't paved, but the landscape was dotted here and there with families living in *gers* or wood cabins, and Dergui had insisted we stop at all of them, indulging at each home in bowls of warm yogurt and plates of hard cheese. He'd even banged on the tiny door of someone's *ger* until they made meat pancakes for us. There, three generations of women had welcomed all four of us inside as they pressed dough into half-moon shapes and stuffed them with coarsely chopped mutton.

By this point, we could hardly imagine that the Gobi had more to offer. After our trip to the ruined monastery, Dergui had made a point of showing us the lighter side of Gobi life. We'd ridden cantankerous camels with humps so floppy it looked like we were straddling saggy old pairs of breasts. We'd climbed to the very top of a sixty-mile-wide length of sand dunes and used a grocery box to sled down them, skidding effortlessly on top of the punishing heat of the roasting sand. Dergui had even found a supermarket to supplement our dwindling food supplies, and Tobie and Meg and I had spent a long time gazing at the unlikely combination of live chickens, transistor radios, peanuts, and jars of Russian cherry compote. But little did we know that we were about to experience the most unusual site the Gobi has to offer. The very best was yet to come.

"Butter," Dergui bellowed one afternoon, squinting into the silver heat through the windshield. He pulled over to the side of the windswept road. Using his sleeve to carefully wipe the window clean, he got back in. Earlier that day, one of the rear window jambs had rattled and broken off. In order to prevent the rest from suffering the same fate, Dergui had protectively sealed shut all of the van's windows, and it was now very, very hot.

"*Mahs-lo!*" he said again, "Butter!" and we sped off in our little oven on wheels.

None of us had any idea what Dergui meant. But by this point in our journey, we'd come to expect the unexpected. After all, Dergui certainly seemed to have a knack for finding it. He'd even managed to treat us to the Gobi's only rainforest, a lush tropical garden labored over by an enterprising and very tanned old nomad, who'd clearly spent a fortune on a garden sprinkler and its water supply. At dusk, we stopped again to make camp. We were halfway to somewhere, but still we didn't know where. I'd forgotten to bring a translation dictionary to the Gobi, and so had Meg and Tobie. Still though, Dergui kept reminding us about "butter."

"Tomorrow," he said with emphatic urgency. "Butter!"

Suddenly, and with a fistful of cash, he marched up a small hill to a *ger* not far from where we'd begun to set up for the night.

"Call off your dogs!" we heard him shout in Mongolian as he approached the compound. Two vicious-looking dogs were loudly grumbling about his arrival, barking and snarling. At a safe distance, we watched with interest.

An old man emerged from the *ger*, called off his dogs, and led Dergui down a dirt path toward a slender stream. Together, they dug into the earth. Filling a paper sack with what they'd found, Dergui offered the man his fistful of cash and then pointed at us. The man nodded, and Dergui returned to our campsite, beaming.

"*Mahs-lo?*" I asked. "Butter?"

"*Bish!*" Dergui laughed uproariously, "No! Butter tomorrow!" he roared, still laughing.

"Tonight, *tooms!*" he declared triumphantly, hoisting the sack over his head. "Potatoes!" He and the old man had picked potatoes and beets from a tiny garden, and we were about to make a stew.

Tobie deposited a miniature keg of beer, a gift from Guenther the German brewmaster at Chinggis Khan Brewery, into the nearby stream to chill its contents. Meg and I peeled the potatoes and beets for boiling while Dergui built a fire from pieces of bayanzag scrub. We couldn't find any salt, but we did manage to discover leftover packets of ramen seasoning stuck in a puddle of grease in the van's chassis. I poured the salted seasoning into a pot, and we all hunched over it and waited.

Impatiently checking on our stew, we stirred it, waited, and stirred and waited some more. Nibbling greedily on scalding, crispy raw beets, we sampled them over and over again to see if they'd softened enough.

Finally, dinner was ready. Watery and cloudy from starch, the stew was deep red in color and smelled of absolutely nothing. Carefully ladling the boiling mixture into metal bowls, we took turns serving ourselves the first fresh hot vegetable meal we'd eaten since our gas stove had spluttered and died a few nights earlier. For a long time, no one spoke. When someone finally did, it was to ask for seconds.

The next morning, Dergui greeted us early. Dawn was rising over the edge of the distant horizon. "Butter!" he reminded us as he built a fire and we rubbed our eyes. At the beet farmer's stream, I freshened up, splashing cold water onto my face and under my arms. Pressing my fingertips along my eyebrows, I savored the last of the water's rivulets trickling down my cheeks, thin streams of chilled tears. The old beet farmer's unblinking guard dogs stopped by, growling a guttural warning for us to venture no farther.

After a breakfast of leftover stew and frothy mugs of chilled beer, we all lay down for a time in the scrubby, vast expanse, staring up at the endless cobalt sky. Suddenly, with a breathy, roaring yawn, Dergui sat up and stretched. Draining the last third of his beer, he patted his paunch with his fat fingers and belched absentmindedly.

"We go to butter!" he shouted just before he wobbled off to urinate.

Off we went, finally, to discover whatever "butter" was. Slowly and circuitously, we'd begun to make our way north again, back to Ulaanbaatar. But that was the very last thing on our minds.

A few hours later, at a rocky outpost in a national park, we realized that Dergui hadn't been saying "butter" at all; he'd been saying "ice." It was an honest mistake; in Mongolian, the two words sound alike.

Gurvan Saikhan National Park, the most popular national park in the Gobi, is also one of the most popular in Central Asia. Nearly 15 percent of Mongolia is classified as protected by the Ministry of Nature and Environment. During independence in 1990, a proposal was floated to turn the *entire* country into a national park. The government, at an impasse with those in favor and those against, finally agreed to transform roughly a third of the country into protected national park regions.

Today, however, with mining revenues whispered to make up at least a quarter of the country's annual budget, mining company initiatives have taken precedence in recent years over environmentalism. This is especially true when mining companies are trying so hard to please the Mongolians that they pay off a fifth of the Mongolian national debt, which supposedly happened recently with a Canadian company's gold interest in the country.

Just inside the entrance to Gurvan Saikhan, we hopped on rented horses, which led us down a narrow footpath flanked by a rocky stream. Trotting into a valley that converged so tightly that we eventually had to continue on foot, we hopped off and tethered our horses.

Then, without any warning at all, the air grew cold. Confused and shivering, we made our way toward the chill's source and rounded a bend to confront nothing less than winter itself. What we saw was what you'd least expect to see in the dead of summer: ice—an entire canyon of ice!

During the frigid Mongolian winter months, the Gobi's Yolyn Am ice canyon grows to thirty feet thick and fifteen miles long, longer even than the island of Manhattan. Then, in summer, it partially melts, shrinking to a fraction of its former size. Still measuring an impressive fifty feet or so in length, the canyon forms a little chamber, an icebox of sorts, into which visitors can crawl and stay for as long as they like. Which is just what we did, spending the entire afternoon marveling over the profoundly strange nature of not only our day but our entire trip. Obviously, this last Gobi adventure had been Dergui's grand finale, for good reason.

Then, after getting back on our horses, we reluctantly headed back to where Dergui was waiting for us. It was time to go home. And not just to Ulaanbaatar, but back to New York. At least that's where I was headed. Although Meg would accompany me on the long train journey from Mongolia to China, we'd part ways in Beijing. Tobie would stay behind in Mongolia for a few more weeks.

CHAPTER 29

Homeward Bound

For the first time since Mongolia became a market economy, budget income will decline in the coming fiscal year. If we do not make any appropriate changes in reducing budget expenditures, the new tax law will yield no positive results. So, we have decided to begin to work to reduce expenditures.

—Interview, Mr. Bayartsaikhan, Ministry of Finance, *MM Today* broadcast

"Roll, Patricia, roll," Batma said, showing me what to do with the boiled knuckles she'd presented to me. Meg and I had just returned from our trip to the Gobi, and we were spending our last day in Ulaanbaatar. The next afternoon, we'd board a train bound for China. As a parting gift, Batma had collected and cleaned eight livestock knuckles and had hand-sewn two tiny silk drawstring pouches to store them in—a pouch for Meg and a pouch for me.

I obeyed, rolling the knucklebone dice just as Batma had instructed. This was the Mongolian way to read a horoscope, and Batma wasn't about to let me leave the country without making sure she was satisfied with my future.

"Oh," was all she said as she frowned and pointed from the dice I'd rolled to the note card she was holding.

Written in English, the card was entitled "Complicated Fortune Telling" and it explained the implications of the knuckles landing in certain positions. Apparently, my toss of the dice had been particularly inauspicious. I'd rolled one of the two worst outcomes: "Your work and deeds won't have any success," it warned, making sure to capitalize the last word for effect. It seemed only marginally better than "With much gossips and bad quarrels." Mongolian fortunes don't mess around and Batma looked genuinely worried.

"I can try again?" I asked.

"Again," she agreed.

Once more, I rolled the knucklebones, and Batma examined the note card.

"One will come or come back soon," she read from the card, and we both exhaled, heaving a collective sigh of relief. Obviously it was crucial to leave Mongolia with tradition's blessing, rather than its curse. After I finished packing, I put the knucklebones in my pocket and went for a walk. It was time to finally visit Gandan Khiid monastery.

Although I'd spent a summer passing through Gandan almost every day, I'd waited until my very last day in Mongolia to actually go inside its interior temples. Savoring this moment had definitely been the right thing to do. It was as if I'd needed to understand something about myself before I could understand anything about Mongolia, especially when it came to Gandan Khiid. Gandan Khiid, the only monastery left standing truly intact after Choibalsan's and Stalin's purges, is a true testament to the determination of spirit that is part of the very soul of every Mongolian I'd met thus far on my journey. That lesson wasn't lost on me.

"No photo!" a little robed raisin of a man shouted at me as I paid for my ticket. Stepping into the hushed quiet, I stopped and stared in awe at an enormous Buddha statue, his heavy-lidded stone eyes gazing at a point somewhere just beyond me. Silently, I walked clockwise around the perimeter of the Buddha's dais, spinning the worn metal prayer wheels as I went. Prayer wheels are like spinning tops, but much larger, the size of oil cans. They're inscribed with flourishes of traditional script and skewered with wooden rods to stand upright. It is believed that as long as they remain spinning, the wheels pray for you, not unlike lighting a candle in a church and letting it burn long after you have left.

I continued to make my way clockwise around the temple. At the back wall, I faced a crowd of angry-looking painted wooden faces. Pausing for a moment, I wished them well and asked that they protect me from harm's way as I headed back home to Manhattan. From behind the wall, I heard the resonant thrum of a low, guttural chant. Making my way out of the temple and sneaking around back, I sought the source of the chant.

The security guard shook his head at me until he saw my Mongolia TV anchor badge, which I'd worn just in case I'd find myself facing a moment like this one.

"*Hut-lugch? Mongol Televit?*" he asked.

"Yes, sir," I said.

Grinning broadly, he clapped his hand on his knee. "*Mongol Televit!*" he declared, and jutted his chin in the direction of that resonating chant, granting me passage.

The chanting grew ever louder as I followed a narrow garden path toward a set of wooden doors. There was no handle, so I knocked, leaning gingerly into one of the doors. It creaked loudly and suddenly cracked. Splinters and thick chips of peeling paint flew in every direction, and I found myself tumbling into a room cloaked entirely in varying shades of red and gold.

Young student monks from the Buddhist University of Mongolia sat on cherry-colored velvet cushions, draped in flowing robes of burgundy and mustard undergarments. From the look of the books in their laps, they'd been studying Buddhist scripture. The monks stared at me and I stared back, but only for a moment. I'd made quite an entrance. Legs spread wide, like a basketball player waiting to be called up from the bench, one of the monks smiled, revealing beneath his robes a pair of high-top sneakers.

"*Uchlarai.*" I said. "Excuse me, I'm sorry." I put their door back together and left as quickly as I'd entered. Still, the chanting went on, and I hunted for its source. Creeping up another flight of stairs, I followed the vibrations. They were so earthy and tactile that I could have shut my eyes and still found their source.

Down a bare cement hall, a door was ajar and I inched toward it. The chanting grew ever louder. Sitting at a polished wooden primary school desks, a dozen or so young boys with shaved heads faced a blackboard. All of them, even their instructor, were dressed identically in robes of deep red. Eyes half-shut, they were reciting hymns, growling melodiously and in resonant unison.

I'd finally discovered the source of the thrumming and chanting. Closing my eyes, I listened and my entire body vibrated in time with their mantras.

Quietly I made my way outside again, inhaling the pallid dust in the temple's square, taking one last look at the towering temple and bright blue sky that served as its backdrop. It was time to go.

Back at home, Meg and I collected our luggage, bid a fond farewell to Batma and her family, and headed downtown. Together, we'd booked passage on the Trans-Mongolian sleeper car, traveling eastward from Ulaanbaatar to Beijing. The journey would last thirty-six hours, and both of us would spend much of it in silence, trying to figure out what was *next*.

"Patricia!" Gandima called out, just as Meg and I were about to board. "I must give this to you!" she shouted breathlessly as she ran toward me.

Back at the station a week earlier, Gandima and I and the rest of the MNB staff had already said our good-byes, and I certainly hadn't expected to see her again.

"Open it!" she cried, pushing a flat, wrapped parcel into my hand.

I tore at the wrapping and then smiled broadly. Gazing up at me was Genghis Khan, his face painted onto a canvas of rawhide. Easily the most ubiquitous souvenir available for purchase in Mongolia, Gandima had worried that I'd already bought one for myself. I hadn't, and I hugged her.

"Gandima, thank you," I said, my eyes welling up. "For everything."

"One day, you will come back here," she predicted.

Just then, the train whistle blew a final call, and Meg and I boarded, waving to Gandima until we pulled out of the station. Inside the tiny, carpeted train car, I sat and stared at the scenery slowly trundling past, wondering what on earth I would do once I got home.

CHAPTER 30

One Step Backward, Two Steps Forward

Currently, the Mongolian government is comprised of thirteen ministries, thirty agencies, eighteen offices serving the prime minister, president, and Parliament; and nearly 6,000 budget organizations. While budget income has been increasing annually since 1991, expenses have also been rising each year.

—Voiceover, English news, *MM Today* broadcast

And then, suddenly, I was back in New York.

Right away, I noticed that absolutely everyone seemed to be in a hurry. All around me, people were frantically typing on their smartphones, plugged into life and obligations. I was still unplugged and found all this very disconcerting. For the first time, I felt out of place in my own home.

My taxi arrived in front of my apartment building. I got out, and the doorman on duty just stared. I was dirty. My clothes were dirty. My backpack was enormous and dirty.

"I live here," I said, offering him my name and unit number as proof, and he let me pass.

Once inside my apartment, I inhaled its familiar scent deeply. Removing my pack, I sat down at the kitchen counter. While I'd been gone, a friend had collected my mail. A stack of it now sat in front of me. I didn't have much else to do, so one by one, I began opening bill after bill.

And then the phone rang.

Of course, it was always going to. If you've ever read Paulo Coelho's *The Alchemist*, you know that there's a day of reckoning. On that day, you'll be asked to decide between the certainty of the past or faith in the future.

"Hello?" I said reluctantly. I didn't think anyone knew I'd returned, and I was more than happy to keep it that way, at least until I knew how to answer the obvious question: "So, what are you going to do next?"

"You're back!" my old Credit Suisse boss said into the phone. In fact, it wasn't exactly my boss I was talking to—it was my boss's boss, and I couldn't help but feel flattered to hear from him at all.

"So," he said. "What are you going to do now?"

Of course, I didn't know, and I said so.

"You should talk to J.P. Morgan," he said authoritatively.

As I fingered the stack of bills in front of me and looked around my apartment at all the *things* I'd managed to accumulate, I found myself agreeing with him. "You're right, I *should*," I said, wincing at the last word.

Telling myself I would only meet J.P. Morgan just this once, I found myself in a series of interviews. After that, things happened quickly. Although I told myself I was powerless to stop what was happening, the truth is that I was looking forward once more to the feeling of responsibility.

A short time later, J.P. Morgan hired me. I was back in my old job, selling Foreign Exchange structures to hedge funds. Mongolia, and all that had happened to me while I was there, suddenly seemed like a lifetime ago, and that was just the way I wanted it, because it was the easiest way to handle it.

"There's no meaning in life but money," Les said to me early one morning soon after I'd started work. "It's the joke that only bankers will ever understand."

By this point, because I'd been out of the market for nearly a year, I'd been assigned to work with a colleague on some of the larger accounts I'd brought with me to J.P. Morgan. It was early 2007, the housing crisis was brewing, and markets were volatile and roiling. I'd need as much help as I could get, especially at a large and aggressive bank like J.P. Morgan. But although Les was my colleague, helping anyone at all appeared to be the last thing on his mind.

If someone were to create a caricature of the slickest, most soulless banker, Les would be it. About forty years old, he had greased-back hair and wore Ferragamo ties and designer suits. He lived in a loft in TriBeCa, owned a house in Connecticut, and commuted between the two in a flashy sports car.

On Monday mornings, he would regale the junior staff with stories of weekend nights spent with models, fine tequila, and rare cigars. Les could've been Patrick Bateman, the main character in Bret Easton Ellis's *American Psycho*—he even looked like him. In fact, "Patrick Bateman" is what everyone called him, right to his face. And Les, for his part, would smile, clearly pleased with his nickname and his image on the trading floor. He was very good at what he did; Les had earned the right to enjoy his eccentricities.

Whenever Les would pontificate, he would take his time doing so. Halfway into a nugget of wisdom, he'd pause, deep in thought, accentuating concentration with his bulging eyes. Then, straightening his silk tie, he'd wink capriciously and repeat the same maxim every single time: "There's no meaning in life but money."

For Les, this was probably true. Not long ago, so the rumor went, his wife had left him for a younger man and had taken half his net worth in the divorce settlement.

Every morning, as soon as I arrived on the floor at six–thirty sharp, I'd take off my watch and place it on the desk in front of me, counting down the minutes until I could leave: 285 minutes until lunch and 645 until quitting time. Rain or shine, I always made sure to go for a walk at lunch, something that was vaguely frowned upon, especially since I chose a restaurant so far away from the building that I'd spend a guilty half hour getting there and back. Whether or not Les noticed, I never knew, but he hardly seemed to care. Somehow, I'd gotten sucked back into all of this. And so I willed myself to wait . . . for just one more bonus, just as I had before.

"Is this call being recorded?" a familiar voice inquired into the phone one afternoon.

"Phil, is that you?" A client for nearly a decade, since I'd begun my banking career, Phil had become a kind of mentor but not the kind of mentor that most bankers would want. Years earlier, when he was in his twenties, Phil been given one shot at his dream to become a musician. Taking well-intentioned advice from all the right people saying all the wrong things, he gave up on himself as the musician and instead pursued the corporate world. Some thirty years later, he still wondered what might've happened, if and only if. He'd offered me wise counsel based on his own experience with a truncated future, and needless to say, I dreaded the conversation I was about to have.

"Yes, we're being recorded, but go ahead, say what you want."

"What in the hell are you doing?" he demanded.

I knew what Phil meant, but I didn't know how to answer. Phil was the only person in banking who knew what had happened to me just a few weeks earlier. I almost wished I hadn't confided in him.

Just before committing to J.P. Morgan, I'd decided to give one last shot to my dream of becoming a foreign correspondent. "It's now or never," I thought, goading the universe into action. With that, I sent my resume and a tape of my anchoring experience to CNN. Not to just anyone at CNN, but to Jon Klein, then the president of CNN USA. Half of me was desperate for him to call; the other half was desperately hoping he wouldn't. If he didn't call, I could return to the safety and comfort of my old job and old life—and do so without any regrets.

But, incredibly, he did call, and a few days later, I was sitting in his office. "So," he'd said after politely introducing himself as if I didn't already know who he was. "Why Mongolia?"

"My dream is to be a foreign correspondent," I'd said. "So I went to Mongolia to follow my dream."

"But what now? What do you want to do? Why are you *here*?" he asked pointedly.

He'd asked me as if I knew, so I told him as if I knew. But at that point, everything that had happened in Mongolia felt as if it had happened a lifetime ago. It just didn't seem real anymore. So I took a deep breath and told him about my faded dream, leaving out the part about it being faded.

"Because I want to go to Baghdad," I said, and I meant it. For years, I'd watched Christiane Amanpour report live from war zones, and still I wished I could do the same.

"Okay," Jon Klein had said so simply that shivers ran down my spine.

Okay?

"Tony Maddox," he'd said, printing Tony's name and number on a piece of paper. "Call Tony by the end of this week. He runs CNN International, and he'll be expecting you."

Outside, it was snowing. For a long time, I stood on the corner of Fifty-Seventh Street in Manhattan, thinking. At some point, I'd have to choose between dreams and reality. Clearly, that time was now.

The following week, CNN flew me to Atlanta, and I was sitting across from Tony Maddox, executive vice president of CNN International. "Why Mongolia?" he'd asked, just as his New York counterpart had done. "And now?"

"And now," I'd said, pausing to nervously lick my lips. "I'd like to go to Baghdad. To work as a correspondent for CNN."

"Everybody wants to go to Baghdad," Tony said gently but without any hesitation. "Right out there in our newsroom," he went on, pointing to it. "There's a line of people paying their dues to get to where you want to be. Are you ready to do what it takes to get there? To move to Atlanta? Can you handle working nights and weekends? Are you ready to give up everything for your dream?"

Suddenly, I wasn't ready. All I could think about was everything I'd ever worried about: mortgage, bills, obligations, uncertainty. Air caught in the back of my throat, and I panicked. I couldn't believe that I wasn't willing to go the distance, but . . . I wasn't willing to go the distance.

Tony knew. "Patricia," he'd said, "I see people like you in my office every day. From recent journalism school grads to seasoned foreign correspondents. Everyone, all of you, wants to be a part of the action. Eventually that happens, but in a different way for each person. What I'm trying to say is that this might not be for you. But listen, *you must follow your dream still, wherever it takes you.*"

At that point, as I was saying good-bye to him and to CNN, I was hardly considering his advice. Boarding a return flight to New York, I decided to accept J.P. Morgan's offer. My dream was over, I thought, and it was time to return to reality once and for all.

Now, sitting on the trading floor a few weeks later, on the phone with Phil, the client, I tried to explain all of this to him. Still, I winced at his reaction. It was what I'd been expecting, but I certainly didn't want to hear it.

"You're telling me you've gone, literally, to the ends of the earth to follow a dream, and you aren't going to follow through?" he asked incredulously.

"I gotta go," I said, and put the phone down. All around me, traders and salespeople had begun to shout at each other, in particular Les, who was spluttering, red-faced, into his phone, flecks of hot spittle landing on his desk as well as on those of us sitting next to him.

The currency market was rife with rumors, and regardless of their accuracy, those rumors were still moving the market to which I'd returned. That morning in particular, the first cracks in the foundation of the housing market had begun to appear. The rumors hadn't become news yet because no one was sure what was going on. The number crunchers were busy crunching numbers, and with those results came gasps from analysts.

Because most of us on the trading floor had worked through at least one global financial crisis, we were accustomed to bracing ourselves for impact. And we did just that, spending a lot of time on conference calls trying to figure out what was false and what was fact, and then calling our clients to alert them of what we weren't yet sure we knew.

The crisis itself was still abstract, so no one was predicting the collapse of the American housing market followed by fears of the Great Depression repeating itself. Instead, everyone was shrugging his or her shoulders, wondering if the analysts had gotten their models right. As for me and everyone else on the trading floor, we were simply too busy to think about anything but work. Frankly, it was a welcome distraction.

"Price up a one-month forty-delta yen," a former Credit Suisse hedge fund client said to me one morning. "In size," he added, and my stomach knotted, just as it always had. That the client was asking for a price "in size" was a gift. When a salesperson starts a job at a different bank, it's always a risk whether or not his clients will continue to do business with him, and that risk can cost him his job if he's guessed wrong. Bringing in big business, especially new business, would create a stir.

Next to me, with his phone in the crook of his neck, Les watched. I opened my options pricing model and started to input the details of the option quote the client had requested. The most important and sensitive ingredient in the model was the price of the yen, which at that moment and for the past few weeks had been fluctuating wildly.

"Dollar-yen quote *in size,* please," I spoke into the microphone on my desk. Although the yen trader was only sitting a row away from me, rules at J.P. Morgan required salespeople to request quotes from their seats, rather than in person. It was just as well; the yen trader had a temper that I was afraid to confront.

"Who the fuck is your client?" the trader snapped at me, shouting so loudly that I could hear him down the mike and from his seat. When salespeople don't trust their colleagues on the trading floor, they'll hide their client's identity. Although it doesn't always work, it helps to prevent the traders from front-running the client's order and prevents fellow salespeople from telling their own clients what someone else's client is doing.

However, when you're new to a firm and your trader is a bully, you make sure you give him the requested information. After I revealed the client's identity to him, he gave me the quote: 120.48. Plugging the trader's quote into my model, I called the client back with the price for the option he was interested in buying. Just as I did so, the dollar began to creep higher against the yen.

"Mine," the client said. "I'll buy two hundred fifty million dollars' worth."

Of course, a deal of this size should've been great news, but the yen was nowhere near the 120.48 I'd shown him. Trouble was, we'd already agreed on the price, and it was my responsibility to cover the bank's hedge, which was no less than one hundred million dollars. Every one one-hundredth move in the yen's price would risk the bank, and the yen trader specifically, about eight thousand dollars.

"Where is the yen now?" I asked the trader.

It was up to 120.56.

I could barely breathe, and my skin had begun to crawl in that way it does when you're facing some sort of spectacular public shame. "Buy one hundred million," I said to him.

At first, the yen trader was quiet, which meant that he was about to show us his worst.

"What the fuck do you think you're doing?" he said after he'd made a special trip to my desk to ask me this. He was fat, sweating, and splotchy-purple with rage. Few situations on a trading floor result in total silence, but this situation had managed to result in just that. Absolutely everyone was watching the newest salesperson go head-to-head with one of the most seasoned traders.

I caught Les's eye, silently pleading for help. Quickly, he turned away.

"I'm sorry," I began, trying to explain that whatever money I'd made on any trades that day I'd give back to him to make up for his loss.

"I just lost sixty-six thousand dollars because of *you*," he interrupted before he stormed off. There was no time for any more discussion. There was barely time to cringe.

"Where is the Mexican peso?" another hedge fund was asking, and if I had any hope of righting my wrong, it would have to be immediately.

The hedge fund manager inquiring about the Mexican peso was one of the biggest and most powerful in the business and still is. He was also generous, willing to allow the bank to make money if he made money. Generosity doesn't appear often on a trading floor, and generous clients are fought over bitterly.

But this particular hedge fund was at odds with J.P. Morgan, on account of one of the London salespeople's supposedly ripping him off in a very large metals trade. Weeks earlier, I'd been on a business trip in London, learning just what had happened between one of the savviest money managers in the world and one of the most senior salesmen at J.P. Morgan.

"He ripped my *fucking eyes out* on a five hundred million–dollar cross," the hedge fund manager explained when I'd flown to the United Kingdom to meet with him. He didn't offer any more detail, and I didn't want any. It hadn't taken me long at J.P. Morgan to learn that there was no upside to getting tangled in their toxic political quagmire. Unfortunately though, this time I wouldn't have a choice.

"Buy me three hundred million dollars against the Mexican peso," the hedge fund had instructed, not long after our meeting, and I immediately went to work. Once I'd finished executing his trade, I sent out the trade confirmation. It would spell the end of my career.

"What the *fuck* do you think you're doing?" the salesman screamed down the telephone line, without even saying hello, just a moment later. Secretive and greedy, he was so short that I'd actually been instructed never to wear heels in his presence.

"I thought I'd *forbidden* you to trade with *my* account!" he shrieked.

The salesman was right. He had forbidden me from doing just that. But, ever since the salesman's dispute with the fund, the fund had refused to trade with him and had insisted on trading with me. I was caught in the middle, and, at that moment, I had no choice but to follow the client's orders. The only time I've ever heard of a salesperson refusing to execute for a client was during 9/11, when New York trading floors were being evacuated.

Now, for the second time, I looked for help to Les, who was gaping at me as he eavesdropped on my conversation with the salesperson. Quickly though, he turned his attention elsewhere, busying himself with a paper clip.

Incredulous that I was having such a combustible confrontation with one of the most senior salespeople at the company, I tried to simply reason with him. After all, I was resurrecting business that he'd lost, and he'd actually be the one to get paid for it, not me. Of course, he was never going to see it that way. At J.P. Morgan, rules were more territorial than practical.

As I listened to the salesman continue to screech at me from his cell phone in London, Mongolia and everything that had happened there came flooding back to me. From living with a Mongolian Mormon family and anchoring the news to reporting on and writing about other people following their dreams—I was reminded why I'd left banking the year before.

Suddenly, I began shaking. Voice trembling, I could barely continue my conversation with the London salesman, so I decided not to. I put the phone down on my desk and hung up on him. With my head in my hands, I asked myself what on earth I was doing back here in banking.

Of course, I knew the answer. Although I'd returned for the paycheck, and not for the kill, I'd gotten sucked back in. It had happened so quickly that I'd barely noticed it had happened at all.

Right then, I stood up and made for my boss's office. It was time to go. This time for good.

"Just stay until the end of the year," my boss said. "For one more bonus." He'd make it worth my while, he promised. For just a moment, I was tempted once again, but I willed it away. This time, it was time—to finally take a real leap of faith.

Back on the trading floor, I cleared out my desk and handed over my security badge and Blackberry. Les watched but still said nothing. Finally, I made my way around the room, shaking hands with the few people I'd gotten to know during my short time there.

"You've made the right decision," a senior saleswoman stage-whispered to me so loudly I wondered if she was talking to just me or to all of our colleagues. Exceptionally well-versed in economics and strategy, this particular saleswoman was a career banker, someone who'd really sunk her teeth into what the industry was all about. Or so I'd thought.

"A long time ago, I had a dream," she went on, still in a voice loud enough for everyone to hear. "So go find yours, before it's too late." Only a few years older than me, the saleswoman looked a lot older. Dark circles ringed her eyes and fine papier-mâché creases lined her face. She didn't look just tired; she looked as if she'd sold her soul.

I thanked her and walked out. Just as I did, Les turned to look at me but only briefly. He was on the phone and didn't bother to say good-bye.

EPILOGUE

After leaving banking, I went to work for CBS News in New York. While there, I got a chance to watch and learn as some of the world's biggest news was being made and produced: the election of President Obama, the global financial meltdown, the bombing at the Marriott Hotel in Islamabad. I was even called up to *60 Minutes* to help Lesley Stahl's team produce a story on credit derivatives. In short, my dream was coming true, but the very best was still to come.

On a whim, I flew to Hong Kong to meet a friend at the Hong Kong Sevens, an annual rugby match that is more costume party than sport. Dressed in an ill-fitting Snow White costume (a last-minute purchase), I met a man dressed as Hugh Hefner (admittedly, not a last-minute purchase). He was a New Zealander living in London. In a crowd of forty thousand people, we met and *really* liked each other. And then we immediately lost each other. Incredibly though, the following day, at the sold-out rugby final match, my friend and I finagled tickets and found ourselves seated . . . right next to my Hugh Hefner. We fell in love, got married, and had a baby girl.

And then the big call came, this time from Sinovision English, the English-language arm of the Chinese television station. They were looking for someone to report on stories of people following dreams. I was hired, and I got a chance to interview celebrities and artists who'd overcome extraordinary obstacles to pursue their passion. This was truly a dream come true. But again, the best was still to come.

Later, along with my director at the network, we formed Morpheus Pictures LLC, an independent film company that plans to chronicle the journeys of people achieving their dreams. Our first film is currently being produced, and it'll take us right back to where it all started for me—Mongolia. And this is where the journey, the real dream, begins again. Still . . . the best is yet to come.

ACKNOWLEDGMENTS

Whenever you find yourself in hot pursuit of something that you're sure about but no one else quite yet understands, you end up with a debt of gratitude owed to all the amazing people who suspended doubt, believed in you, and granted you a shot. For this, I have so many people to thank that I barely know where to begin, so I'll begin at the beginning.

I'd like to thank my mom, for planting the seed of this "book" in my head. And then for nagging me about it until I got started. I'd like to thank my dad for putting a globe on his desk, just out of reach, knowing that would do the trick to get me interested in following in his own adventurous footsteps. I'd like to thank my three brothers—Joe, Tim, and Danny—for doing it better, saying it more eloquently, and usurping my firstborn monopoly on our parents' attention. Without them, maybe I never would have left home at all.

With deep admiration, I'd like to thank Magee Hickey for giving me that "shot" here in New York. Likewise, I'm forever grateful to Gandima

Rentsendorj in Mongolia for believing in me and giving me a chance I didn't deserve. And without Tobie and Meg and "Evan" and Batma and her family, this book wouldn't have happened at all. My gratitude to all of them for so graciously allowing me to write their stories and their descriptions from my own perspective. And a very big thanks indeed to my former banking colleagues, 99 percent of whom are the most wonderful, caring people on the planet. They must be, if they continue to support me and keep in contact with me despite my pestering them to follow their own dreams.

Humbly and with endless gratitude, I'd like to thank my agent, publisher, and editors. Doug Grad is my first agent, and hopefully he'll be my last, too. Anyone who takes frantic phone calls with his serenity and wisdom simply must become your agent—maybe your physician, too. Beaufort Books, my publisher, and Tracy Ertl of TitleTown have taken a huge chance on me. I'm honored to have such dynamic, inspiring people in my court. My many thanks to them and their teams. Also a huge thank-you to Claire Gerus, and Sandy Smith, the editors without whom this book would not be what it is—Claire and Sandy offered just the tough, constructive love that it, and I, needed.

Finally, I'd like to thank my husband and my friends for their endless support and patience over the years. In particular, Meghan for her existential wisdom that encouraged me to leave banking and pursue my own path. Meghan believed in me from the start, as well as when the going got tough. It's a true friend who does, and she's a keeper. Netta read, reread, and read-some-more the manuscript, and then even treated me to fine sushi while talking me through her assessment. Finally, I'm grateful to my husband, Jesse "Bunkle" Phillips, for his infinite (and often hilarious) support and patience throughout this mentally tumultuous process. Not only did he coin the term "consonant omelet," he challenged me to be a better writer and a better person. But don't tell him I said that last part.

Thank you, all of you. I'm so very lucky to have each and every one of you in my life.

CPSIA information can be obtained
at www.ICGtesting.com
Printed in the USA
LVOW12s2035230117
521865LV00004B/4/P